THE FINAL
SCULPTURE

THE FINAL
SCULPTURE

★

PUBLIC MONUMENTS AND
MODERN POETS

★

Michael North

CORNELL UNIVERSITY PRESS

ITHACA AND LONDON

Cornell University Press gratefully acknowledges a grant from the Andrew W. Mellon Foundation that aided in bringing this book to publication.

First published 1985 by Cornell University Press.
Published in the United Kingdom by Cornell University Press Ltd., London.

Excerpts from *The Poems of W. B. Yeats, a New Edition,* ed. Richard J. Finneran, copyright 1924, 1928 by Macmillan Publishing Co., Inc., renewed 1952, 1956 by Bertha Georgie Yeats; copyright 1940 by Georgie Yeats, renewed 1968 by Bertha Georgie Yeats, Michael Butler Yeats and Anne Yeats; © 1983 Anne Yeats, are reprinted with the permission of Macmillan Publishing Co, Inc., New York, Michael Yeats, and Macmillan London Limited.

Excerpts from *The Cantos of Ezra Pound,* copyright © 1934, 1937, 1940, 1948, 1956 by Ezra Pound, and *Personae,* copyright 1926 by Ezra Pound, are reprinted by permission of New Directions Publishing Corporation and Faber and Faber Ltd.

Excerpts from *The Collected Poems of Wallace Stevens,* copyright © 1954 by Wallace Stevens, and *Opus Posthumous,* ed. Samuel French Morse, copyright © 1957 by Elsie Stevens and Holly Stevens, are reprinted by permission of Alfred A. Knopf, Inc., and Faber and Faber Ltd.

Excerpts from "Boston Common" from *Short Poems* by John Berryman, copyright © 1948, renewed © 1969 by John Berryman, and excerpts from "For the Union Dead," "Buenos Aires," and "The Neo-Classical Urn" from *For the Union Dead* by Robert Lowell, copyright © 1960, 1963, 1964 by Robert Lowell, are reprinted by permission of Farrar, Straus and Giroux, Inc., and Faber and Faber Ltd.

Excerpts from *Lord Weary's Castle,* copyright 1946, 1974 by Robert Lowell, are reprinted by permission of Harcourt Brace Jovanovich, Inc., and Faber and Faber Ltd.

International Standard Book Number 0-8014-1725-2
Library of Congress Catalog Card Number 84-17011
Printed in the United States of America
Librarians: Library of Congress cataloging information appears on the last page of the book.

Contents

5

Illustrations

Preface

My interest in the subject of this book began with one of Wallace Stevens' smallest poems, "The American Sublime," and grew into a consideration of one of his longest, *Owl's Clover*. That Stevens took the public monument seriously enough to wrestle with it at such length indicated that some essential aspect of his own ambition for poetry was concerned in the struggle. And I soon realized that monuments rarely appear in modern poems without some struggle because they vividly represent contradictions in the poetry itself. In one sense, this book is an entry in the protracted debate over modern poetry's "lost audience" and in the even muddier debate over the politics of modern poets. But it is the conflict *within* certain modern poets that concerns me, the contradiction between hermeticism and public ambition, between the poem as self-contained object and as seed of a new culture. These controversies take place first in the poets themselves, and the result is not sterile debate but major poetry.

There is nothing absolutely necessary about the roster of poets considered, but those included have been chosen for what I hope are good reasons. Yeats and Pound seem to me the preeminent modern examples of the kind of imaginative writer who hopes to build a culture to receive his own work partly by calling attention to other works of art. In Yeats and Pound the conflict between such culture-building and the privacy of the poet appears particularly sharp, and thus the monument is called upon to play a particularly ambiguous role. For Yeats and Pound as well, the visual arts seem to provide a prototype and example as they do not for Eliot, another culture-building poet. Stevens, for his part, takes the monument as an example both of what is strong and of what is weak in American art and literature, and his difficulties with this analogy led me to consider the idea that poets working with American materials suffer in a different way from the conflicts of Yeats and Pound. Thus there are really two introductions in this book, one of which, Chapter 7, attempts to give an American background to the poetry on monuments of Stevens, Berryman, and Lowell. In these cases the conflict between modernist aesthetics and the desire for didactic impact is exacerbated by a particularly American queasiness about the idealization characteristic of monuments. And yet Stevens, Berryman, and Lowell call upon the monument as example just as insistently as do Yeats and Pound.

I feel as well that there is some connection between their experiences and the controversies that now break out over each new piece of public sculpture. Nearly every community is by now familiar with the limited possibilities of the argument about whether some object can be called art. As perverse as they are, these arguments constitute almost the only discussions of artistic matters that involve the public at large. The fact that the public cares with such intensity, that it demands to be memorialized (as, for example, the Vietnam veterans have) while repudiating virtually every serious attempt to do so, suggests an ambivalence about more than art. To probe this ambivalence further would be an important project, the terms of which can only be touched on here.

A considerable portion of this book was written while I held two Summer Research Fellowships granted by the College of William and Mary. Thanks are due to the college for this support and to the department of English for clerical and research assistance. Chapter 1 originally appeared as "The Paradox of the Mausoleum: Public Monuments and the Early Aesthetics of W. B. Yeats" in *The Centennial Review* 26 (Summer 1982). Chapters 2 and 3 appeared in somewhat different form as "The Ambiguity of Repose: Sculpture and the Public Art of W. B. Yeats" in *ELH* 50 (Summer 1983), copyright © 1983 by The Johns Hopkins University Press. Chapter 5 appeared as "The Architecture of Memory: Pound and the Tempio Malatestiano" in *American Literature* 55 (October 1983), copyright © 1983 by Duke University Press. Portions of Chapters 8 and 9 appeared in considerably different form as "Public Monuments and Public Poetry: Stevens, Berryman, and Lowell" in *Contemporary Literature* 21 (Spring 1980).

I am especially grateful to Joseph Cary for his advice in the earliest stages of this work. Thanks are due as well to James Clinch, Paul Wellen, and Kim Sands for their help in preparing the manuscript.

MICHAEL NORTH

Williamsburg, Virginia

Works Abbreviated in the Text

WALTER PATER
Greek Studies (GS)
Plato and Platonism (PP)
The Renaissance (R)

W. B. YEATS
Autobiographies (A)
Essays and Introductions (EI)
On the Boiler (OB)
The Poems (P)
A Vision (AV)

EZRA POUND
Ezra Pound and the Visual Arts (VA)
Gaudier-Brzeska (GB)
Guide to Kulchur (GK)
Letters (L)
Literary Essays (LE)
Personae (PE)
Selected Prose (SP)

WALLACE STEVENS
Collected Poems (CP)
Letters (LS)
Opus Posthumous (OP)

ROBERT LOWELL
Lord Weary's Castle (LWC)

THE FINAL
SCULPTURE

This it is that answers when I ask,
This is the mute, the final sculpture
Around which silence lies on silence.
This reposes alike in springtime
And, arbored and bronzed, in autumn.

—Wallace Stevens,
"Yellow Afternoon"

Introduction

A tiresome battle, repeated in city after city, now takes place whenever a piece of modern sculpture is installed outdoors. The lines of this battle are so well drawn, the arguments on both sides so infinitely repeatable, that the conflict has come to seem a fated one. Both opponents and admirers of contemporary sculpture, as well as those who create it, agree that it cannot function in public spaces as representational sculpture did in the nineteenth century. Even Sam Hunter, in defending the General Services Administration's Art-in-Architecture program, has declared: "contemporary monuments can no longer plausibly celebrate national heroes, patriotic or personal virtue, or great historical events. Both the mythologies and the sustaining artistic conventions for such themes have vanished."[1] Yet sculpture continues to be installed outdoors, on the kind of site once occupied by conventional monuments, and the squabbles that almost inevitably occur tell a great deal about the current relationship of art, art theory, and the general public.

1. Sam Hunter, Pref. to Donald W. Thalacker, *The Place of Art in the World of Architecture* (New York: Bowker; London: Chelsea House, 1980), p. ix. Thalacker's book is a survey of the GSA's public art program. A similar survey of the National Endowment for the Arts's program is John Beardsley's *Art in Public Places* (Washington, D.C.: Partners for Livable Places, 1981). For a good example of the debate over contemporary public monuments, see *The Public Interest*, 66 (Winter 1982), 3–24. For a survey of the classical monument and a call for a return to its standards, see Philipp Fehl, *The Classical Monument: Reflections on the Connection between Morality and Art in Greek and Roman Sculpture* (New York: New York University Press, 1972).

These controversies seem to reflect a conviction on both sides that truly public art is now impossible, that the very phrase "public art" has been made a contradiction in terms. The National Endowment for the Arts, for example, carefully calls its program "Art in Public Places" to avoid the question whether the art itself is public or not. This distrust of public art is at bottom a distrust of the very concept of the public. As Amy Goldin says, "I think the reason there is so little genuine public art today is our own disbelief in the reality of the public world itself. Nowadays almost anything big and/or public is suspect."[2] The public monument has succumbed to the modern habit of equating the public with the false, the meretricious, the propagandistic. And yet, as Douglas Davis says, "The twentieth century has been obsessed by the dream of a public art."[3] Both in literature and in the arts, the anonymous, collective style mythologized by Ruskin has remained a kind of visionary goal. Especially for certain poets of the twentieth century, public monuments have been a powerfully ambiguous model, fascinating and repellent at the same time. In their poetry they reenact over and over the controversy of the modern monument, erecting structures that seem to advertise their own impossibility.

Contemporary sculpture seems to lack three basic attributes that turn an ordinary piece of art into a monument. It does not commemorate any event or person from the past; it is not didactic; it does not embody public agreement either in style or in message. The myth behind current arguments over contemporary monuments is that sculpture once clearly possessed these three attributes, but has since abandoned them. But this is to consider contemporary sculpture in a severely restricted frame of reference, in comparison only to the realistic and literary productions of the nineteenth century as exemplified by the Albert Memorial. In fact, sculpture has often been ambiguous in just these three areas: its relationship to the past and the future; its status as referential object; its relationship to the public. What many current controversialists seem to ignore is that sculpture has held a public place in the

2. Amy Goldin, "The Aesthetic Ghetto: Some Thoughts About Public Art," *Art in America*, May–June 1974, p. 34.

3. Douglas Davis, "Public Art: The Taming of the Vision," *Art in America*, May–June 1974, p. 84.

past partly by virtue of its ambiguity, not because it is the simplest of the arts, but because it is able to satisfy conflicting desires.

The clearest and most obvious cliché to emerge from the controversy over contemporary outdoor sculpture is the idea that monuments and modern art, and therefore modernity in general, are diametrically opposed to each other. This position is accepted most readily by artists whose works occupy public places and by groups like SITE, which take public space as the medium of their work. James Wines, founder of SITE, says, "The age of monuments (whether art, architecture, or urban spaces) is finished and most attempts to perpetuate the tradition are pretentious and extraneous."[4] The nonrepresentational style of modern sculpture is only part of the reason for this judgment. Even more important, perhaps, is the idea that modernism in the arts looks forward and is devoted to change, while the monument looks back into a frozen moment in the past. In 1938, Lewis Mumford declared the monument dead on these grounds: "Instead of being oriented, then, toward death and fixity, we are oriented to the cycle of life . . . the notion of material survival by means of the monument no longer represents the impulses of our civilization." Therefore, Mumford decided, "The notion of a modern monument is veritably a contradiction in terms: if it is a monument it is not modern, and if it is modern, it cannot be a monument."[5]

Actually, sculptors began to face this problem at least a century before Mumford's pronouncement. Devoted for so long to exact copies of the antique, sculpture began to suffer from anachronism early in the nineteenth century. The embarrassed debate over Horatio Greenough's monument to Washington, who was represented as an undraped, seated Zeus, shows a conflict between sculptural tradition and contemporary American reality as early as the 1840s. Greenough's *Washington* is a good example of how sculpture had become antique in the pejorative sense, completely dependent as it was on antiquity for its methods of idealization. For this reason, among others, Théophile Gautier, at about the time Greenough was delivering his statue of Washington, declared

---

4. James Wines, "De-Architecturization," in *Esthetics Contemporary,* ed. Richard Kostelanetz (Buffalo: Prometheus Books, 1978), p. 278.

5. Lewis Mumford, *The Culture of Cities* (New York: Harcourt, Brace and World, 1938), p. 438.

sculpture dead in France, comparing the salon entries of 1841 to a group of unclaimed bodies in a morgue.[6]

There are, however, different varieties of respect for the antique, some of them academic and conservative, and some paradoxically modern. The hold of neoclassical style in sculpture is broken partly by appeal to a prior antiquity. The great archaeological–artistic finds of the eighteenth and nineteenth centuries, the Parthenon marbles, the Venus de Milo, the Winged Victory of Samothrace, showed up neoclassical touchstones like the Apollo Belvedere as late, decadent, and Hellenistic. Neoclassical finish came to be associated with a derivative sophistication, while roughness and damage, no matter that it was an effect of long neglect, with the authenticity of great age. Perhaps the only piece to survive this change of taste was the Belvedere Torso, a battered hulk of muscles, which did so primarily because it was half-destroyed.[7] Romantic taste in sculpture, replacing Winckelmann's favorites with fragments and unrestored ruins, is *more* archaic, not less so, than former fashions. This quasi-puritanical appeal to older books of scripture is a feature of many modern movements. The African sculpture crucial to the development of Epstein and Gaudier-Brzeska, as to that of Picasso, seems even more ancient than the Parthenon figures that replaced the Apollo Belvedere. As modern sculpture advances, its taste in antecedents works steadily back in time, and the aura of authenticity that attaches to the antique is not limited to sculpture alone. Pound's "Papyrus," an archaeological fragment from Sappho, represents a taste for the unrestored analogous to that which saved the Winged Victory from being fitted with a pair of arms.

Mumford's definition of modernism as forward-looking is obviously partial and his dichotomy of the modern and the monumental polemical rather than accurate. In fact, monuments are frequently erected not to the past but to the future. The revolution of 1848 and the establishment of a new republic convinced Gautier that he was wrong about sculpture. There was a general rage for

6. Elizabeth Gilmore Holt, ed. *The Triumph of Art for the Public* (Washington, D.C.: Decatur House, 1980), p. 373.

7. The most complete consideration of changing tastes in sculpture is Francis Haskell and Nicholas Penny, *Taste and the Antique: The Lure of Classical Sculpture, 1500–1900* (New Haven: Yale University Press, 1981).

monuments in 1848: "'Statuomania,' as it had already come to be called, was in point of fact considered as an inherent feature of modern urbanism and liberal and secular society." Gautier followed this fad, declaring that Republican art would be "civic, large-scale—even colossal—and nobly collective and anonymous," that is to say, monumental.[8] In this context, monuments are inherently modern, even, according to Godefroy Cavaignac, "revolutionary."[9] In 1870 the process of revolution was commonly compared to that of forging or casting a monumental statue, with Paris as "the furnace in which the fusing metal is bubbling, the burning mould from which will emerge the great statue of Liberty."[10] Clearly, many monuments are counter-revolutionary, with Dürer's 1525 design glorifying Victory over the Peasants as the most lurid example. But monuments are often prospective as well as retrospective. As John Berger says, "Nothing less is involved than the commemoration of the present values of that society addressed to its future. . . . A State can be judged by the future its sculpture sets out to promise it."[11]

Monuments can be associated with revolutions in art as well as in politics. The chief polemical tract of modernism in architecture, Le Corbusier's *Towards a New Architecture,* is full of pictures of ancient monuments. In fact, much of the polemical intent of the book is contained in its juxtaposition of photographs of modern grain elevators and automobile parts with pictures of the Parthenon. Under the heading "Automobiles," Corbusier discusses the Parthenon; a page of photographs of grain elevators contains a text about "the Pyramids, the Temple of Luxor, the Parthenon, the Coliseum, Hadrian's Villa."[12] Obviously, Corbusier borrows the prestige of such monuments so as to attach it to modern implements thought purely functional. But he also sees these great mon-

8. Maurice Agulhon, *Marianne into Battle: Republican Imagery and Symbolism in France, 1789–1880,* tr. Janet Lloyd (Cambridge: Cambridge University Press, 1981), pp. 70 and 71. The statement preceding Gautier's is Agulhon's.

9. Agulhon, pp. 4 and 192. It should be noted that Cavaignac's "Monuments révolutionnaires" was published in 1834, on the heels of a previous wave of statuomania.

10. Agulhon, p. 138.

11. John Berger, *Art and Revolution* (New York: Pantheon, 1969), p. 75.

12. Le Corbusier, *Towards a New Architecture,* tr. Frederick Etchells (New York: Brewer, Warren, and Putnam, 1927), p. 29.

uments of the past as inherently modern: "Phidias would have loved to have lived in this standardized age. . . . His vision would have seen in our epoch the conclusive results of his labours."[13] Corbusier envies in the works of Phidias the most conventional aspects of the monument—its scale, its classical simplicity, its anonymous style—and wants to import these features into modern design. And to the extent that it has been formed by Corbusier's ideas, modernist design is synonymous with, not inimical to, the monumental.

This is, to be fair, an aspect of modernism that Mumford dislikes and disclaims. Mumford opposes the monumental wherever it rears its head: "The deflation of our mechanical monuments, then, is no less imperative than the deflation of our symbolic monuments." He sees and despairs that "the machines and utilities that have helped foster the dense occupancy of cities often take on a monumental character."[14] In this context, "monumental" is an adjective pertaining not to time but to size, another aspect of the monument that seems to Mumford and others anti-modern in that it retains the authoritarian bombast of the past. Mumford pleads against gigantic size because it fossilizes, obstructs, and prevents change. In sculpture, the academic convention that great size is appropriate only for noble or elevating subjects seems to solidify the relationship Mumford sees between sheer size and conventional pieties of the past, with size itself as a reactionary force. This is an equation also suggested by Quatremère de Quincy in comments on the Arc de Triomphe, whose designer, Chalgrin, he commends for understanding that "sufficient solidity is not enough, there must be an over-sufficiency so that people will feel that there is really enough. This over-sufficiency is for them the guarantee of the durability of buildings, and without that guarantee there can be no feeling of grandeur."[15]

Tocqueville's sarcasm at the expense of Washington, D.C., is based on the disparity he saw between the size of the capital and the modesty and youth of the country's achievements, and he names "gigantic splendour in the erection of their public monu-

13. Le Corbusier, p. 145.
14. Mumford, pp. 441 and 440.
15. Elizabeth Gilmore Holt, ed., *From the Classicists to the Impressionists* (New York: New York University Press, 1966), p. 263.

ments" as one of the least attractive characteristics of the new country.[16] But Tocqueville has simply uncovered an aspect of sheer size that was to surface in his own country in 1848. For societies like the United States and France in the mid-nineteenth century, size was progressive, not reactionary at all. It became a commonplace in the 1840s to observe that "bourgeois sculpture was on a small scale while progressive sculpture was grandiose." Thus Théophile Thoré observed in the *Encyclopédie nouvelle:* "Sculpture has sunk to the level of busts and statuettes; in so doing it has lost its sense of social purpose. Its regeneration will no doubt have to wait for signs of a new religion and new politics which will give it new fertility."[17] Gautier in 1848 called for "armies of painters," and huge new buildings designed for "the gigantic life of the future."[18] Clearly, size was one aspect of the monumental that made it most appropriate, at that time at any rate, as a symbol of the future.

Tocqueville also associated colossal size with democratic art because size seemed best to express the collectivity on which the democracy depends. The equation is an obvious one, but what disquieted Tocqueville gave heart to his revolutionary contemporaries. Charles Blanc, who directed the Bureaux des Beaux-Arts under the Second Republic, lamented that under Louis-Philippe "there was room only for art in miniature. Physical greatness was as impossible as moral greatness; space was out of fashion, so was enthusiasm."[19] Blanc was simply expressing in an official capacity the idea common to Thoré, Gautier, and many others of the time: "Clearly, the gigantic is considered revolutionary."[20] The revolutionary aspect of the monumental statue is best expressed in a bizarre project by Charles Duveyrier, who in 1833 planned a Saint-Simonian city whose main public building was to be a gigantic statue of a woman. The folds of her robe were to be promenades, her train an amphitheater, and so on. Here monument and utopia

16. Alexis de Tocqueville, *Democracy in America,* tr. Henry Reeve (New York: Random House, Vintage, 1945), II, 56.

17. Agulhon, p. 58. The preceding statement is Agulhon's.

18. T. J. Clark, *The Absolute Bourgeois: Artists and Politics in France, 1848–1851* (Greenwich, Conn.: New York Graphic Society, 1973), p. 31.

19. Clark, p. 57.

20. Agulhon, p. 58. The Duveyrier project is described on p. 57.

merge, as they often did in the eighteenth century for the visionary French architect Boullée, who could memorialize Newton sufficiently only in a structure suggestive of infinity. Nor is this association of sheer size with a revolutionary utopia limited to the eighteenth or nineteenth century, as Colin Rowe shows in comparing the utopian schemes of Ledoux to the planned cities of Le Corbusier.[21] Colossal size, which stands in the minds of Mumford and Quatremère for permanence, solidity, fidelity to the past, indicates for those of different persuasion change, revolution, future greatness.

The relationship of the monument to time, which might have seemed its clearest and least ambiguous attribute, is in fact troubled and uncertain. Neither its capacity to memorialize nor its size prevents the monument from serving the modern at whatever period it may arise. Nor are these associations with the modern any more necessary than associations with the past. In general, however, modern sculpture has moved closer to rather than further from the monumental. Once the old relationship of the statue to the human body is broken, the main constraint on size is lost, and sculptures can be as large as the sculptor likes. A very common way of criticizing sculpture in the early decades of this century was the size test applied by R. H. Wilenski: if a piece benefited by "enlargement to a colossal scale" then it was a successful piece.[22] Wilenski believed that enlargement displays the essential formal organization of a sculpture and ruthlessly exposes fussiness or unnecessary detail. The drive toward abstraction, toward cleanness of form, is therefore also a drive toward the monumental. Wilenski's test is the basis of the art of Claes Oldenburg, who displays the formal beauty and humor of everyday objects by enlarging them to massive size. Batcolumn in Chicago, a colossal and beautiful Louisville Slugger, is a joke directly out of Towards a New Architecture: the modern, machine-made implement given the size and grandeur of the Parthenon. It is an absolutely modern monument and is anything but pure sport, illustrating as it does one more step in a

21. Colin Rowe, "The Architecture of Utopia," in The Mathematics of the Ideal Villa and Other Essays (Cambridge: MIT Press, 1976) pp. 206–223.

22. R. H. Wilenski, The Meaning of Modern Sculpture (New York: Stokes, 1933), pp. 130 and 163. Pound frequently applies this test to sculpture himself.

history beginning with Boullée and continuing with Corbusier and Wilenski.

Batcolumn bothers people, however, who have no particular reverence for baseball. It runs athwart the second major rule for monuments: that they should make reference to something, that they should assume a more didactic function than most art. As an anonymous writer opined in *The Civil Engineer* of July 1839: "A public monument is a book opened for the perusal of the multitude; unless it declares its meaning fully, plainly, and sensibly, the main use is lost."[23] Not only do modern works of sculpture decline to declare themselves in this fashion, but it is also becoming possible in current criticism to see the monument as the perfect example of nonreferential art. Michel Foucault's whole purpose in *The Archaeology of Knowledge* is to transform what the past thought of as documents, declaring their meaning as clearly as *The Civil Engineer* would like, back into monuments, which represent "discourse in its own volume," opaque, nonallegorical, and nonreferential. These are "silent monuments, inert traces, objects without context, and things left by the past," facts not given in earnest of something else, but existing in their own dumb actuality.[24] Similarly, Roland Barthes is fascinated by the Eiffel Tower because "as a matter of fact, the Tower is *nothing* . . . it participates in no rite, in no cult, not even in Art; you cannot visit the Tower as a museum: there is nothing to see *inside* the Tower."[25] Barthes and Foucault are not being merely fanciful in treating monuments in this way. In fact, the relationship between the statue and its message is fluid and problematical, and it is so easy to strip the message from the sculpture that monuments often function as images of mute mystery.

So closely are statues associated with didactic intent that one of the more common tropes in sculptural appreciation is that of

23. *The Civil Engineer*, July 1839, p. 251, as quoted in Ellen Eve Frank, *Literary Architecture: Essays toward a Tradition: Walter Pater, Gerard Manley Hopkins, Marcel Proust, Henry James* (Berkeley: University of California Press, 1979), p. 254.

24. Michel Foucault, *The Archaeology of Knowledge*, tr. A. M. Sheridan Smith (London: Tavistock, 1972), pp. 138–139 and 7.

25. Roland Barthes, *The Eiffel Tower*, tr. Richard Howard (New York: Hill & Wang, 1979) p. 7.

sculpture as text, even as scripture. The language of *The Civil Engineer* is anticipated by the abbé Barthélemy, who declared of the Capitoline collection in 1756: "This is no longer just a collection: it is the dwelling place of the gods of ancient Rome; the school of the philosophers; a senate composed of the kings of the East. . . . A whole population of statues inhabits the Capitol; it is the great book of antiquarians."[26] The equation could also be reversed, as it was by Galileo, who compared the *Orlando Furioso* to "a regal gallery adorned with a hundred classical statues by the most renowned masters."[27] The great sculpture collections, by embodying the best of the classical past, teach innumerable messages. No statue may indicate a single clear message, but the whole is a kind of encyclopedia, a key to life as it was lived in the perfection of ancient times, and thus a guidebook or even a scripture.

Even the most ordinary, decorative works thus have the capacity to carry a great weight of philosophy, and any statue can become a public monument almost despite itself. In 1794 the revolutionary government of France proclaimed that the Louvre "was the rightful home for such masterpieces of art as could be seized from conquered territory. . . . Certainly, if our victorious armies penetrate into Italy, the removal of the Apollo Belvedere and the Farnese Hercules would be the most brilliant conquest."[28] When the Papal States surrendered to Napoleon in 1796, a hundred works of ancient art were ceded to France, among them busts supposed to be of Lucius Junius Brutus and Marcus Brutus. Obviously, revolutionary France deserved these latter as the home of republicans and tyranicides, but what could possibly justify a similar claim to statues of Apollo and Hercules? These statues, though not didactic monuments in any sense, acquire political importance as symbols of the perfection of ancient institutions, a perfection only resurrected in 1793. In the same way, Hitler laid claim to the *Discobolus,* using it as a symbol of athletic Germany in Leni Riefenstahl's *Olympia.* And Michelangelo's *David,* according to Marianne Doezema, acquired a place in the conflict between

26. Haskell and Penny, p. 64.

27. Francis Haskell, *Patrons and Painters* (New Haven: Yale University Press, 1980), p. 103.

28. Haskell and Penny, p. 108. See pp. 199–200 for Hitler's interest in the *Discobolus*.

Medici and anti-Medici factions in Florence and was stoned as a result.[29]

Such occurrences have a dual significance, however. They show how pervasive and strong is the idea that all sculpture should mean *something* and that that meaning should most probably be political. But at the same time France and Germany's expropriation of perfectly innocent works exposes the extreme tenuousness of the connection between statue and text. The equestrian statue of Marcus Aurelius in Rome has been known at various times in history under the names of Antoninus Pius, Commodus, Constantine, Hadrian, Septimius Severus, Theodoric, Lucius Verus, and simply as a heroic peasant, "il gran villano." The statue probably owes its survival to the idea that it represents Constantine, though modern appreciations of it, including Henry James's, are inseparable from the personality of the great Antonine.[30] The entire assembled sculpture collection of the Western world was subject to such dislocation of identity in the eighteenth and nineteenth centuries, when Roman names were removed under the influence of Winckelmann's idea that the great statues were Greek works, and then again when modern scholarship established that they were probably Roman copies after all. Some of these shifts are certainly trivial, but there is something about a statue and its combination of didactic power with a certain inevitable generality of reference that makes it a kind of wild card in the world of politics. When the Brazilian junta accuses Oscar Niemeyer of forming his monument to Juscelino Kubitschek in the shape of a hammer and sickle while Niemeyer insists he has rendered a palm tree, both the power and the elasticity of the monument as a political symbol are exposed.[31]

In fact, the names and myths attached to statues often endure longer than the stone itself. In *The Great Code*, Northrop Frye observes that "the supremacy of the verbal over the monumental has something about it of the supremacy of life over death."[32] Frye

29. Marianne Doezema, "The Public Monument in Tradition and Transition," in *The Public Monument and Its Audience*, ed. Marianne Doezema and June Hargrove (Cleveland: Cleveland Museum of Art, 1977), p. 11.

30. Haskell and Penny, p. 252. For James's appreciation see *The Art of Travel*, ed. Morton Dauwen Zabel (Garden City, N.Y.: Doubleday, 1958), p. 323.

31. *New York Times*, September 9, 1981.

32. Northrop Frye, *The Great Code* (New York: Harcourt Brace Jovanovich, 1982), p. 200.

stands Horace's famous boast on its head, suggesting that the text might serve the statue as a model of immortality. During the Renaissance, the common method of identifying newly discovered statues was to search through Pliny or Pausanias under the assumption that the sculptures described in their works would inevitably come to light. But Pliny and Pausanias turned out to be more durable than stone and very few of the old attributions are now accepted. It took several centuries for Western scholarship to admit that not a single authenticated work by any of the Greek masters—Phidias, Polycleitus, Myron, Praxiteles—is known to have survived.[33] Sculpture has indeed immortalized these names but only by inserting them in guidebooks and appreciations, and the respect still paid to them is part of an intense nostalgia for a myth of timelessness simply invested in the wrong medium.

Similarly, the monument without a text is weak and defenseless, no more proof against time than an ordinary stone. Mumford senses this, reminding his readers "of the fact that stones that are deserted by the living are even more helpless than life that remains unprotected and unpreserved by stones."[34] The standard image of such desolation is, of course, Ozymandias, abandoned and broken in the desert. But this figure also suggests the appeal of the mute statue to the Romantics and their heirs. Without its text the statue is dumb, but the suspense it endures is more poignant, more powerful even, than communication. Because it is so easily stripped of explanations, the statue is a convenient example of nonreferential art, of language halted and therefore preserved. Revisiting the United States early in this century, Henry James stopped at a head of Aphrodite in the Boston Athenaeum, and ruminated:

The little Aphrodite, with her connexions, her antecedents and references exhibiting the maximum of breakage, is no doubt as *lonely* a jewel as ever strayed out of its setting; yet what does one quickly recognize but that the intrinsic lustre will have, so far as that may be

33. This is a somewhat controversial point. Wilenski develops at some length a polemical proof of it, while Haskell and Penny follow minutely and meticulously as the attributions are changed and stripped off. Their catalogue in *Taste and the Antique* is the best guide to these changing attributions.
34. Mumford, p. 434.

possible, doubled? She has lost her background, the divine creature— has lost her company, and is keeping, in a manner, the strangest; but so far from having lost an iota of her power, she has gained unspeakably more, since what she essentially stands for she stands for alone, rising ineffably to the occasion.[35]

The Aphrodite, like Ozymandias, is in "a desert," but her loneliness and loss of reference double her power. James is dabbling a bit in a paradox appealing to Proust, Ruskin, Pater, and Yeats, and thus central to modern use of the monument in literature. For all its public reference, its redolence of Greece and democracy, the monument is also a powerful image of secrecy, especially since it is so often observed in a setting like that of James's Aphrodite, in the bare lack of context provided by a museum. Where Mumford might find the work weakened by such an installation, James finds it strengthened precisely because the threads of reference and communication are broken, for the same reason that Valéry finds the power of words increased when their purpose as communication is thwarted. Pater captures this paradox perfectly in praising the "inexpressive expression" of a figure by Myron, which seems to indicate so much, but of such an indefinable nature that it can never be exhausted.[36]

The paradox also affects modern ideas about the place of sculpture in history as an index of culture. Neoclassical art history made sculpture one of the most associational of the arts. For Winckelmann, a good deal of the value of all sculpture was due to association, since he felt that the artistic achievements of Greece were inseparable from her political institutions, her geography, even her climate. Winckelmann indulged in a great deal of circular reasoning, arguing that perfection in sculpture comes only from a convergence of political and physical facts in a distinct period of history, then using purely subjective standards of beauty to place works in this period, thus reinforcing his original estimate of its fertility for genius. His was the first suggestion that antique sculpture be

35. Henry James, *The American Scene* (Bloomington: Indiana University Press, 1968), p. 253.

36. Walter Pater, *Greek Studies* (London, 1895; rpt. Oxford: Blackwell; New York: Johnson Reprint, 1967), p. 289. All further references to this work will appear in the text, accompanied by the abbreviation *GS*.

arranged in some kind of historical order so that different styles could represent not just artistic variations but the rise and fall of whole civilizations. It is partly due to Winckelmann that so many cultural histories rely on sculpture as a major category of evidence, using it as a social diagnostic, an unfailing key to the health of the society that produced it. Ruskin says of the stones used in building that they "write various legends, never untrue, of the former political state of the mountain kingdom to which they belonged, of its infirmities and fortitudes, convulsions and consolidations, from the beginning of time."[37]

Monuments are intriguing, in this analysis, because they are microcosmic summations of entire cultures. Yeats follows both Ruskin and Spengler when he makes sculpture his primary symptom of historical change in the "Dove or Swan" section of *A Vision,* and Pound repeats Ruskin's statement a dozen different times, most notably in the Usura Canto.[38] But Winckelmann's view of artistic history was defunct by the time Pound repeated it, and both Pound and Yeats disagreed with the precise artistic evaluations on which it rested. When pure mechanical representation is no longer the goal of art, history can hardly be seen as the progress of mechanical ability toward a representational end. But it seems possible for certain writers to accept Winckelmann's graph of culture while seeing each of its various installments not as associational but as absolute in its value. Pater follows both Winckelmann and Hegel in assigning each of the arts to a grand period of world history, sculpture going to the Greeks: "Sculpture corresponds to the unperplexed, emphatic outlines of Hellenic humanism; painting to the mystic depth and intricacy of the middle age; music and poetry have their fortune in the modern world."[39] At the same time that he finds art indicative of whole civilizations, sculpture of Greek life particularly, he commends art that is not "self analytical," that remains mysterious and aloof and therefore absolute.

37. This statement, quoted by Proust, is requoted by Ellen Eve Frank, p. 146. For Winckelmann's role in historical scholarship, see Haskell and Penny, pp. 103–105.

38. For nineteenth-century examples of this practice relevant to Yeats, see Richard Jenkyns, *The Victorians and Ancient Greece* (Cambridge: Harvard University Press, 1980), p. 75.

39. Walter Pater, *The Renaissance,* ed. Donald L. Hill (Berkeley: University of California Press, 1980), p. 75. All further references to this work will appear in the text, accompanied by the abbreviation *R.*

The basis of Pater's version of art history is contained in his attempt to preserve the associationalism behind Winckelmann's periodization while arguing that truly successful art contains all its own value. The result is analysis of nonreferential works of art that refer to whole civilizations in which nonreferential art was a way of life. The versions of art history in the works of Yeats and Pound are based on the same paradox, which is supportable only because sculpture is so ambiguous itself.

These versions of history begin to touch on the last and most important attribute of the monument, the one most often found lacking in contemporary outdoor sculpture, its public nature. Winckelmann's method of periodization presupposes a golden age, an age propitious for great art because artistic success was valued both by the people and by political institutions. The catalogue of the Salon of 1795 maintained that the esteem for art was so general in Greece that when a monument was planned "men and women of all classes hurried to show themselves unveiled to the sculptors and were glorified if they were chosen as models for masterpieces which should surpass those owned by rival cities."[40] In this myth all Greek art works are public monuments because respect for art is one of the chief characteristics of the Greek state and people.

Versions of this myth are at the heart of nineteenth-century academic practice in sculpture, and of neoclassical aesthetics in general. Perhaps the neatest accomplishment of the academic tradition is its replacement of nature by an anthology of antique statues, on the theory that nature is portrayed more clearly and perfectly there than in the raw. Stories like that in the 1795 Salon catalogue underlie this idea, which holds basically that the Greeks, having the most beautiful bodies to choose from and the freest opportunities for choice, have already completed the process of selection from nature indispensable to art. Antique statues are the democratic representatives of nature. Copying such works and displaying the copies opened up the possibility, under academic dogma, of recreating the perfect civic system they represent.[41] Public monu-

40. Holt, *Triumph of Art for the Public*, p. 48.
41. In *Idea,* tr. Joseph J. S. Peale (Columbia: University of South Carolina Press, 1968), Erwin Panofsky describes the genesis of this idea in the aesthetics of G. P. Bellori, p. 71. See Charles W. Millard, "Sculpture and Theory in Nineteenth Century France," *Journal of Aesthetics and Art Criticism,* 34 (1975), 15–20, for a summation of the academic debt to Winckelmann and for the idea that copying ancient works might perfect contemporary institutions.

ments thus become a kind of political nostrum as well as the highest form of art, a pure expression of mankind as a whole.

The prestige of the Greeks is such that this aspect of academic dogma survives the death of neoclassicism and the discrediting of academic art. Oscar Wilde, for example, begins "The Critic as Artist" with Ernest's offer of a Greek statue as example of a perfect relationship between art and audience: "The sculptor hewed from the marble block the great white-limbed Hermes that slept within it. The waxers and gilders of images gave tone and texture to the statue, and the world, when it saw it, worshipped and was dumb."[42] Another version of this myth is the popular story given currency by Winckelmann that Greek women always slept with a beautiful statue nearby so as to conceive beautiful children. This fable is for Wilde, Pater, and Yeats a central myth of the preeminence of art in perfect societies.

Why should this one aspect of a discredited tradition persist, often in oddly distorted forms, in the works of artists utterly opposed to neoclassicism? Clearly, Wilde uses the myth to argue waggishly that the estranged status of the artist in Victorian England is the fault of society, which has become unaccountably unwilling to make monuments of its statues. Belief in these golden ages also confesses an uneasiness about the difference from society at large that writers like Wilde insist on for themselves. Arguing against any idea that this is a myth of pure aggrandizement, of megalomaniacs seeking the power they lack, is the repeated emphasis on anonymity as one of the chief features of the best monuments. The anonymous Gothic workman is, of course, one of the clichés of the nineteenth century. Yeats's Byzantium is peopled by anonymous workers in mosaic and gold, and Gautier insists "the great works of art are almost all collective. No one knows the names of those who built and chiselled the cathedrals."[43] There is certainly nothing remarkable in Gautier's statement except the fact that it was made by the writer who stands at the very beginning of the Art-for-Art's-sake idea. Nor is this simply a fantasy of writers. The search for an anonymous visual style is, as Jack Burnham

42. Oscar Wilde, "The Critic as Artist," *Complete Works of Oscar Wilde* (Garden City, N.Y.: Doubleday, Page, 1923), v, 117–118. For the statue in the bed-chamber, see Chapter 3 below.
43. Quoted in Clark, p. 31.

points out, general among visual artists early in this century.[44] Jacob Epstein, for one, admired African sculpture for exactly the same reason Gautier admired the cathedrals and Wilde Greek monuments: because it is collective and anonymous in its style.[45] In modernist dogma, the anonymous engineer replaces the anonymous Gothic craftsman, and the goal of industrial standardization becomes the recovery of what Hermann Muthesius called in 1914 the "universal importance" enjoyed by the arts "in ages of harmonious civilization."[46] The myth of the public monument has an amazing staying power, growing even stronger in an era when artists defend their individual prerogatives from any interference, especially from the public.

Yet the very location of these collective, anonymous monuments in the past allows for certain evasions. The approach to public concerns by way of a golden age allows writers to handle civic subjects without being contemporary, that is, without stooping to journalism. They can be "public" without any overt appeal to an actual, living, reading public. At the same time, the evocation of an anonymous style has a way of placing art beyond intention, of giving it some of the necessity of a natural force. The anonymous style is beyond style itself since it is not really a willed creation or a response to individual whim but an expression of certain immutable laws, as inevitable as the polygons in a honeycomb. Thus Pater sees the genius of Greek art as a kind of anti-style, both collective and general, that "purges from the individual all that belongs only to him, all the accidents, the feelings and actions of the special moment" (*R,* p. 51). Greek art, by showing the "supreme types of humanity" frees art from "the commonness of the world" (*R,* p. 172). It may be utterly collective and cooperative, and it may involve the will of even the most ordinary citizen, but the goal of the anonymous style is to put art above accident, idiosyncrasy, and the everyday.

Pater's idealism is revealing because it shows how the monu-

44. Jack Burnham, *Beyond Modern Sculpture* (New York: Braziller, 1968), pp. 114–115.

45. Jacob Epstein, *The Sculptor Speaks* (told to Arnold J. Haskell) (London: Heinemann, 1931), p. 89.

46. Quoted in Nikolaus Pevsner, *Pioneers of Modern Design* (Harmondsworth: Penguin, 1960), p. 37.

ment erected by the perfect Greek state has a way of becoming an absolute form of art, an art separate from, not indicative of, human intention. More modern writers and artists carry this association even further. In 1925, Jane Heap, coeditor of the *Little Review,* commended the anonymous style as expressed in the engineering of modern machinery: "The artist works with definite plastic laws. He knows that his work will have lasting value only if he consciously creates forms which embody the constant and unvarying laws of the universe."[47] The language of science and technology has been called in, but the effect is the same, to grant necessity, inevitability of an unearthly kind, to the work of art. One source of such language is Le Corbusier, who shows in *Towards a New Architecture* how the great anonymous monuments of the past achieve a pure and eternal geometry. Mies van der Rohe defines a new kind of monument when he calls modern architecture "the will of the epoch translated into space."[48] The will of the epoch, the collective, anonymous will of a time, is translated immediately and naturally, it is presumed, without the intervention of personalities, into a building. As Colin Rowe observes, "Form became now, not the result of choice, but an imperious necessity of evolution or an unavoidable effect of social change; and, in this way, the architect could depersonalize his taste, and then interpret it afresh as a prophetic intuition."[49] In other words, modern architecture seeks to be monumental, in the sense intended by the Salon catalogue of 1795. The result is not, however, something representative of the body politic but rather an expression of laws above and beyond any collection of people. The art that results is an absolute art, obeying its own laws, the laws of form and beauty, and responding to nothing outside itself. Anonymity severs form from human reference as it removes it from human hands so that the myth of the Greek polis, as powerful for Corbusier as it is for Winckelmann, issues in an art theory of a fundamentally Symbolist nature.

Thus even the most straightforward aspect of the public monument, its public nature, can be equivocal and ambiguous. This is

47. Jane Heap, "Machine-Age Exposition," in *The Little Review Anthology,* ed. Margaret Anderson (New York: Hermitage House, 1953), p. 342.
48. Rowe, p. 126.
49. Rowe, p. 127.

true even of conventional works executed in the heyday of the heroic monument. Friedrich Gilly's design for a shrine-monument commemorating Frederick the Great, designed in the 1790s, served as model for many later constructions, some of which, like the monument to Victor Emmanuel II in Rome, have become synonymous with retrograde bad taste. But even Gilly showed some unease about the exact status of his work in the city of its installation, a dilemma that is apparent in his description of the intended site. The shrine will be placed in a frequented, popular spot, at the intersection of certain major streets, and will be provided with promenades and amenities, yet it is also "removed from the bustle of business establishments," a removal to be desired because it protects the shrine from being "desecrated through profane and scandalous scenes."[50] The difficulty Gilly faced was how to make his monument central to the life of the city and yet apart from it. The spot was to be both popular and sacred, crowded and empty. The dual imperatives, that the ideals Frederick represented to Gilly live at the center of society and that they yet retain the difference from ordinary life that constitutes the ideal, can never quite be harmonized, only compromised.

The situation of the modern monument, therefore, simply exacerbates a situation as old as the monument itself. Outdoor sculpture is such a potent issue in the current art world because it exemplifies one of the most basic aspirations of modern art: to elude the museum and all the sanctity and privilege it represents.[51] Placing a piece of sculpture at a public intersection is a way of finally obliterating the barriers between the art object and the non-artistic world. And yet, even such works, sitting astride everyday life, bring with them some of the aura of the museum and an inescapable reminiscence of Gilly's taste for the exclusive. Richard Serra, whose public works have caused controversy in a number of cities, describes the function of one of his more recent pieces, "Tilted Arc," at the Javits Federal Building in New York, in resolutely anti-artistic terms. The piece, a tall, slightly curved wall of Cor-Ten steel 120 feet long, has as its objective "dislocating the

50. Holt, *From the Classicists to the Impressionists,* p. 260.

51. This desire has been described in a number of recent articles by Calvin Tompkins in *The New Yorker*. See, for example, "The Natural Problem," March 29, 1982, and "The Urban Capacity," April 5, 1982.

decorative function of the plaza" and "actively bringing people into a sculptural context."[52] Serra's work is supposed to circumvent the architect's desire to have a large, pretty plaza devoid of people, a sacred space admirable for its emptiness. The wall is a truly public monument because its purpose is to make people consider and inhabit a common space in an artistic way. Serra accomplishes this aim, however, by striking directly across the space with a tall steel wall, which makes crossing the plaza a great deal more difficult. It could therefore be argued that he has simply substituted one form of decorativeness for another, because the sculpture makes the plaza itself into a work of art purely by removing it from use, by making simple passage across it impossible. Despite his desire to bring people into the art work and to remove the work itself from the decorative context of the museum, Serra succumbs to a contradiction essentially identical to Gilly's.

These contradictions are pushed to their ridiculous extreme in another contemporary work situated in New York, this one by Dennis Oppenheim, entitled "Protection Piece." The installation comprised twelve chained police dogs who prevented, for a short period of time, the use of a particular plot of land in Battery Park. Oppenheim chose a plot frequented by park-users to make the point more poignant. He describes the piece as "infecting the land with an air of preciousness, yet there was nothing there. . . . The piece is really about pure concentration, protection, making by keeping away."[53] "Protection Piece" is the purest of art works because it includes nothing but a barrier; it is a monument created by forcing people off the site. As Oppenheim says, the art is made by keeping away, the aura created by demarking and forbidding. This seems an anti-monument, the least public monument of all, but in fact Oppenheim has ludicrously pushed to its limit one aspect of Gilly's dilemma. Nothing vulgar will ever disturb the precincts of this shrine. Nothing more than a boundary is needed to make this work of art because art is created where anything is removed from use. The public monument, always a difficult prop-

52. Richard Serra, as quoted by Grace Glueck, "Serra Work Stirs Downtown Protest," *New York Times,* September 25, 1981.
53. Wines, p. 276.

osition, becomes even more so when art is defined by its distance from all who might see or use it.

The ambiguous, almost contradictory, ambitions shared by artists as different as Friedrich Gilly and Dennis Oppenheim also characterize the literary monuments of some of the twentieth century's greatest poets. W. B. Yeats, Ezra Pound, and Wallace Stevens are modern heirs of a tradition Richard Stein describes in *The Ritual of Interpretation*. Stein considers the Victorian genre of literature about art, literature whose subject is the aesthetic impulse and whose call is to a salvation found in the appreciation of great art. Visual art, in Stein's analysis of Ruskin, Pater, and Rossetti, serves to mediate between the private and the public, and art criticism tries to teach a large audience how to experience moments of intense vision that seem personal in nature. As Stein says, the external work of art "helps to clarify the problematic relation of artist and audience which haunts Romantic and post-Romantic writers. The external artifact mediates between the writer interpreting it and his audience, creating a middle ground on which the most elusive personal vision can become accessible and convincing."[54] Public monuments are perhaps the most perfect example of Stein's rule. Because of their special status they can perform the mediation between poet and audience even more efficiently than other art works. What seems difficult and ambiguous in the definition of the monument is in fact its greatest strength because the ambiguity allows the monument to be dual, to be both an idiosyncratic and secretive talisman and a public inspiration. When Yeats writes of the statue of Cuchulain in the Dublin Post Office, or Pound of the Tempio Malatestiano, or Stevens of a statue in the park, they are practicing the ritual Stein describes in an even more complex way than did Ruskin in a Gothic cathedral or Pater before a Greek statue.

The more overtly public nature of the art works used by these poets helps to advance a political dream also shared with the late Victorians. As Stein says, artistic appreciation serves where religious and political ideas once stood in making possible "a com-

54. Richard L. Stein, *The Ritual of Interpretation: The Fine Arts as Literature in Ruskin, Rossetti, and Pater* (Cambridge: Harvard University Press, 1975), p. 11.

munity of belief."[55] The public monument both advances and symbolizes this community. "The Statues" is both a call to Ireland to gather around its heroic arts and a recipe for an art of political salvation. *The Cantos* constitutes an anthology, a storehouse of valuable art worthy of worship, and a call to worship. There is, as Stein suggests, an almost inevitable relationship between inter-art analogies and social utopianism. When Yeats, Pound, and Stevens assimilate the visual arts to the literary and try to create great unified and unifying monuments, they express their hopes for a unified culture. The monument is the structure made to house both art and society, where each preserves the other in the repetition of worship.

This cultural utopianism is also served by the monument's peculiar status in time. The literature of art, as Stein defines it, preaches a future based on appreciation of the art of the past. The monument is a perfect embodiment of this mediation between future and past and as such plays an important part in the revolutionary antiquarianism of poets like Yeats and Pound. Yeats evades contemporary rhetoric by preaching through stories from the past. The monument is a favorite symbol of his not just because he feels the past is more attractive, but because heroic legend is both distant and near, relevant to the Troubles and yet abstract and formal. Pound is almost a perfect parallel to the French revolutionaries of the nineteenth century who tried to forecast the society of the future by careful monumentalization of the past, "remembering," as he says, "that a 'memorial' should speak not to the present but the future."[56] In both cases, the monument, as a work of art with a special relationship to time, becomes an especially efficient example of the literature of art.

Most important of all, however, is the monument's odd status as both didactic and nonreferential. For every modern writer with aspirations to social relevance, the prevailing horror of propaganda requires either compromise or dishonesty. Whether these aspirations are quite precise, as Pound's were, or simply the product of anxious concern, as with Stevens, they must clash with the almost

55. Stein, p. 32.
56. Ezra Pound, *Ezra Pound and the Visual Arts,* ed. Harriet Zinnes (New York: New Directions, 1980), p. 94. All further references to this work appear in the text.

absolute taboo against the polemic. Monuments, despite their reputation, offer a possible compromise. Didactic and yet abstract, they present the alluring possibility of a polemic without rhetoric. Simply as works of visual art, they seem to neutralize the tendency of language to become abstract. As monoliths they represent the concrete at its least compromised. Yet because of their status in culture, they represent a splendid hybrid: nonreferential art with a message. Therefore the monument represents these poets' hopes for a public art faithful to the modernist revolution. Their claim is that modernist prohibitions against rhetoric make monuments more durable, not less so, but the vacillations of their works make the difficulty of the project clear. That it issues in some of the greatest work of Yeats, Pound, Stevens, and Robert Lowell indicates the value of the project and the depth of the hope behind it— that aesthetic appreciation of a certain intensity can function in a public way as the social cement once offered by belief.

PART

−I−

W. B. Yeats

CHAPTER

—I—

The Paradox of the Mausoleum

I

One of Yeats's earliest lyrics is about a room full of statues, and his mature poetry is often decorated with similar figures in marble or bronze. Sculpture is an important feature of all his Cities of Art, the tool of historical description in *A Vision,* and the metaphor he uses over and over for the beauty of Maud Gonne. It is a central metaphor in such poems as "Michael Robartes and the Dancer," "Nineteen Hundred and Nineteen," "Meditations in Time of Civil War," "Among School Children," "Byzantium," "The Statues," and "A Bronze Head," to name only the most prominent examples. But sculpture has an ambiguous significance in Yeats's work, especially in its monumental aspect, because of the peculiar quasi-public nature of the art. Monuments are, in Yeats's poetry, both central and secretive, and they serve both to solidify society, as in "The Statues," and to mock it, as in "Among School Children." This ambiguity is not an accidental effect. Sculpture is so common a metaphor in Yeats's work precisely because of its ambiguous nature, because it is the art of public memorials and at the same time the one whose subject matter is almost entirely composed of isolated, musing individuals. The nature of the art itself and the tradition of criticism associated with it offer Yeats the opportunity to resolve a central difficulty in his aspirations for poetry.

The tactile and visual qualities evoked in Yeats's earliest poetry are primarily soft ones: pallor, mistiness, dimness. Pound's famous metaphorical figure, "dim lands of peace," may not have come from Yeats, but it uses two of the early Yeats's favorite words, and it describes the locale of most of the early poems. In the midst of this dim peace, however, stands a figure whose tactile qualities are quite hard and definite, the statue that appears in *The Island of Statues, The Wanderings of Oisin,* and some of Yeats's most important descriptions of his ideal art. One of Yeats's very first poems portrays a group of statues as the indigenous population of a dim land of peace:

> I've built a dreaming palace
>> With stones from out the old
> And singing days, within their graves
>> Now lying calm and cold.
>
> Of the dreamland marble
>> Are all the silent walls
> That grimly stand, a phantom band
>> About the Phantom halls.
>
> There among the pillars
>> Are many statues fair
> Made of the dreamland marble
>> Cut by the dreamer's care.
>
> And there I see a statue
>> Among the maids of old
> On either hand, a goodly band
>> So calmly wise and cold.

This is the prefatory poem to the playlet now included in the *Variorum Plays* as *Time and the Witch Vivien,* which is dated January 8, 1884, when Yeats was eighteen.[1] The basic metaphor of "dreamland marble" is an odd one, because it combines the

---

1. *The Variorum Edition of the Plays of W. B. Yeats,* ed. Russell K. Alspach (London: Macmillan, 1966), pp. 1279–1281. The *Variorum* does not print the prefatory poem, which is found in Richard Ellmann, *Yeats: The Man and the Masks* (New York: Macmillan, 1948), pp. 33–34, and reprinted here by permission of the Estate of William Butler Yeats.

vagueness and evanescence of dreams with the solidity of stone. Pater complains about the "hard realism" of sculpture, the inescapable fact that a statue represents the body more completely in space than any other art form, but Yeats uses marble as if it were cloud, or the light pearl embellished so lavishly on his early poems (*R*, p. 51).

Obviously, ancient marble is a material whose romantic associations are quite different from its physical attributes. The ancient statues are dreamlike because they are calm, cold, and enigmatically wise. The dreamer has certain unspecified cares, and because of these he cuts in marble a world beyond care, not without it, because there is something slightly sad about the statues, but removed from care because it is removed from time. There is a slight ambiguity in the poet's attitude toward the ancient world, which seems to have been a "singing" one, but whose denizens are silent and far from gay. The poet's dream is not really of the old world, in any case, but of figures from that world who now inhabit a moment of timelessness, the moment of the grave. They achieve the attributes of calm and coldness by their distance from their rightful time and all the complications of it and in this way become eternal, cheating death by having nothing to do with life. Calmness, coldness, and wisdom are the qualities an adolescent most aspires to in the confusion of adolescent life, and marble is a version of his own skin with all the imperfections and nerve ends removed.

The statues inhabit the "one dead, deathless hour" carved "in ivory or in ebony" to which Rossetti consecrates himself in the prefatory sonnet to *The House of Life*.[2] The resemblance between Rossetti's sculptural metaphor and Yeats's suggests that more than the adolescent imagination is at work in his poem. In fact, the statue was a favorite subject of the Pre-Raphaelites. The Pygmalion story enjoyed a tremendous vogue in the late Victorian period, as Richard Jenkyns shows, listing Thomas Woolner's twelve-book poem on the subject, as well as the series of paintings by Burne-Jones, and G. F. Watts's "The Wife of Pygmalion." A late example of this mode is Olive Custance's insipid "The White

---

2. Dante Gabriel Rossetti, *The House of Life*, ed. Paull Franklin Baum (Cambridge: Harvard University Press, 1928), p. 59.

Statue": "I love you, silent statue . . . To press warm lips against your cold mouth."[3] Custance's fervor does expose one of the basic ambiguities in Victorian handlings of the Pygmalion story: it is Pygmalion in reverse. There is very little difference between the woman in the last panel of Burne-Jones's series and the statue of the first, and, in fact, the statue closely resembles Burne-Jones's other women even before its transformation. The story is popular not because of a desire to create full-blooded women out of stone but because of a desire to find women with the finish of sculpture. Jenkyns describes the vogue as an example of Victorian sublimation, sin falling away from desire as flesh becomes stone. But the true motive, and what attracts the young Yeats to the subject, is that the figure solves all the complications of life by presenting a calm, cold, and wise ideal before which the artist can fall. The statue is a sexual image of equal purity and power, and it solves the problem of sex not so much by avoiding flesh as by freeing the male from his own will, by reducing him to a celebrant. Neither sin nor frustration nor disappointing conquest is possible when the goal is not consummation but worship, and love can never come to an end when it is suspended at the first moment of attraction. The statue brings freedom from desire, and thus the calmness, coldness, and wisdom that are its attributes.

One of the best expressions of this ideal, as it affects the appreciation of art, is Pater's *The Renaissance,* which Yeats may have read as early as his seventeenth year.[4] Discussions of sculpture occupy a very large part of the articles collected to form *The Renaissance,* and its appeal for Pater rests largely on its freedom from complication: "That white light, purged from the angry, blood-like stains of action and passion, reveals, not what is accidental in man, but the tranquil godship in him, as opposed to the restless accidents of life. The art of sculpture records the first naive, unperplexed recognition of man by himself . . ." (p. 170). Freedom from passion, from restlessness, from perplexity are just what the dreamer wants when he carves in dreamland marble. "This serenity is, perhaps, in great measure, a negative quality: it is the absence of any sense of want, or corruption, or shame" (p. 176).

3. Jenkyns, pp. 141–144. Custance's poem is quoted in *Decadence and the 90s,* ed. Ian Fletcher (London: Arnold, 1979), p. 29.
4. Ellmann, *Yeats: The Man and the Masks,* p. 136.

"Unperplexed" is a word Pater returns to, but he also sees the essentially negative nature of the desire to be free of perplexity and approves completely of it only when the desire has become strong enough to achieve "passionate coldness" (p. 183), a term the mature Yeats was very fond of.

In this early poem, though, there is none of the very slight sense of doubt that creeps into Pater's hymns to Greek sculpture. In 1884, Yeats is closer to the mood of Morris, whose early prose romances "The Story of the Unknown Church" and "The Hollow Land" equate sculptured figures with a promised land of peace. At the end of their long search, the hero and the heroine of the latter work find the gates of the Hollow Land and on them two sculptured figures "like faces we had seen or half seen in some dream long and long and long ago." The faces are in fact their own, freed of all the intricacies they lay aside to enter the Hollow Land.[5]

II

The exact significance of statues to late Victorians whose work Yeats admired is pertinent because the statue continues to appear in Yeats's juvenilia and in important pronouncements showing his early attitude toward poetry. A fragment from the tailpiece to *The Island of Statues,* also written in 1884, is now the first of Yeats's collected poems. The whole play is a much more sophisticated version of the dreamland of *Time and the Witch Vivien* and suggests some of the basic difficulties Yeats was to face in later poems. *The Island of Statues* is set in Arcady, that land of stereotype where low-born bumpkins jostle the romances of noble lovers. In this case, Almintor, a hunter, determines to win the love of Naschina, a shepherdess. To do so, he must prove his intrepidity by crossing to an island where groweth "the goblin flower of joy."[6] Those who choose the wrong flower, however, are turned into statues, a

---

5. William Morris, *Early Romances* (London: Dent, 1973), p. 271.

6. W. B. Yeats, *The Poems,* ed. Richard Finneran (New York: Macmillan, 1983), p. 461. All further references to the poetry of Yeats are to this edition and appear in the text with the abbreviation *P*.

forest of which now woods the island. All this is the work of an Enchantress, who presides over the island until such time as it is visited by one for whom another person will willingly die. Almintor chooses incorrectly and stiffens up, to be saved by Naschina, whose power over the Enchantress is ratified when one of the comic pawns of Arcady dies for her sake.

The plot summary does not seem to offer a very promising field, but there is some interest in Yeats's deliberately ambiguous handling of the statues. The island, more Arcadian than Arcady, owes its existence, Yeats says, to Spenser and Shelley and perhaps Jonson. As he says in the *Autobiography*, on Spenser's islands "certain qualities of beauty, certain forms of sensuous loveliness were separated from all the general purposes of life . . . ."[7] This is the kind of island wished for in "The White Birds," "Where Time would surely forget us, and Sorrow come near us no more" (*P*, p. 42). It is appropriate that the island should be studded with statues, which represent in Morris the land of enchantment and in Pater and Rossetti freedom from time and sorrow. The statues are not goddesses, however, but men in love, who, having made a single misstep in their search for the "goblin flower of joy," are immobilized.

Underneath the fairy-tale trappings of flower and lady love is a different story altogether, in which the island represents not a threat to happiness or a place to win one's love but a solution to baffled passion. The Enchantress attempts to seduce Naschina, who is disguised as a boy, with a promise:

> Here no loves wane and wither,
> Where dream-fed passion is and peace encloses,
> Where revel of foxglove is and revel of roses.
> . . . O whither, whither, whither
> Wilt roam away from this rich island rest?
> [*P*, p. 475]

The word "peace" figures largely in her blandishments, signifying

7. W. B. Yeats, *Essays and Introductions* (New York: Macmillan, 1961), pp. 3 and 570, and *The Autobiography* (New York: Macmillan, 1953), p. 188. All further references to these works appear in the text, with the former designated by the abbreviation *EI* and the latter by *A*.

that what draws men to the island and holds them is less desire to win love than to be free of it. As a statue, one is at peace, at rest, fed on dreams that never die. It is helpful to recall a later poem, "The Secret Rose," in which those who find the *right* flower

> dwell beyond the stir
> And tumult of defeated dreams; and deep
> Among pale eyelids, heavy with the sleep
> Men have named beauty.
>
> [*P*, p. 69]

The Enchantress is in fact the first of those women of the Sidhe who seduce mankind into throwing everything away for a dream. And as Richard Ellmann says in his comments on "The Song of the Happy Shepherd," Yeats sustains a deep ambiguity about dreams, which on one hand are held out as the only good and on the other disparaged as the stuff of an insubstantial world.[8]

This ambiguous attitude toward dreams contributes to the rather odd ending of *The Island of Statues*. Though Naschina frees all the men from their paralysis by vanquishing the Enchantress, she does not free them from the island. Most have been statues so long that the lovers they set out to win have died. They are in an oddly posthumous position that seems to have had a fascination for Yeats, whose father once painted a scene of an old beggar returned to the town of his birth to find a statue of himself (*A*, p. 50). The men are in the anachronistic position Oisin is in after his three hundred years of wandering from island to island, and their solution is simply to stay on the island. Though failures in the quest, they have achieved a kind of immortality through failure and have outlived Ulysses, Aeneas, and even Pan. They are as ancient as Greek statues and curiously sexless, no less in subjection to Naschina, who becomes their queen, than they were to the Enchantress. Edward Engelberg argues that Naschina brings sin and reality to the island, but Almintor's last words describe it as a "charmed ring," and no island can be as sinful as the real world if it contains only a single woman and not many men.[9] Just as they

8. Ellman, *Yeats: The Man and the Masks*, p. 38.

9. Edward Engelberg, "'He Too Was in Arcadia': Yeats and the Paradox of the Fortunate Fall," in *In Excited Reverie*, ed. A. N. Jeffares and K. G. W. Cross (New York: St. Martin's, 1965), pp. 69–82.

have been forgotten by their own time, the men seem to have forgotten the original motives that took them to the island and evince no desire, no aspiration, no curiosity, none of the restlessness that might take them from it again. In other words, they have achieved in life the state of the dreamer in Yeats's early poem, slightly sad, but calm and wise and cold.

The situation of the men on the island betrays one of the fascinations of the statue for Yeats: its removal in time. The men are physically young, with the statue's appearance of eternal youth, yet they are in actuality quite ancient and have all the sad wisdom of age. They very much resemble the persona Yeats creates for himself in early lyrics such as "He Thinks of His Past Greatness When a Part of the Constellations of Heaven": "I have drunk ale from the Country of the Young / And weep because I know all things now." They resemble even more the persona he creates for the woman of his early lyrics:

> White woman that passion has worn
> As the tide wears the dove-gray sands,
> And with heart more old than the horn
> That is brimmed from the pale fire of time:
> White woman with numberless dreams . . . .
>
> [P, p. 63]

Beauty is both white and worn, perfect and distressed, young and old. Both white woman and poet seem made of the dreamland marble that is attractive because it is cooler, smoother, and more enduring than flesh. Yet such beauty must always exist in a temple or on an island, because one of its basic attributes is removal from the present. Exile is a sad condition but a soothing one as well; one has learned one's lesson about the impossibility of present joy, and one retires to the island. The young poet gains the perspective and stillness of age without losing the purity of youth through an experience that brings wisdom but not corruption. Perplexity is solved but not at the cost of physical decrepitude. The statue is attractive, and becomes a symbol of the kind of beauty favored by the early Yeats, because it solves all the convoluted discords of youth without sacrificing its physical beauty. By having nothing to do with life, poet and beloved cheat death and occupy the "one dead, deathless hour" forever.

But even at the age of nineteen Yeats was aware of the irony of cheating death by rushing past it into posthumous contentment. When the moon rises over the final tableau of *The Island of Statues,* Naschina casts no shadow. She has lost her earthly existence and has taken the place of the Enchantress. Furthermore, she has herself become a statue in a rather roundabout way. In leaving Arcady for the island, she tells Antonio, "if I return no more, / Then bid them raise my statue on the shore. . . . A white, dumb thing of tears" (*P*, p. 470). It violates the fiction of the play to assume that obedient Arcadians have erected this statue, believing that Naschina has failed, but such a violation does point out what is either a subtlety in Yeats's presentation or a flaw in the play's construction. For it is possible that while Naschina is the only human being on an island of former statues she is also the only statue in an Arcady of human beings. The men become statues by failing in their quests for joy, but Naschina may have become one by succeeding. The Arcadians have been instructed to come and sit before this statue to "tell sad histories, till their eyes / All swim with tears" (*P*, p. 470), and the possibility that they are doing so at the very moment Naschina loses her shadow exposes the loss she incurs in the human world. By staying on the island she removes herself from the midst of men, leaving behind a stone image of herself like a voodoo fetish, an image that coexists with her though it should signify her death. If she were ever to return to Arcady she would, like the old beggar in J. B. Yeats's painting, have the unpleasant experience of seeing herself commemorated in stone.

Such a reading of the play depends rather too much on filling gaps most probably left by haste or carelessness. But the situation recurs in *The Wanderings of Oisin* in a way that makes the disadvantages of life as a statue perfectly plain. Published in 1889 and Yeats's first public success, *The Wanderings of Oisin* has three islands, each removed from "the general purposes of life," two of which are populated by statues. The appeal of the islands, the appeal Niamh uses to spirit Oisin away from the Fenians, is that of "never-anxious sleep" where

> men have heaped no burial-mounds,
> And the days pass by like a wayward tune,
> Where broken faith has never been known,

And the blushes of first love never have flown. . . .

[*P,* p. 357]

Niamh herself is white, pale, and as peaceful as the white woman of the lyrics. Though the second island, that of Victories, contains a temple full of statues, the third, the Island of Forgetfulness, is truly the Island of Statues. There the "huge white creatures" are "weary with passions that faded when the seven-fold seas were young"; and yet weariness brings peace, and Oisin lies down for a century of it. The poignance of the poem, however, comes when Oisin wants to return to the Fenians and finds himself three hundred years out of step, returned to find himself a purely commemorative figure as if seeing his own statue in the square. The cost of the dream-life of statues is separation from the life of one's people, as if one could go to the island only at the price of becoming a stiff marble figure on the mainland. Though still a young man, Oisin has become the "weather-worn, marble triton" grown "old among dreams" of "Men Improve with the Years," a poem of thirty years later.

III

The statue occupies such a central position in Yeats's poetry of this period because it offers a set of associations pertinent to the basic conflict in the poems between the private dream and the public world of the Fenians. On one hand a statue is preeminently private: solitary, silent, and self-enclosed. On the other, sculpture is, as Jacques Lipchitz says, "an art for crowds," the only open-air art, the art of public memorials.[10] And, in fact, much of Yeats's political life of the nineteenth century is an attempt to fuse these two seemingly opposed aspects of sculpture. Many of the projects he created or discussed with Maud Gonne were for public monuments, and the most interesting of these is the Castle of Heroes, which she describes in "Yeats and Ireland":

10. Quoted in Berger, p. 67. See Berger's discussion of the essentially public nature of sculpture, pp. 62–75.

One of our early dreams was a Castle of Heroes. It was to be in the middle of a lake, a shrine of Irish tradition where only those who had dedicated their lives to Ireland might penetrate; they were to be brought there in a painted boat across the lake and might only stay for short periods of rest and inspiration. It was to be built of Irish stone and decorated only with the Four Jewels of the Tuathe de Danaan, with perhaps a statue of Ireland, if any artist could be found great enough to make one which we doubted.[11]

It is an exquisite recognition to find here, in this project for a temple to Ireland, none other than the Island of Statues, complete with the little boat borrowed from Shelley's *Alastor* to get Naschina from shore to shore. Maud Gonne's account sounds very much like Yeats himself: "All trivialities were to be excluded from the Castle of the Heroes; only things combining beauty and utility were to be admitted to its furnishings. In austere comfort those setting forth on some great task for Ireland might through lonely meditation on Ireland harmonize their individual effort with national endeavour." Here is a public monument that is not public but secluded, not frequented by crowds but occupied by lonely individuals, not hortatory, as many monuments are, but meditative and occult. The operative word retained from *The Island of Statues* is "lonely," for somehow the dedicatee is to merge himself with the nation through seclusion and lonely meditation.

Yeats felt very strongly in these years that Maud Gonne's beauty "seemed incompatible with private, intimate life."[12] This feeling certainly affected his own poetic ambition, as he relates in an episode in the *Memoirs* not included in the formal *Autobiography*. Seeing on her table Swinburne's *Tristram of Lyonesse, and Other Poems* (1882), Yeats proclaimed to Maud his desire to "become an Irish Victor Hugo." Though Swinburne was always anathema to Yeats, and Hugo not much better, one poem that appears in *Tristram of Lyonesse*, "The Statue of Victor Hugo," reads like a prescription both for the kind of poet Yeats had insincerely proclaimed himself and the kind of art he attempted to create in the Castle of Heroes:

11. Maud Gonne, "Yeats and Ireland," in *Scattering Branches,* ed. Stephen Gwynn (New York: Macmillan, 1940), pp. 24–25.

12. W. B. Yeats, *Memoirs,* ed. Denis Donoghue (New York: Macmillan, 1972), p. 41. See the same page for the anecdote recounted below.

Since in Athens God stood plain for adoration,
    Since the sun beheld his likeness reared in stone,
Since the bronze or gold of human consecration
    Gave to Greece her guardians' form and feature shown,
Never hand of sculptor, never heart of nation,
    Found so glorious aim in all these ages flown
As is theirs who rear for all times' acclamation
    Here the likeness of our mightiest and their own.[13]

This, the first stanza of one of the many poems Swinburne wrote about statues of famous compeers, is a perfect example of the rhetorical Swinburne Yeats always despised. Yet, the ideal expressed in it is a public one, the statue held up for glory the kind of statue to be placed in a public monument, the poet to be immortalized in stone the kind of poet Yeats had told Maud Gonne he wanted to be.

Obviously, the Castle of Heroes was never to be this kind of florid monument but instead was to fulfill the public ambition of Swinburne and Hugo with quite different materials. The Island of Statues, with very few changes, is to occupy the culturally central place described in "The Statue of Victor Hugo," and Yeats is somehow, through "lonely meditation," to become "the likeness of our mightiest and their own." The statue, which represents all that is separated from life, free of its complications, identical in fact with the island protected by water from the problems of the mainland, is now made the central expression of a culture. The whole project confronts directly the question John Berger raises when he asks whether there can be "truly public monuments which are mysterious, problematic, or obscure."[14]

Yeats's brilliance, ultimately nothing more than obstinate faithfulness to his own standards, is to insist that monuments can be truly public *only* if they are mysterious, problematic, or obscure. He does not abandon the dream of rest that is the subject of *The Island of Statues,* nor does he search for some compromise between the private world of dreams and the public. Always, he insists, as he did during a controversy about a monument to Parnell, "The good sculptor, poet, painter, or musician pleases other men in the

---

13. *The Poems of A. C. Swinburne* (New York: Harper, 1915), V, 215.
14. Berger, p. 128.

long run because he has first pleased himself. Work done to please others is conventional or flashy and, as time passes, becomes a weariness or a disgust."[15] It is the private that is enduring, eternal, as it is in *The Island of Statues,* not the composite ideal proclaimed as enduring in Swinburne's poem. Yeats justifies this claim by means of research into antiquity, into an Irish past that truly represents Ireland although its romantic trappings, its women of the Sidhe, give it the distance so seductive to the eighteen-year-old poet. Irish legends are the natural material for Yeats in the 1890s first of all because they are old, and age gives them the composed, peaceful, hieratic quality characteristic of the statue, which the denizens of the early poetry acquire by becoming statues. The broils, the complications, the perplexity of contemporary politics are resolved by the cool wisdom of ancient figures. Yet because these figures stand at the dawn of Irish history, they are more basic to it than contemporary squabbles. They are more fitting to serve as symbols of Ireland for the same reason that the dreamland marble appealed to Yeats at the very beginning, because they are enduring, eternal, changeless, beyond life. In this way, the statue that is the very symbol of isolation comes to the center of the public stage, and Yeats throws his energy into schemes for monuments, literary and sculptural, that possess their contemporary significance because they exist in the past.

It is not surprising, then, that Yeats spent so much time on the feckless task of erecting a monument to Wolfe Tone or that he believed that such a monument would serve as a rallying point for the various factions of the Irish Renaissance. Ireland achieves unity in these projects by facing the past, and the distance of the past removes any taint of the rhetorical, the journalistic, or the bombastic Yeats so much despised. Of course, Yeats incurred a great deal of criticism for his concentration on the past. There was also the weakness pointed out by Engelberg: "For the very act of restoration was, of course, intensely personal, and for a single poet to undertake the conscious burden of what had once been the collective and unconscious pattern of a culture was to court all the passionate pain of effort and the strain of conflict characteristic of

15. Quoted by Malcolm Brown in *The Politics of Irish Literature* (Seattle: University of Washington Press, 1972), p. 378.

the lone voice."[16] But only in antiquity can the private and the public be brought into even a proximate relation, and thus the ancient monument came to have a central importance in Yeats's aesthetic of the 1880s and 1890s.

IV

Yeats tells in the *Autobiography* of spending days in the 1880s in the British Museum compiling books of Irish fairy stories. The most important find he made there, however, was the remains of the Mausoleum at Halicarnassus: "The statues of Mausolus and Artemisia at the British Museum, private, half-animal, half-divine figures, all unlike the Grecian athletes and Egyptian kings in their near neighborhood, that stand in the middle of the crowd's applause, or sit above measuring it out unpersuadable justice, became to me, now or later, images of an unpremeditated joyous energy, that neither I nor any other man, racked by doubt and inquiry, can achieve. . . ." These two statues, retrieved from the ruins of what was long considered the first, eponymous mausoleum, are obviously related to the statues of the early poems. Like statues on an island, they stand aloof from the crowd, receiving neither its applause nor its homage. They are private and, as half-animal, half-divine, mysterious. Above all, they are beyond "doubt and inquiry," and Yeats's ascription of such peace to them recalls Pater's adjective, "unperplexed." Here is the rest, the simplification, and the privacy of *Time and the Witch Vivien* and *The Island of Statues*. But Yeats goes on:

> And that yet, if once achieved, might seem to men and women of Connemara or Galway their very soul. In our study of that ruined tomb raised by a queen to her dead lover, and finished by the unpaid labour of great sculptors, after her death from grief, or so runs the tale, we cannot distinguish the handiwork of Scopas from that of Praxiteles; and I wanted to create once more an art where the artist's handiwork would hide as under those half-anonymous chisels or as

16. Edward Engelberg, *The Vast Design: Patterns in W. B. Yeats's Aesthetic* (Toronto: University of Toronto Press, 1964), p. 58.

we find it in some old Scots ballads, or in some twelfth or thirteenth-century Arthurian Romance. [*A,* p. 92]

The very character of the sculpture seems to have changed in mid-paragraph. Now it seems that the people of Connemara and Galway all have private, half-animal, half-divine souls and, having such, might sympathize with or join in a work of art absolutely collective in nature. The slight disdain for the crowd apparent in the first half of the paragraph gives way to a myth of collective, half-anonymous art. This change is accomplished by shifting the perspective from the individual figures to the Mausoleum as a whole and to the legend that clings to it, to the idea that a great artist like Scopas might lose himself in a collective style. When Yeats says that the figures of Morris' romances are to him "the likeness of Artemisia and her man," the derivation of the latter myth becomes clear. The Mausoleum is Yeats's version of Morris' world of traditional handicrafts and ultimately of Ruskin's Gothic cathedral. In the *Memoirs* Yeats places *Unto This Last* at the very beginning of his intellectual development, and his political vision of Ireland was always, as Ellmann says, influenced by Ruskin and Morris.[17] Here an ideal of art and society come together, as they do in Ruskin, in the symbol of a magnificent building, the very house a culture makes for itself.

The crucial difference, of course, is that Ruskin finds his ideal of society in a cathedral while Yeats finds his in the Mausoleum. The difference occurs not just because of the vast dissimilarities between the personal religions of the two men. A cathedral is in regular and recurrent use; one of its beauties, the light entering through stained glass, is appreciable only from within. The Mausoleum, of course, as a tomb, is not meant to be entered. Furthermore, the structure itself was built as a modified Egyptian pyramid, on a sheer stone foundation seventeen meters high. The significance of the two buildings follows from this physical difference. The cathedral is a place of worship whose direction is mainly prospective; its physical layout suggests heaven and directs the eye there. The Mausoleum is a place of worship only for the brief time that Artemisia honors her husband and the workers

17. *Memoirs,* p. 19; Ellmann, *Yeats: The Man and the Masks,* pp. 112–114.

honor her, and even then the direction of worship is commem-
orative. The physical place it is meant to suggest is, of course, the
earth itself. Those within the cathedral are unified with respect to
the church triumphant yet to come, those around and about the
Mausoleum in respect to a single event in the past. But what might
seem a relative weakness in the social cement offered by the
Mausoleum is in fact its chief attraction for Yeats. Like his own
Castle of Heroes, the Mausoleum brings society together in wor-
ship of the past. Just because it *is* the past, because Artemisia and
Mausolus are dead, the ideal can also seem, as Yeats says in the first
half of his appreciation, private, mysterious, aloof from the crowd
that worships it.

What seems an open contradiction in Yeats's description of the
figures is in fact an exploitation of the ambiguities of public sculp-
ture, one that will characterize all his attempts to mingle the pri-
vate imagination with the public. The heroic statue seems to place
a human body at the intersection of every gaze, but the process of
idealization inseparable from public sculpture has a double effect.
The public statue is simultaneously near and remote, placed at the
very center of civic life and yet raised above it. As Pater says,
sculpture mimics the human body more completely in space than
any other art, yet the body mimicked is inevitably harder, cleaner,
more durable and more nearly perfect than our own. The statue
seems to be a human being, but refuses to become one; it gestures
but it never moves. It lives as an exemplary figure in the midst of
the crowd and yet exists purely by virtue of its difference.

On one hand, then, Yeats uses the statue as a symbol of private,
self-contained life, free of all the nervous disabilities of real life.
Mausolus and Artemisia are particularly useful for this purpose
precisely because they are funerary figures. The kind of calm,
peaceful life lived on the Island of Statues is really lived only by the
dead, as Yeats confesses in such poems as "He Wishes His Beloved
Were Dead." A further advantage, and a rather curious one, is the
dismal condition of the statues. It is likely that Yeats saw a restored
version of the Artemisia quite different from the ruin now on
display, but even in 1880 the Mausolus was weathered and half-
consumed, as if half the head had been clubbed away. Such de-
struction has the effect of increasing the mysteriousness of the
figures, giving them a visible distance in time. The fragmentary,

Artemisia and Mausolus. Two statues discovered at a site long considered to be that of the eponymous Mausoleum. Courtesy of the Trustees of the British Museum.

damaged nature of the works is part of their appeal for Yeats not just because it bestows the romance of age but because the damage removes the figure one step further from precise representation and thus into that half-animal, half-divine world where Artemisia and Mausolus live alone.

On the other hand, the statues take the place of Naschina's statue on the shore, around which the Arcadians gather to moralize and cry. As beloved figures, Artemisia and Mausolus become ideals for the crowd and their tomb the best expression of the people they ruled. The gap between these two conceptions of sculpture, and ultimately of art, is also bridged by the depredations of time. In his description of the Mausoleum, Yeats indulges in an unobtrusive anachronism of a kind most likely inherited from the Pre-Raphaelites. The archaism of the Pre-Raphaelite Brotherhood is contradictory in that it values the old because of its age, because of its distance from the nineteenth century of locomotives and steam, and yet constructs golden ages of art in which it was logically impossible for the art to be appreciated in this sense. That is to say, the term pre-Raphaelite can exist only after Raphael, and much else, so that contemporary admirers of Giotto can hardly have admired him because he had not followed a path not yet invented. As John Dixon Hunt says, "That Memling would have spoken to and for his own age did not occur to Rossetti who valued him for qualities inaccessible, as it seemed, to the Victorian age."[18] Yeats admires the statues of Artemisia and Mausolus because time, by chipping away bits of the figure, has rendered them odd, otherworldly, altogether different from contemporary reality. He then reasons backward, anachronistically, to imply that the works were admired in their own time for these same reasons, doing so in order to be able to argue that Connemara or Galway men and women should be able to appreciate such art today. The private air, in other words, is available only to the present, after many centuries, yet Yeats makes it a quality of the work in its contemporary setting and in so doing creates a golden age in which groups of half-anonymous artists formed a public that created mysterious, private art.

18. John Dixon Hunt, *The Pre-Raphaelite Imagination* (Lincoln: University of Nebraska Press, 1968), p. 23.

What Yeats has done, consciously or not, is to exploit the very situation that so vexes Oisin on his return to reality, to use the paradoxical old–young existence of the statue to argue that art may be simultaneously current and remote. The same thing is accomplished, of course, by many of the theories of symbolism Yeats took up in the 1890s, by the concept of Anima Mundi, for example, in which the world soul is very ancient in its collective aspect and contemporary in its personal one. But the statue appears in Yeats's poetry before he acquired any systematic symbolical ideas, and his images of that peculiar construct, mysterious and obscure public art, continue to be sculptural. Nothing else, finally, can approach the task Yeats assigns to art in "The Statues," to stand in the midst of the public gaze and yet remain aloof, austere, and utterly self-contained. The insistence that such a feat is possible is the source of Yeats's greatest poetry, and the figure that stands behind these poems, or directly in them, is a late Victorian one of which only Yeats was able to see the real possibilities.

−2−

The Ambiguity of Repose

I

The bronze and marble statues of Yeats's mature poetry also have a public significance that makes them true monuments. In fact, Yeats takes one of the traditional aspects of sculpture, its calm stillness, and uses it as his very definition of the public. In "Poetry and Tradition," he uses this terminology to describe an art held in perfect balance between contrary aspirations: "For the nobleness of the arts is in the mingling of contraries, the extremity of sorrow, the extremity of joy, perfection of personality, the perfection of its surrender, overflowing turbulent energy, and marmorean stillness" (EI, p. 255). The balance between the assertion of personality and its surrender, between the concrete integrity of the particular and the spiritual power of the universal, is struck in the freestanding statue of a human being, whose vitality is composed and eternalized by the stillness of the medium. Most of all, "marmorean stillness" represents the compromise of individual forms so that they may become public, traditional, and enduring. The best example of such a compromise is "that ancient canon discovered in the Greek gymnasium, which, whenever presented in painting or sculpture, shows a compact between artist and society" (A, p. 304). The Polycleitean canon represents an eternal norm that each individual figure approaches, the "marmorean stillness" that composes and eternalizes the energy of the particular. The stillness of the statue thus represents a perfect equipoise of public and private life.[1]

Yeats's interest in the canon centers not on the realistic statuary itself, but on the abstract proportions never quite visible within it. In fact, there is almost an opposition between the actual figure, and the hunger for realism that it represents, and the formal measurements of the canon. In "Certain Noble Plays of Japan," Yeats says, "In half-Asiatic Greece Callimachus could still return to a stylistic management of the falling folds of drapery, after the naturalism of Phidias, and in Egypt the same age that saw the village Headman carved in wood, saw set up in public places statues full of an august formality that implies traditional measurements, a philosophic defense" (*EI,* p. 225). Two different styles are being opposed here: naturalism, which is a popular style, used in Egypt for the statues of familiar local figures, and a more hieratic, stylized set of conventions which are used for the religious figures of Egyptian rulers. Only the second are truly public because the standardization of their forms overcomes the idiosyncratic and temporary. This distinction can partially explain Yeats's seemingly inconsistent attitude toward Phidias, disparaged here only to be praised in a later poem, "The Statues." Yeats was never interested in the Phidias who supposedly brought the human form to perfect representation in stone. He was intrigued by Phidias as a representative of "traditional measurements," of a kind of abstract formality he often found in Egyptian or Japanese forms. These share a kind of formal composure, the "stillness and silence" Yeats associated with Byzantine mosaics, and thus escape the triviality of the purely individual.

The most perfect example of this ideal of art is a face Yeats saw on his trip to Sweden to receive the Nobel Prize, "the face of Princess Margaretha, full of subtle beauty, emotional and precise, and impassive with a still intensity suggesting that final consummate strength which rounds the spiral of a shell. One finds a similar beauty in wooden busts taken from Egyptian tombs of the

---

1. Among the more complete discussions of Yeats's attitudes toward the art of sculpture are the following: Thomas R. Whitaker, *Swan and Shadow: Yeats's Dialogue with History* (Chapel Hill: University of North Carolina Press, 1964), pp. 235–245; F. A. C. Wilson, *Yeats's Iconography* (New York: Macmillan, 1960), pp. 290–303; Engelberg, *Vast Design,* pp. 108–204.

Eighteenth Dynasty and not again until Gainsborough paints" (*A*, p. 328). The combination of a Swedish princess, an Egyptian bust, and a Gainsborough painting is an odd one, but the very oddity should make it plain that Yeats's definition of beauty here is only partially visual. Rather, he senses in the bearing of the princess the whole royal life behind her, something implied also in the bearing of Gainsborough's sitters, and in the very stiffness that distinguishes the royal from the common in Egyptian sculpture. Above all, the three contain a "still intensity," the energy created in and by stillness, by the impassive, unanxious face of a princess, by the hauteur of the Egyptian bust. The security of wealth and position, the security of a tradition, and the geometric quality of Egyptian art have in common the quality of stillness.

The special nature of that term, and the habit of finding examples of it particularly in sculpture, Yeats almost certainly derived primarily from Pater. In *The Renaissance*, Pater finds the particular success of sculpture in its ability to distance and abstract itself from the commonplace: "It unveils man in the repose of his unchanging characteristics . . . reveals, not what is accidental in man, but the tranquil godship in him, as opposed to the restless accidents of life" (*R*, p. 170). For Pater, the aesthetic stillness of the form becomes the spiritual repose of its subject, the human figure pacified and strengthened by the removal of all extraneous material. Pater's term for this spiritual peace, *Heiterkeit,* "blitheness or repose," is borrowed from Hegel, who uses it to describe the particular "serenity and tranquility" to be found in the noblest Greek art. Such serenity comes from and in fact is identical with "the negation of everything particular." It is the erasure from the face of the statue of every passing emotion, every expression so intense as to be insupportable for any length of time. It is, in other words, the kind of composure Yeats calls "marmorean stillness" and functions in the same way, releasing the ideal from the convolutions of the temporary.

Pater couples *Heiterkeit* with the term *Allgemeinheit,* "generality or breadth," a term he claims to find in Winckelmann and Goethe "to express that law of the most excellent Greek sculptors . . . which prompted them . . . to abstract and express only what is structural and permanent" (*R*, p. 51). As Donald L. Hill points out in his edition of *The Renaissance,* neither Winckelmann nor

Goethe uses the term *Allgeimeinheit* to describe Greek sculpture, and the term is derivable again from Hegel (*R,* p. 341). Winckelmann does say, along with most other neoclassical critics of plastic art, that "stillness is the state most appropriate to beauty," for the rather interesting reason that any object—his example is the sea— is most itself when still.[2] Thus the still is the typical, and if one wants to express the general ideals of an age or a culture one must express them through stillness. *Heiterkeit,* the happy, peaceful repose of the figure, becomes *Allgemeinheit,* the centrality or typicality of it, the quality that allows it to express the very essence of its culture. The stillness of sculpture, even the constriction of it, certainly has this significance for Yeats, who once recalled "a passage in some Hermetic writer on the increased power that a god feels on getting into a statue. I feel as neither Eliot nor Ezra do the need of old forms, old situations."[3] The statue represents tradition, eternal standards that bring power through limitation, as the god feels the statue around him almost like a suit of armor.

Yeats and Pater follow in a tradition begun by Winckelmann, finding in the placid, untroubled faces of Greek statues an indication of the health and serenity of Greek society. For Pater especially, the Greeks inhabit the happy boyhood of the race, and show the perfection of their lives most clearly in the repose of their statues. On the other hand, Pater recognizes quite different associations in the same repose: "Again, the supreme and colourless abstraction of those divine forms, which is the secret of their repose, is also a premonition of the fleshless, consumptive refinements of the pale, medieval artists. That high indifference to the outward, that impassivity, has already a touch of the corpse in it" (*R,* p. 179). This contradiction, the dangerous touch of the corpse in the absolute serenity of repose, troubles Pater but also attracts him slightly, a tendency especially visible in "The Age of Athletic

2. Johann Joachim Winckelmann, *History of Ancient Art,* tr. G. Henry Lodge (Boston: Osgood, 1872), IV, 113. An interesting passage in Robert Langbaum's *The Mysteries of Identity* (New York: Oxford University Press, 1977), connects Winckelmann and Goethe, through Pater, to Rilke, Yeats, and Lawrence. According to Langbaum the stillness of Greek sculpture, in Winckelmann's terms, came to be "a model for unified identity, with no division, between inner and outer, self and body" (p. 67).

3. Quoted in Richard Ellmann, *The Identity of Yeats* (New York: Oxford University Press, 1954), p. 240.

Prizemen," since it makes the cheerfulness of the Greeks poignant because fleeting.

Other nineteenth-century readers of Winckelmann embrace the contradiction and in so doing pass on to Yeats a meaning of stillness that is almost exactly the opposite of the one presented in Winckelmann's own work. Mario Praz has suggested an acquaintance with Winckelmann's thought appears in the writings of Théophile Gautier, which Yeats knew through Balzac if from nowhere else.[4] Gautier, in his more Parnassian moments, elevates the statue to the pinnacle of art, making sculpture and verse identical in their ability to present a clear, hard outline to the confusion of time: "Marble and verse are materials equally difficult to work, but the only ones that eternally preserve the form entrusted to them."[5] This is the ideal presented in "L'Art," where "le buste/Survit à la cité." If Parnassianism advocates a white and eternal ideal, however, Gautier, like Balzac and Baudelaire, is also fascinated by the statue of the hermaphrodite, by the equivocality and ambiguity of it. And he describes one figure, the "marbre de paros" of "Le poème de la femme," which is simultaneously a dying woman, "mort de volupté," and an eternal statue.[6] The statue is thus both pure and unassailable, the most durable and eternal of the arts, and equivocal, disturbingly ambiguous, deathly. These two aspects of sculpture are at the heart of Baudelaire's "La beauté," in which the statue inspires in the poet "un amour / Éternel et muet ainsi que la matière." Sculpture despises "mouvement qui déplace les lignes," and its uncompromising stillness is both the ideal and the despair of mortal artists.[7]

Yeats himself is much closer to later French artists and poets who follow Gautier and Baudelaire without much of the rigor of the latter. Yeats was particularly taken with Gustave Moreau, to

4. Mario Praz, *The Romantic Agony* (1933; rpt. London: Oxford University Press, 1970), p. 414. In *On Neoclassicism* (London: Thames & Hudson, 1969), Praz states that Winckelmann himself is slightly morbid, and ascribes his worship of white, still statues to a fascination with death (p. 61).

5. "Le marbre et le vers sont deux matières également dures à travailler, mais les seules qui gardent éternellement la forme qu'on leur confie!" Quoted in Enid Starkie, *From Gautier to Eliot* (London: Hutchinson, 1960), p. 28 (my translation).

6. Théophile Gautier, *Émaux et camées* (Paris: Flammarion, n.d.), pp. 230 and 17.

7. Charles Baudelaire, *Oeuvres complètes* (Paris: Louis Courand, 1930), p. 33.

whose work he was introduced by Charles Ricketts about 1896. A reproduction of Moreau's *Licornes* hung in Yeats's study for many years.[8] Moreau's basic aesthetic attitudes grow naturally out of Baudelaire's. Following Baudelaire's demands to purge the natural, the accidental, as makeup covers blemishes, Moreau formulated a doctrine called the Beauty of Inertia.[9] Just as Baudelaire's figure of beauty despises movement, Moreau's figures achieve a cold and static quality from being frozen in a single, unnatural pose. Inertia, heaviness, reverie, become the essential qualities of beauty because they oppose the vivacious, accidental qualities of life. What moves is corrupt, earthly, transient, so what refuses to move must be eternal. Praz notes the resemblance between the Beauty of Inertia and Winckelmann's stillness; though he is aware of all the ambiguities of Moreau's doctrines, it is not his purpose to observe that inertia and stillness have precisely contradictory meanings. For Moreau, inertia opposes the natural. The body achieves its triumph over time by borrowing the durable qualities of artificial, nonliving materials. For Winckelmann, of course, stillness is nature itself. Stillness is the state in which the natural shows itself at its most unsullied. To Winckelmann, then, repose connotes health, joy, serenity, to Moreau sickness, ennui, and death. Yeats himself veers to Moreau's side of the paradox when he says in "Certain Noble Plays of Japan," "It is even possible that being is only possessed completely by the dead, and that it is some knowledge of this that makes us gaze with so much emotion upon the face of the Sphinx or of Buddha" (*EI*, p. 226). The "stillness and silence" that should lie at the center of a culture is, in this analysis, possessed only by its corpses.

The contradiction is an important one because it affects Yeats's

8. D. J. Gordon, *W. B. Yeats: Images of a Poet* (Manchester: Manchester University Press; New York: Barnes and Noble, 1961), pp. 96 and 98.

9. See Praz's discussion in *Romantic Agony*, p. 303. In "The Painter of Modern Life," Baudelaire praises makeup because it makes the human face into that of a statue: "une unité abstraite dans le grain et la couleur de la peau, laquelle unité, comme celle produite par le maillot, rapproche immédiatement l'être humain de la statue, c'est-à-dire d'un être divin et supérieur." *Critique d'art* (Paris: Armand Colin, 1965), p. 477. In Charles Baudelaire, *Selected Writings on Art and Artists* (Harmondsworth: Penguin, 1972), E. Charvet gives this translation: "an abstract unity of texture and color in the skin, which unity, like the one produced by tights, immediately approximates the human being to a statue, in other words to a divine or superior being" (p. 427).

attempts to postulate a kind of art that might accomplish that
fusion of individual and society he found in the Polycleitean canon.
The statue, which at times represents the ideal that gives a society
its cohesion, reappears in his work of the same period as the Fatal
Woman, the Woman of the Sidhe whose seductive powers are
based on the relief from society that she offers. In *The Only Jeal-
ousy of Emer* (1919), Fand, the Woman of the Sidhe, is identical to
the "statue of solitude" met at the end of the play.[10] In this play, as
in *The Island of Statues,* the statue represents the land of dreams,
removal from real life, and the solitude of life away from family
and country. In many ways, *Emer* seems a rewriting of *The Island
of Statues,* with the paralyzed Figure of Cuchulain as Almintor,
stiffened into a statue. Fand is the Enchantress, yet another version
of Niamh, who takes Oisin away to an island covered with statues
called the Island of Forgetfulness.

In a draft of *The King of the Great Clock Tower,* Yeats says,
"love's image is a woman made of stone."[11] The image, however
beautiful it may be, is a predatory one, with the hieratic stiffness of
a figure from Moreau and a significance like that of Moreau's
Inertia, removal from life into a sickly repose. Behind this image
lies the brutal reversal of the Pre-Raphaelite Pygmalion myth by
the disciples of that movement. Instead of coming to life in re-
sponse to the sculptor's love, these women freeze and paralyze
their lovers, until they become stone themselves. Swinburne's
Faustine, for example, is "carven" and statuesque, and if she
comes to life it is to snatch the poet away, to dominate him and
imprison him as Fand does Cuchulain.[12] Praz points out how often
the Fatal Woman appears as a statue, in Mérimée's *Venus d'Ille,* for
example, and in Heine's "Florentine Nights."[13] Gautier asks of the
courtesan who stares out from Thomas Couture's *Romans of the
Decadence,* "What kisses could make that marble flesh blush, what
arms bend those insatiable thighs? Ah, all the love, all the gold and
all the blood in the world could not succeed in satisfying her, that
beautiful creature with the Sphinx's glance, a statue's bosom, that

10. W. B. Yeats, *Collected Plays* (New York: Macmillan, 1953), p. 193.
11. Quoted by Wilson, p. 127.
12. Swinburne, I, 116–122.
13. Praz, *Romantic Agony,* pp. 218 and 287.

beautiful Messalina. . . ."[14] Moreau conceived his own *Messalina* as "a rose-coloured statue . . . a living and terrible statue."[15] The figure of Salome is the best example of this predatory woman, and she is in all depictions influenced by Moreau, "heavy as lead, the image of an idol," to use Arthur Symons' description. Symons in fact calls Moreau's Helen "an image of stone" in his article on Moreau, published in 1905, long before *Emer* or *King of the Great Clock Tower,* but the practice of seeing the Fatal Woman as a statue is so pervasive a direct line to Yeats need not be drawn.[16] He describes Maud Gonne over and over again as a statue and takes as the typical image of the beautiful woman of Phase 14, of which Helen is his chief example, "the 'Eternal Idol' of Rodin: that kneeling man with hands clasped behind his back in humble adoration, kissing a young girl a little below the breast, while she gazes down, without comprehending, under her half-closed eyelids."[17] This woman, with her stiff pose, blank eyes, and downcast face, is the image of Inertia, the deadly ideal that seduces Oisin, Cuchulain, and Yeats away from all that is connected with humankind at large. Corpselike herself, she reduces the lover to a corpse by robbing him of his will and immobilizing him in a dream world.

This woman, all of whose plastic characteristics resemble quite closely the Egyptian art to which Yeats compares the Princess Margaretha, replaces the princess with what seems to be a completely contradictory image. But Yeats has the wonderful conviction that even this woman, indifferent and deathly as she is, can function as the central image of a healthy society. The true oddity, and perhaps the genius, of Yeats's mature discussions of the public statue is that they take the inert figure of Moreau and draw from it the healthful, central repose of Winckelmann. In "The Tragic Generation," Yeats discusses his acquaintance, through Symons,

14. Quoted by Albert Boime, *Thomas Couture and the Eclectic Vision* (New Haven: Yale University Press, 1980), p. 168.

15. Quoted by Pierre-Louis Mathieu, *Gustave Moreau* (Oxford: Phaidon, 1977), p. 117.

16. Arthur Symons, "Gustave Moreau," in *Studies in Seven Arts* (New York: Dutton, 1925), p. 51.

17. W. B. Yeats, *A Vision* (1937; rpt., New York: Collier, 1966), p. 133. All further references to this work will be in the text, accompanied by the abbreviation *AV.*

with Verlaine, Mallarmé, and Villiers de l'Isle Adam, and he says, "Certainly I had gone a great distance from my first poems, from all that I had copied from the folk-art of Ireland, as from the statue of Mausolus and his Queen, where the luminous circle is motionless and contains the entire popular life." The Mausoleum is his symbol of all that Winckelmann, Hegel, and Pater see in the statue, the traditions of an entire people composed into a single, still circle by the stone image of one man, and Yeats sees the literature of French Symbolism as inimical to, or at least quite different from, this ideal. But with characteristic second thoughts, he says, "and yet why am I so certain? I can imagine an Aran islander who had strayed into the Luxembourg Gallery, turning bewildered from Impressionist or Post-Impressionist, but lingering at Moreau's 'Jason' to study in mute astonishment the elaborate background, where there are so many jewels, so much wrought stone and moulded bronze" (A, p. 193). The Aran islander, Yeats's version of the common man, suddenly has more in common with the statuesque decor of Moreau than with Impressionism, in which Yeats once sensed "a new sympathy for crowds" (A, p. 335). In the course of a paragraph, Yeats transforms the art of Moreau, which he confesses has very little to do with the Irish folk, into the only art for the Arans. The "moulded bronze," the heavy decor so necessary to the Beauty of Inertia, takes the place of Artemisia and Mausolus at the center of a culture, and Inertia is transformed back into stillness and centrality, the *Allgemeinheit* of Pater, symbolized here by Yeats's motionless circle. It is a leap such as the one D'Annunzio takes when he wills the Vittoriale, full of all the kitsch of the Decadent movement, to his country as a shrine for the Italian people.

The beauty of the transformation is that it allows Yeats to take the products of Symbolism, with all their hermeticism, privacy, and obscurity, and use them as if they were available for popular consumption. He exploits the heritage of the Symbolist statue, using it as if it were in fact the statue praised so strongly by Pater in *The Renaissance* and *Greek Studies,* to draw from it a public significance it was created to deny. It is no wonder that the statue plays such an important role in Yeats's aesthetic discussions, that it is a feature of all his Cities of Art, and thus the key to his definition of the public place of art. Only the statue can offer him a metaphor that dissolves the gap between public and private, obscure and culturally significant. On his trip to Sweden, Yeats discovered yet another version of the Mausoleum in the town hall of Stockholm, "decorated by many artists, working in harmony with one another and with the design of the building as a whole, and yet all in seeming perfect freedom. . . . These myth-makers and mask-makers worked as if they belonged to one family." He found in the "representations of great Swedes, modelled naked as if they had come down from some Roman heaven" a perfect combination of "multitude and unity" (*A,* pp. 337–338). The artists are both myth-makers and mask-makers, an odd designation that seems to make them simultaneously public, as they create and live the myth of their country embodied in the town hall, and private, as they create the mask that Yeats makes antithetical to the popular in "Certain Noble Plays of Japan." Also "myth-makers and mask-makers" are the members of his own pantheon of great artists, "men of aristocratic mind, Blake, Ingres in the 'Perseus,' Puvis de Chavannes, Rossetti before 1870, Watts when least a moralist, Gustave Moreau at all times, Calvert in the woodcuts, the Charles Ricketts of 'The Danaides,' and of the earlier illustrations of *The Sphinx.*" These aristocratic men, Yeats says, "have imitators, but create no universal language . . . and not one of them can be mistaken for another." What is more, their art is the direct opposite of Impressionism, with its "sympathy for crowds" (*A,* p. 335). It is hard to see how the same term can be applied to a group of unnamed artists who work together as a family on a single, unified design and a group of artists who are quite different from one another, alike only in that they have nothing to do with any style available to a large public. One longs to see the building produced by Blake, Ingres, Puvis de Chavannes, Rossetti, Watts, Moreau, Calvert, and Ricketts working all in harmony. But the leap of faith that sees such men as anonymous Gothic workmen is absolutely necessary to the poems of Yeats's maturity.

II

The leap is taken again and again in Yeats's mature poetry as he uses the ambiguous nature of sculpture itself and the contradictory

traditions behind the word "repose" to place the "statue of soli-
tude" at the center of collective life. One such transference takes
place in "Michael Robartes and the Dancer." In this poem,
Michael Robartes teaches the dancer the proper business of being a
woman, using Michelangelo's *Morning* and *Night* as his texts.
These two statues, from the Medici Chapel of San Lorenzo in
Florence, enjoyed a tremendous vogue in the nineteenth century.
But like all works of art, they mean very different things to differ-
ent observers, and their interest in this poem lies in the way Yeats
uses a very complex set of associations. They are, of course,
sepulchral figures, surmounting the tombs of the Medicis, and as
such lie in a kind of tormented posture that Praz associates with the
Beauty of Inertia. Praz also notes how their peculiar combination
of womanly beauty and death affects Heine's "Florentine Nights,"
in which Maximilian "professes his love for representations of
women in sculpture (especially Michaelangelo's *Night*) and in
paintings, and also for women already dead."[18]

The connection with the dead is also made by Pater, who, in an
essay that exercised a very strong influence on "Michael Robartes
and the Dancer," puts the San Lorenzo sculptures in a particular
Florentine tradition: "They must often have leaned over the lifeless
body, when all was at length quiet and smoothed out. After death,
it is said, the traces of slighter and more superficial dispositions
disappear; the lines become more simple and dignified; only the
abstract lines remain, in a great indifference. They thus came to see
death in its distinction" (*R*, p. 74). Here, sculpture and death have
the same effect in that they pacify their subject to reveal its essential
characteristics. Repose of this kind is deadly rather than blithe, and
yet death has an odd kinship with the canon as another means of
revealing the abstract lines within superficial dispositions. There-
fore, when Michael Robartes teaches the dancer the lesson of
Michelangelo's *Morning* and *Night,* he is teaching by the example
of the corpse, schooling her in a kind of repose inimical to life. The
dancer in "The Double Vision of Michael Robartes" is in fact
dead, and only the dead have the complete self-absorption, the
total indifference to the trivial aspects of life that Robartes recom-

18. Praz, *Romantic Agony,* p. 303. Julius Kaplan reprints Moreau's own manu-
script note on Michelangelo in *Gustave Moreau* (Greenwich, Conn.: New York
Graphic Society, 1974), p. 143.

mends when he tells the dancer to look "upon the glass / And on the instant . . . grow wise" (*P,* p. 175). The turn away from controversy, from learning, from all that is represented in the poem by the dragon from which the lady is rescued, is ultimately a turn toward death.

What Yeats does, however, is to take these qualities and to make them an index of health. He does so by exploiting an ambiguity inherent in Pater's attitude toward Michelangelo, an ambiguity inherent in the idea of repose. One part of Robartes' dialogue is certainly suggested directly by Pater's discussion of the San Lorenzo monuments, a passage in which Pater says, "Michaelangelo is so ignorant of the spiritual world, of the new body and its laws, that he does not surely know whether the consecrated Host may not be the body of Christ" (*R,* p. 75). This suggests to the very un-Catholic Yeats Robartes' retort: "Did God in portioning wine and bread/Give man His thought or His mere body?" (*P,* p. 176) It also suggests the whole line of Robartes' reasoning:

> While Michael Angelo's Sistine roof,
> His 'Morning' and his 'Night' disclose
> How sinew that has been pulled tight,
> Or it may be loosened in repose,
> Can rule by supernatural right
> Yet be but sinew.
>
> [*P,* p. 176]

Pater's term, "repose," is Yeats's standard of beauty in life, not because it suggests physical relaxation—the figures in the San Lorenzo chapel are much more sinewy than relaxed—but because it suggests a state of perfect fusion of body and thought that Pater finds in sculpture, a fusion possible because sculpture expresses thought only through the body. Robartes says

> That blest souls are not composite,
> And that all beautiful women may
> Live in uncomposite blessedness.
>
> [*P,* p. 176]

Pater was in fact not fond of the Adam of the Sistine ceiling but found in the tradition that culminates in the San Lorenzo chapel an art like that of the Elgin marbles: "that balance and completeness which expresses so well the sentiment of a self-contained, independent life" (R, p. 59). This is the same balance and completeness that Pater calls *Allgemeinheit,* the aspect of repose that corresponds to the naive good health of the Greeks. That it can also be derived from Michelangelo's dark and contorted figures, figures which Pater also associates with the repose of death, indicates the malleability of his terms. Yet Pater's ideas are useful to Yeats because of their inherent ambiguity, because of the fact that in their fusion of the ennui of Moreau with the good health of the Greeks they offer Yeats a state of uncomposite blessedness, good health, and balance that one reaches by turning one's back on life itself. To approximate a statue is to approximate a corpse and yet, at the same time, to reach a perfect state of physical well-being. The result is a poem in which a sepulchral monument is used to teach a dancer how to move.

The figures of the San Lorenzo chapel are perfect instances of the ambiguity of sculpture in that they inhabit a public building and commemorate the leaders of a very active civic dynasty and at the same time, as individual works of art, represent for a whole line of admirers the most private, even the most deathly, emotions. Yet the existence of these dark sepulchral figures in a civic setting is reproduced in some of Yeats's finest political poems, notably "Nineteen Hundred and Nineteen" and "Meditations in Time of Civil War." The basic image of both poems is the vulnerability of conventional monuments and of the political ideals for which they stand. The "ancient image made of olive wood" which is lamented in the first stanza of "Nineteen Hundred and Nineteen" is the quintessential public monument in that it is exactly coterminous with and identical to the city of Athens (P, p. 207). The willingness of "incendiary or bigot . . . To burn that stump on the Acropolis" shows the weakness of such monuments that exist at the pleasure of the populace (P, p. 208). It also threatens the very myth of civic bliss, of the stable, happy democracy with its highly artistic public life, that takes Athens as its prime example. Even the statuary of "Meditations in Time of Civil War," more secure as the furnishings of an ancestral house, is shaken by war and disorder, too weak to serve its function as copy-book to an aristocracy: "And maybe the great-grandson of that house, / For all its bronze and marble, 's but a mouse" (*P*, p. 200). The statue, which first represented for Yeats a symbol of a happy society working on the mausoleum of its king, is destroyed in these poems, and with it goes some of the faith that art can serve as a focal point of civic life.

But what saves the poems from utter despair is a version of the same ideal, without any of its vulnerability to violence or the crowd. The daughters of Herodias who sweep into "Nineteen Hundred and Nineteen" on horseback represent the worst tendencies of the present age: tumult, terror, violence. Yet no ideal that ignores these is likely to stand. Therefore, very similar ladies on horseback sweep into "Meditations in Time of Civil War" as an antidote to hatred:

> Their legs long, delicate and slender, aquamarine their eyes,
> Magical unicorns bear ladies on their backs.
> The ladies close their musing eyes. No prophecies,
> Remembered out of Babylonian almanacs,
> Have closed the ladies' eyes, their minds are but a pool
> Where even longing drowns under its own excess;
> Nothing but stillness can remain when hearts are full
> Of their own sweetness, bodies of their loveliness.
>
> [*P*, p. 206]

The ladies are beautiful because they bring a more perfect stillness at the center of the whirlwind and thus a version of the peace the monuments were supposed to bring but perfected by the example of Yeats's Symbolist forebears.

The basic components of the vision are derived, as T. R. Henn has shown, from Moreau's *Licornes*.[19] The stillness of Yeats's women is certainly derived from Moreau's languid figures. Even the half-closed eyes, a feature of Yeats's earliest poetry that goes back to the Pre-Raphaelites as well as Pater, are connected in Yeats's mind to Moreau. How close Yeats comes to reproducing

---

19. T. R. Henn, *The Lonely Tower* (London: Methuen, 1950), p. 242. In *The Whole Mystery of Art* (London: Routledge & Kegan Paul, 1960), Giorgio Melchiori suggests a source in the endpapers of *The Dome,* which show male angels riding unicorns. These decorations, however, lack the closed eyes so important to Yeats's symbol.

75

the thought as well as the visual imagery of Moreau can be seen in the artist's description of his own *Messalina:* "Her expression is vague, an inward smile gives her features a tinge of mystery and disquieting placidity, and the half-closed eye looks inward, pursuing an unknown and unfathomable dream."[20] The isolation of the closed eye and the "disquieting" repose it symbolizes is something Yeats, like Moreau, associates particularly with sculpture. In *A Vision,* Salome is seen as a statue, tinted like the "moral double of bronze or marble athlete," and as such represents "mankind shut within the circle of his senses" (*AV,* p. 273). The women who appear at the end of "Meditations in Time of Civil War" have the same closed eyes, the eyes of Salome dancing, the eyes of statues who have nothing whatsoever to do with outward reality, just as the brazen hawks of the end of the poem represent "the eye's complacency." Their drowning under excess is the quintessential Moreauvian action, the languid drooping of the body under encrustations of ornament, the inertia that approximates the corpse.

Yet these women are meant to satisfy the claims that the poems make on art, to provide the very things the traditional monument is meant to provide. All the crucial terms of "Meditations in Time of Civil War" and "Nineteen Hundred and Nineteen" are resolved in these stanzas. The minds of the women become a pool drowning in its own excess, and this is surely the fountain of "Ancestral Houses," with its effortless flowing, its ability to "choose whatever shape it wills," its "self-delight," completed and perfected to become even more self-contained. Yeats's dismissal of the fountain is "Mere dreams, mere dreams," yet the ladies represent the strength of dreams, protected behind their closed eyes (*P,* p. 100). The search for sweetness, carried on throughout the poem, is also ended here. There is a connection between Athens' famous ivories and bees and the bees Yeats prays to in "The Stare's Nest by My Window": "O honey-bees, / Come build in the empty house of the stare" (*P,* p. 205). The empty house is both Yeats's own, the emptied ancestral house at Coole Park, and the Acropolis, despoiled of its stump of olive. Yeats's prayer is that sweetness might return to these sacred places, broken by the civil wars. But sweetness comes, the final vision seems to say, from within only. The

20. Mathieu, p. 117.

empty house, which represents the discontinuity of culture, is re-
filled through a private kind of power as the women turn away
from all that is outside themselves and Yeats turns back to familiar
images, the "demonic images" that sufficed the younger poet.
What these women have to offer is the same stillness that Niamh
offers Oisin, and yet the more mature Yeats seems certain that
such stillness is stronger than bloodshed, that it can provide all the
benefits of the classical monuments of the past.

In the real world achieving this stillness requires a turning away
from the public altogether, but Yeats's ideal worlds are con-
structed so as to make turning away unnecessary. The Byzantium
poems reenact the conflict of "Meditations in Time of Civil War"
and "Nineteen Hundred and Nineteen" on a higher level of ab-
straction, in a realm outside contemporary affairs, yet the poems
do have a civic significance and a close relationship to Yeats's
earlier ideas about public art. "Sailing to Byzantium" begins in a
world in which "all neglect / Monuments of unageing intellect"
(*P*, p. 193). There is none of the violence of the political poems,
but the opening situation is the same, an antipathy between the
populace and its monuments of timelessness. In one of the earliest
drafts of the poem, the world of Byzantium is represented by
"gold & ivory," the gold and ivory of a statue by Phidias, oddly
enough, indicating that the situation of "Nineteen Hundred and
Nineteen" is still in Yeats's mind.[21] The basic conflict of the By-
zantium poems is between the world of generation and the world
of monuments, between the dying generations and the soul,
studying "Monuments of its own magnificence" (*P*, p. 193). In
"Sailing to Byzantium" the young neglect these monuments; in
"Byzantium" the dome of Santa Sophia disdains "the fury and the
mire of human veins," or all that the young of the earlier poem live
for (*P*, p. 248). The monuments of Byzantium are perfect versions
of the stump of olive on the Acropolis, "self-sown, self-begotten,"
as Yeats says in "Colonus' Praise" (*P*, p. 218). The antipathy is
finally between the blood-begotten and the self-begotten, the for-
mer ignoring the latter in the rush of everyday life, the latter
embittered by the former, by its constant change and decay.

21. Jon Stallworthy, *Between the Lines* (Oxford: Oxford University Press, 1963),
p. 94.

The two poems are about the function of art as monument, about its ability to stand against death. Many of the visual sources of the poems are also monumental, including the sepulchral images discussed by Eugénie Strong, or sculptural, such as the "cast at the Victoria and Albert Museum" Yeats mentions in a note to *A Vision,* or the statue designed by Raphael of a "Dolphin carrying one of the Holy Innocents to Heaven."[22] At the early point in the manuscript when Santa Sophia's dome seems to contain statues by Phidias, the sculptural motif is so strongly present in Yeats's mind as to transfer the scene to the Acropolis. But as Giorgio Melchiori says of the statue by Raphael: "What matters is that the image of the dolphin presented itself to his imagination as a piece of sculpture."[23] The source of the image is less important than the fact that Yeats remembered the image in terms of sculpture, because the important features of the art he postulates in the two poems are sculptural.

The world of sculpture and the world of spirit are, in fact, identical for Yeats, precisely because sculpture always enjoys a state of perfect stillness. As he says in *Wheels and Butterflies:*

> Let images of basalt, black, immovable,
> Chiselled in Egypt, or ovoids of black steel
> Hammered and polished by Brancusi's hand,
> Represent spirits.
>
> [*P*, p. 571]

Sculpture approximates the world of spirit because it is immovable, still, because it enjoy the "glory of changeless metal" (*P*, p. 248). As in "Among School Children," sculpture evades the world of death by keeping "a marble or a bronze repose" (*P*, p. 217). These in fact were the words Yeats originally used to describe the art that breaks all the complexities of mire and blood in "Byzan-

---

22. In Eugénie Strong's *Apotheosis and After-Life,* Yeats found models for the "cocks of Hades" and for the dolphins at the end of the poem, which reappear in "News for the Delphic Oracle." See Ellmann, *Identity of Yeats,* pp. 220 and 284. Ellmann discusses the cast in his note to "News," p. 284. The statue by Raphael is mentioned in a letter to Sturge Moore: W. B. Yeats and T. Sturge Moore, *Their Correspondence, 1901–1937,* ed. Ursula Bridge (New York: Oxford University Press, 1953), p. 165.

23. Melchiori, pp. 212–213.

tium": "The bronze and marble of the emperor."[24] A statue is thus a self-begotten being, an isolated being, whose bronze or marble repose mocks all human generation and all collective life, as Yeats says in hailing the "self-born mockers of man's enterprise" in "Among School Children" (*P*, p. 217). Sculpture suggests a world in which reproduction takes place without generation and thus without death, whose denizens become immortal, as in Moreau's works, by repudiating the vivacity of everyday life.

Byzantium is at the same time, however, the most well known version of the kind of monument first imagined by Yeats when he discovered the Mausoleum. Yeats's interest in Byzantium may first have been piqued by aesthetes like Moreau, since the first mention of it in his work comes in "Rosa Alchemica," a piece of fantasy Yeats says is part Pater and part de L'Isle Adam (*A*, p. 193). But there is an important difference between Yeats's Byzantium and that of the Decadents. For Moreau, the Oriental world is fascinating because it seems to exist at the very end of time, in an ennui perfected through a thousand years of decline. Moreau borrows the decor of Byzantium as Delacroix did before him to lend a deathly stillness to works such as *The Death of Sardanapalus*.[25] Yeats's Byzantium, the Byzantium he describes in *A Vision,* is not decadent but vital, not the Byzantium of 1453 but that of 550. Though Yeats once dated the second poem at the end of the first Christian millennium, he spoke of both together as of a single civilization, like the one he describes in the famous passage that places it "a little before Justinian opened St. Sophia and closed the Academy of Plato" (*AV*, p. 279). Whatever the dating, the crucial difference remains, that for the Decadents of the nineteenth century Byzantium was an image of decay, while for Yeats it represents a golden age of art. Yet the very terms in which Yeats praises Byzantium, its removal from nature, its freedom from time, its perfection of artistic form disdaining mere humans, make it identical to the earlier, decadent Byzantium. This mythical, anachronistic city is in fact Yeats's most thorough attempt to take the art of

24. Stallworthy, *Between the Lines,* p. 127.
25. For Moreau's borrowing from the Byzantine goldsmiths, see Mathieu, p. 141. For Delacroix's use of Byzantine decorations in *The Death of Sardanapalus,* see Frank Anderson Trapp, *The Attainment of Delacroix* (Baltimore: Johns Hopkins University Press, 1971), pp. 82–83.

the Decadence and give it a public place, since his Byzantium is really Pater's Greece with the decorations substantially altered.

Yeats wrote the second Byzantium poem in response to T. Sturge Moore's criticism of the first for using a golden bird, a form as much from nature as a living bird.[26] The second poem therefore makes the work of art much more autonomous, less subject to lowly human processes like enamelling or gold-working. It removes all the processes of art from view so as to keep intact the distinction between blood-begotten and self-begotten, as if works of art could somehow escape the touch of human hands. But in Yeats's prose description in *A Vision,* he gives the picture of "some philosophical worker in mosaic who could answer all my questions" (*AV,* p. 279). Thus the smithies of the Emperor, which work in "Byzantium" like something from "The Sorcerer's Apprentice," acquire smiths, and beyond them a whole society, one that participates as a single organism in the creation of art. This is one of the basic meanings of what Yeats calls Unity of Being: "I think that in early Byzantium, maybe never before or since in recorded history, religious, aesthetic, and practical life were one, that architect and artificer . . . spoke to the multitude and the few alike" (*AV,* p. 279). This dream of unity between an artist and a people is made possible by the same hereditary canons of art Yeats praises in "Certain Noble Plays of Japan": "The painter, the mosaic worker, the worker in gold and silver, the illuminator of sacred books, were almost impersonal, almost perhaps without the consciousness of individual design, absorbed in their subject matter and the vision of a whole people" (*AV,* pp. 279–280). Art, which has as its chief distinction in these poems its radical difference from the "dying generations" becomes in *A Vision* "the vision of a whole people." In the poems, the dome disdains the world of blood and mire, the smithies break the complexities of the world of generation, yet in *A Vision,* those smithies are manned by members of the world that is begotten, born, and dies. What Yeats calls in "Among School Children" "self-born mockers of man's enterprise" are revealed as being themselves the products of man's enterprise.

Unity of Being itself is a usefully ambiguous concept. Its basic

26. Yeats and Moore, p. 162.

visual representation is the "perfectly proportioned human body" and its abstract meaning a kind of life where spirit and matter are not at odds. Behind this is Pater's appreciation of Myron's rendition of the bodies of Greek athletes and the life they represent. For Pater their value is the determination behind them "not to give expression to mind, in any antagonism to, or invasion of, the body; to mind as anything more than a function of the body, whose healthful balance of functions it may so easily perturb;—to disavow that insidious enemy of the fairness of the bodily soul as such" (*GS*, p. 286). The statue of the Greek athlete also embodies a perfect civic life, a perfect balance between individual and society. Yeats says in the *Autobiography*, "I delighted in every age where poet and artist confined themselves gladly to some inherited subject-matter known to the whole people, for I thought that in man and race alike there is something called 'Unity of Being,' using that term as Dante used it when he compared beauty in the *Convito* to a perfectly proportioned human body" (*A*, p. 116–117). The body, in its role as compact between artist and society, is "that ancient canon discovered in the Greek gymnasium" the body of the Greek athlete, which, become a statue, becomes a tradition.

As expressed in the perfect physical specimen, Unity of Being is eminently civic, and represents the centrality Pater calls *Allgemeinheit*. The same Greek statue that represents *Allgemeinheit* is, however, almost simultaneously the figure of Salome, a piece of sculpture herself, who represents in *A Vision* "mankind shut within the circle of its senses." In the portion of *A Vision* devoted to Byzantium, the Greek statue is both the "lovely flexible presence like that of a perfect human body" (*AV*, p. 279), which represents art at one with society, and the "ascetic, called in Alexandria 'God's Athlete,'" who sees on closed eyelids "no representation of the living world but the dream of a somnambulist" (*AV*, p. 280). Unity of Being can mean unity between the self and the world or unity within the self as isolated from the world. This flexibility in Yeats's term comes from the visible symbol he chooses to represent it, the statue of an individual human being, which can be a civic symbol or a version of the corpse, enjoying both an intimate public connection and the privacy of the dead. Obviously Yeats turns to monuments as a subject and model because they are amenable to such ambiguous usage, because they seem to make possible a public art faithful to the most private dream. The public statue's complex critical past, filtered in all its ambiguity through Pater, offers Yeats an image of a society founded on the repudiation of collective life.

— 3 —

"The Statues"

"The Statues" is Yeats's final vision of the public role of art, a poem that makes the highest possible claims for the activities on which he had spent his life. It is also the most extreme example of his lifelong desire to thrust the statue at its most private into the center of civic life. Many readers, including Edward Engelberg, T. R. Whitaker, and F. A. C. Wilson, are stirred by the poem and see it as a vigorous and noble conception of what art can do in the public world. A few, including Harold Bloom, are repelled by it, by the iciness of its idealism and by the openly anti-democratic political ideas that lie behind it.[1] Yeats's ambitions for art always contend with his own mixed emotions, especially when he entertains hopes of its becoming a national art. In an early journal entry he says, "When I try to create a national literature, for all that, do I not really mean to attempt to create this impossible thing after all, for the very reason that I always rouse myself to work by imagining an Ireland as much a unity in thought and feeling as ancient Greece and Rome and Egypt?" The task of unity is so difficult because Yeats distrusts the unity brought by incitement or law, and wants only that brought "by what is interior, delicate and

1. Engelberg, *Vast Design*, pp. 180–204; Whitaker, pp. 235–245; Wilson, pp. 290–303. See also Harold Bloom, *Yeats* (New York: Oxford University Press, 1970), pp. 441–445, Vivienne Koch, *W. B. Yeats: The Tragic Phase* (Baltimore: Johns Hopkins University Press, 1951), pp. 57–75, and Peter Ure, "The Statues," *Review of English Studies*, 25 (1949), 254–257.

haughty."[2] Yeats himself recognizes the impossibility of his
desires. To take what is interior and make it the bond that must
necessarily be exterior to individuals, to take what is delicate and
make it a principle of strength or what is disdainful of the crowd a
motive for the unity of the crowd—these *are* impossible tasks.
They are impossible because Yeats envisions public ideals only in
terms that are defined by their opposition to the public. The same
difficulty lies at the heart of the ideal created in "The Statues," as it
exists in all of Yeats's poems that take a public subject, and it is
only because of the special nature of sculpture that the ideal en-
dures for the moment of the poem.

I

"The Statues" begins in a way that seems almost consciously to
reverse the opening of "Sailing to Byzantium." The young are no
longer playing in one another's arms, indifferent to "monuments
of unageing intellect." Instead, the young realize, from tossing and
turning on their beds, the beauty of monuments:

> Pythagoras planned it. Why did the people stare?
> His numbers though they moved or seemed to move
> In marble or in bronze, lacked character.
> But boys and girls pale from the imagined love
> Of solitary beds knew what they were,
> That passion could bring character enough;
> And pressed at midnight in some public place
> Live lips upon a plummet-measured face.
>
> [*P*, p. 336]

The world of generation and the world of monuments, on whose
opposition the Byzantium poems depend, come to be identical,
unified by Yeats's eugenic ambitions. The very fact that the di-
chotomy is dissolved so easily, in the simple assertion that the
young will embrace the statues that chill the blood of all other

2. W. B. Yeats, *Reflections*, ed. Curtis Bradford (Dublin: Cuala Press, 1970), p.
31.

onlookers, is a hint of how Yeats intends to remove the ambiguity from the concept of repose almost by force.

The idea of repose enters the poem in the first two stanzas by way of the statues' role as eugenic device: "when Phidias / Gave women dreams and dreams their looking-glass" (*P*, p. 337). Yeats must first have encountered this particular form of the idea on Christmas Day, 1888, when Oscar Wilde read to him "The Decay of Lying," which asserts that the Greeks "set in the bride's chamber the statue of Hermes or of Apollo, that she might bear children as lovely as the works of art she looked at in her rapture or her pain."[3] Wilde himself must have borrowed this anecdote rather directly from Pater, who quotes in *The Renaissance* Winckelmann's claim that in Greece "the general esteem for beauty went so far, that the Spartan women set up in their bedchambers a Nireus, a Narcissus, or a Hyacinth, that they might bear beautiful children" (*R*, p. 166). In Pater's chapter on Winckelmann in *The Renaissance*, this esteem for beauty and this peculiar worship of statues are further indications of the "unperplexed youth of humanity" in which the Greeks were privileged to live (*R*, p. 167). The statue mimics in space the mind's new consciousness of itself before that consciousness has even thought to break free from the body that is its symbol. The presence of the statue in the bedchamber also indicates the perfect fusion of individual and society, in that society takes the body of one individual as its civic symbol. The statue is thus the visible image of the compact between individual and society and between art and general life.

Yet, almost simultaneously, the statue to whom the humans bring their love in Yeats's poem blights it with the coldness of the corpse. In *On the Boiler* Yeats says the statues of the Doric studios "gave to the sexual instinct of Europe its goal, its fixed type," and certainly he means that men and women were impelled to find mates who resembled Greek statues.[4] But in the poem, the communion of statue and youth is direct, in a fairly ghoulish way. As Herbert Read says, there is always a tension in a statue between the sexual beauty of the form and the reserve of the pose, a reserve

3. Wilde, v, 39.
4. W. B. Yeats, *On the Boiler* (Dublin: Cuala Press, 1939), p. 37. All further references to this work will be made in the text, with the abbreviation OB.

enforced, Read says, to hold its sexual power in check.[5] Yeats's statues, both cold and provocative, force this tension into the open. The image in the first stanza of boys and girls kissing a stone face is not one of satisfied desire but instead just the sort of balked emotion that would occur if one were to fall in love with a statue of classical reserve. As such, it joins a very large class of statuesque images in Yeats's earlier work, where the statue often represents both ideal beauty and sexual frustration. Many critics have noticed that Yeats often describes Maud Gonne in sculptural terms very similar to those used in "The Statues": "her face, like the face of some Greek statue, showed little thought, her whole body seemed a master work of long labouring thought, as though a Scopas had measured and calculated, consorted with Egyptian sages, and mathematicians out of Babylon" (A, p. 218). The debt of this ideal of beauty to Pater's ideas about sculpture is plain. To approach such an idol sexually, though, is difficult. In the Memoirs, Yeats describes a double vision in which Maud "thought herself a great stone statue through which passed flame, and I felt myself becoming flame and mounting up through and looking out of the eyes of a great stone Minerva." It proves impossible, however, to translate this obvious sexual vision into reality because, as Maud confesses, "I have a horror and terror of physical love."[6] Maud Gonne is thus a kind of classical statue, as measured in her beauty as the statues of Yeats's own late poem, and yet her reserve contradicts her beauty. Though Yeats might become pure flame, the statue is, by its very nature, impenetrable.

This kind of statue, far from helping to give birth to a new race and civilization, paralyzes life by its indifference to the human. It recalls Rodin's *Eternal Idol* as Yeats describes it in *A Vision,* or the statues in "The Living Beauty," "indifferent to our solitude" (P, p. 139). In the final chorus of *The Only Jealousy of Emer,* Yeats says, "He that has loved best / May turn from a statue / His too human breast."[7] But in "The Statues," Yeats turns his lovers back toward the statue, and not to a statue softened in any way but to one whose "plummet-measured face" is deliberately cold.

Yeats himself shows the outcome of such passion in "A Bronze

5. Herbert Read, *The Art of Sculpture* (New York: Pantheon, 1956), pp. 32–33.
6. Yeats, *Memoirs,* p. 134.
7. Yeats, *Collected Plays,* p. 194.

Head," a poem that forms an ironic counterpoint to "The Statues." In the latter, Yeats advises boys and girls to embrace the statue that represents physical beauty, while "A Bronze Head" is about a woman whose perfect beauty eluded him and the world precisely because it was statuesque. Yeats ascribes to the bust of Maud Gonne that is the subject of the poem the aristocratic disdain of his own old age. Her supernatural eye looks out on "gangling stocks grown great, great stocks run dry" and wonders "what was left for massacre to save" (*P*, p. 340). The whole world is a "sty," the "filthy modern tide" of "The Statues" has washed over all, and Maud's supernatural eye seems willing to slaughter all. But what besides willingness to slaughter has wasted her form? The bust is of Maud in old age, "withered and mummy-dead," and worse, become some "great tomb-haunter," a sort of vulture in the distant sky (*P*, p. 340). The slaughterer of all that is common and the vulturine tomb-haunter are the same, the idealism that purifies the human countenance wasting it to nothing in the end. In poems such as "Peace" or "A Thought from Propertius" Maud Gonne becomes Hellenic and Phidian because she is so far above the contemporary world. But in "A Bronze Head" she becomes a tombstone because nothing in the world is good enough for her. "Propinquity had brought / Imagination to that pitch where it casts out / All that is not itself" and the result is not beauty but desiccation (*P*, p. 340). Thus the statue has an oddly complex and discordant significance as a sexual image in these late poems, an image that comes directly from Yeats's lifelong habit of conflating two opposed aspects of sculpture: Winckelmann's benign and beautiful statue in the bedchamber, which seems to preside over the first two stanzas of "The Statues," and Moreau's statuesque woman, who presides at the tomb. The boys and girls he sends to an embrace with the statues can hope for little more satisfaction from that ideal than he found himself.

II

The other important sculptural concept reintroduced in "The Statues" is that of the canon, which is contained in the reference to Pythagoras, whose numbers "moved or seemed to move / In marble or in bronze." Edward Engelberg has already provided a detailed discussion of the relationship between "The Statues" and Pater's *Plato and Platonism,* in which the influence of Pythagoreanism on Plato is a major subject. The basic idea of the canon itself is considered in Pater's *Greek Studies.* Engelberg stresses the importance of motion to the statuesque form, but in *Greek Studies* Pater identifies the canon of Polycleitus, "the *canon,* the common measure, of perfect man" with "the expression of rest after toil . . . the passive beauty of the victor," and calls Polycleitus "the master of rest" (*GS,* pp. 293–294). In *The Renaissance* he compares the statues of Greek youths to Winckelmann's "quiet sea, which, although we understand it to be in motion, we nevertheless regard as an image of repose" (*R,* p. 174). Whatever the actual posture of the statues in question, repose is their essential characteristic because the canon as a system is meant to reflect that typical state, that centrality, Pater always associates with repose.

Erwin Panofsky notes the fact that the canon pertains only to bodies at rest, and this technical stricture agrees with the neoclassical idea that the typical and the still should be identical.[8] The canon represents a purity of artistic form that propagates itself by laying down rules for all later statues to follow, and by extending those rules to society Yeats postulates a perfect state regulated by perfect beauty. Yeats quotes Arnold's definition of culture in *On the Boiler,* and the assumption that he too is calling for a society regulated by "the best that is said and thought in the world" governs most interpretations of "The Statues" that see it as the great advocate of humane culture. In this analysis, the statue seems to be a mechanism for turning society into the palace of pure number.

The norm behind the canon regularizes and tames movement, defeating multiplicity just as the Greek fleet put down the "many-headed foam at Salamis." The standardization of the human form represented by the canon gives mankind some of the abstract independence of pure number and thus the autonomy of art. And yet, at this late stage in his life, Yeats has his own odd definition of number, of measurement, and thus of the canon. In *On the Boiler*

8. Erwin Panofsky, *Meaning in the Visual Arts* (Garden City, N.Y.: Doubleday Anchor, 1955), p. 57. Panofsky, however, sees the Egyptian canon as embracing this limitation, while the Greeks work against it.

he says, "Mathematics should be taught because being certainty without reality it is the modern key to power . . ." (*OB,* p. 29). Certainty without reality is a perfectly legitimate definition of mathematics, which is hard, precise, concrete in a way, and yet ideal, corresponding to no single situation in the actual world. Mathematics appeals to Yeats particularly at the end of his life, when he longs for certainty, a word prominent in the early drafts of "The Statues," and for freedom from intricacy, perplexity, and flux. The desire for a kind of mathematical certainty is present throughout his life, in the diagrams and numbered phases of *A Vision,* for example, yet the example should also be a reminder that numbers have a kind of occult significance for Yeats.

Furthermore, the praise Yeats lavishes on "measurement" here and in such poems as "Under Ben Bulben" must always seem strange to readers who remember the ringing statement from "The Thinking of the Body": "Art bids us touch and taste and hear and see the world, and shrinks from what Blake calls mathematic form, from every abstract thing, from all that is of the brain only" (*EI,* p. 292). Though Blake's law reads "Grecian is Mathematic Form,"[9] Yeats consistently contrasts Greek sculpture to mathematic form, in "The Thinking of the Body" itself and in *A Vision,* where he opposes the Parthenon frieze to art dependent on "measurement." Almost simultaneously, however, Yeats identifies "the human norm, discovered from the measurement of ancient statues" with "that 'perfectly proportioned human body' which had seemed to Dante Unity of Being symbolised" (*AV,* p. 291). Whitaker has identified T. Sturge Moore's *Albert Durer* as the source of Yeats's interest in the Renaissance version of the canon, and has, by linking Blake with Dürer, attempted to show that there is no essential contradiction in Yeats's attitude toward measurement.[10] But Yeats is in this case neither a good follower of Blake nor of himself, since he uses Greek sculpture both to denounce measurement and to praise it. The measurement that goes to create the canon must differ in some essential way from the "mathematic form" denounced elsewhere in Yeats's work.

9. William Blake, *Complete Works,* ed. Geoffrey Keynes (London: Nonesuch, 1957), p. 778.

10. Whitaker, p. 237. See also Hazard Adams, "Yeatsian Art and Mathematic Form," *Centennial Review,* 4 (1960), 74.

The key to unraveling the difficulty is the fact that Yeats sees number in two quite different ways, as certainty and as unreality. The canon has the same usefulness for him that it will have for Ezra Pound, since it embodies a compromise between the certainty of true observation and the unreality of the spirit world. For Yeats, as for many more conventional thinkers, the canon is the point of connection between the basic physical life of mankind and the harmonics of the spheres. Mathematic form that does not touch the larger spiritual realm is of no interest to him. Thus the long discussion of Greek sculpture in *A Vision* seems to contradict what he says in "The Statues." Instead of holding Phidias up as the wellspring of artistic form, as he seems to in "The Statues," Yeats comments languidly, "Phidian art, like the art of Raphael, has for a moment exhausted our attention" (*AV*, p. 269). The sin of Phidian art is "systematisation," a term that sounds suspiciously like measurement, as if Yeats were disparaging Phidias for exactly the qualities praised in "The Statues." Even the athletic statues that mean so much to Pater, which are expressions of the canon itself, receive a very off-handed dismissal because they are typical of an age where everything is "systematised more and more" (*AV*, p. 291).

It helps to realize that these statues represent Phase 22, the decline of the antithetical glory of Greece, and that it is a feature of the phase to "systematise" (*AV*, p. 159). To "systematise" is to use number in a purely practical way. The word denotes for Yeats a kind of witless amalgamation, the collection of a jaybird, and he applies it to both Darwin and *Bouvard et Pécuchet*. Yeats dislikes in Flaubert the impersonal acceptance of all that comes within the novelist's gaze: "he is 'the mirror dawdling down a road' of Stendhal" (*AV*, p. 160). Flaubert's novels are reduced here to a kind of reportage, full of the sort of contemporary curiosity that always repelled Yeats, the kind of outward-facing mirror that might be contrasted to the sage of "The Statues," who realizes that "Mirror on mirror mirrored is all the show." Phidias, post-Phidian sculpture, Darwin, and Flaubert make a strange soup, but what all have in common in the analysis of *A Vision* is an untoward attention to the exterior side of things, a naturalism like that which Yeats says, in accents reminiscent of his brush-off of Phidias, "begins to weary us a little" (*AV*, p. 290). There is, therefore, a kind of mathematic form, even a form to be found in the art of Phidias, that inspires Yeats's disdain. Used to perfect naturalistic representation, mathematics is passive, practical, and disgustingly earthbound.

Other statues, on the other hand, represent a geometrical, and hence mathematical, alternative to naturalism. "Certain Noble Plays of Japan" also casts Phidias in the villain's role, and the "naturalistic drapery of Phidias" is contrasted there to "statues full of an august formality that implies traditional measurements" (*EI*, p. 225). Measurement escapes censure here because its purpose is not to mimic the natural world but to replace it, "to substitute for the face of some commonplace player, or for that face repainted to suit his own vulgar fancy, the fine invention of a sculptor," a mask that lacks "curiosity, alert attention, all that we sum up under the famous word 'vitality'" (*EI*, p. 226). Yeats was very pleased by certain geometric masks that were produced for performances of his plays because they eliminated the possibility of expression and, by reducing local and contemporary suggestions, made it easier to lift the play into a mythic realm. For the same reason, he favors the limited representationalism of Byzantine art and the archaic, stiffer aspect of Greek sculpture that he imagined in the lost work of Callimachus. All might be said to represent a measurement that substitutes a stylized geometry for the human figure or face in order to gain access to a suprahuman world.

Though such art is often puposely anti-Phidian in Yeats's writing of the 1910s and 1920s, its influence is still apparent in the Phidian forms of "The Statues." In *On the Boiler,* Yeats speaks of Greek statues as "faces which are divine because all there is empty and measured" (*OB*, p. 37). This is often taken as a reference to the canon, but the confluence of "divine," "empty," and "measured" should indicate an idea closer to "Certain Noble Plays of Japan." "Measured" could almost take here its secondary meaning, usually only applied to language, of "restrained," because the faces Yeats describes are empty of expression; like the masks of "Certain Noble Plays," they lack curiosity, vitality, alertness, or any indication of interest in the exterior world. They lack, in a word, what Yeats chooses to call "character" in the poem. Like the "Empty eyeballs" of the third stanza, these faces represent the knowledge that "Mirror on mirror mirrored is all the show," and are the very antithesis of the systematising consciousness with its mirror dawdling down the road. And it is exactly this lack of character that makes them divine, not because they show man's most perfect physical form, but because they turn away from all representation of the physical into the emptiness of pure thought. In *A Vision* Yeats compares the drilled eyes of Roman portrait busts—"with their world-considering eyes"—unfavorably to "vague Grecian eyes gazing at nothing, Byzantine eyes of drilled ivory staring upon a vision, and those eyelids of China and India, those veiled or half-veiled eyes weary of world and vision alike" (*AV*, p. 277).

In *Plato and Platonism* Pater shows how the Pythagorean influence on Plato's thought produces a conception of art very close to the Yeatsian mathematic: "art being itself the finite, ever controlling the infinite, the formless."[11] Thus in "The Statues," Greek form defeats "Asiatic vague immensities" by providing a strict canon for reproduction of the human body both in stone and in flesh. But the finite in Pater's terms is not the real, not some concrete example, but the ideal, which is finite because it is unitary as opposed to the sprawling formlessness and multiplicity of the real. The finite, in fact, is the Platonic form, while the infinite is the visible world. Like pure number in Yeats's definition, this form gains its certainty, its precision, because it is unreal, not to be found in any single form on earth. Pater's whole description of the development of Plato's thought strongly resembles the logic of "The Statues" and all of Yeats's ideas in his final years. In his old age Yeats comes to resemble the Plato whom Pater represents as struck with horror at the flux of Heraclitus, and for whom "such pleasant or innocent words, as 'manifold,' 'embroidered,' 'changeful,' become the synonyms of what is evil" (*PP*, p. 25). As Yeats turns more and more to the problem of flux, he turns more and more against representations of flux in space, against variety, disorganization, against the manifold. The reaction Pater notices in Plato is Yeats's reaction in *On the Boiler*: "It is by the irresistable influence of art, that he means to shape men anew; by a severely monotonous art however, such art as shall speak to youth, all day long, from year to year, almost exclusively, of the loins girded

11. Walter Pater, *Plato and Platonism* (London: Macmillan, 1910), p. 60. All further references to this work will be in the text, accompanied by the abbreviation *PP*.

about" (*PP,* p. 25). Yeats intends very literally to shape men anew by holding the passions of the young to a single, severe standard.

Behind this desire, Pater discerns the ultimate Platonic formula, "a compromise between the One which alone really is . . . and the Many, which most properly is not" (*PP,* p. 46). The doctrine of the flux teaches Plato, Pater says, that what is in constant change has no real existence, while the doctrine of Parmenides replaces it with pure being, the One which exists because it persists through change. In this way the ideal comes to be finite, precise, almost concrete, while the real world seems only a moiling, undifferentiated mass, so undistinguished as to seem unreal. The same basic belief lies behind Yeats's conception of number. Only the world of pure number is certain, *because* it is unreal. "Certainty without reality" becomes less a paradox and more a tautology. The "multiform, vague, expressive sea" Yeats speaks of in *On the Boiler* is vague because it is expressive, because it reflects the multiplicity and mess of the actual world. Number creates the despised mathematic form if it simply reproduces the accidents of this world, but when it is "measurement" its purpose is to escape those accidents, to leave the manifold behind so as to elude flux. The final conclusion of a belief in number is that life as seen on earth does not really exist, that as the "Dreamer of the Middle Ages" in "The Statues" sees in his empty eyeballs, "knowledge increases unreality." Pater recognizes in *The Renaissance* that the idealization of sculpture "is a train of reflexion which must end in defiance of form, of all that is outward, in an exaggerated idealism" (*R,* p. 164), and this is where Yeats's idealization of the human form has paradoxically ended.

III

The same basic contrast between the one and the many informs the political message that "The Statues" is supposed to carry. The basic political fable of the poem is an old one: Greek humanism defeats the Asian hordes at Salamis and Marathon, though it is the Greek sculptors who "put down / All Asiatic vague immensities, / And not the banks of oars that swam upon / The many-headed foam at Salamis" (*P,* p. 337). Again, a number of direct verbal parallels to Pater have been drawn, including the statement that Greek statues express "the temper which made the victories of Marathon and Salamis possible" (*GS*, p. 260). These battles are simply the military versions of the artistic and intellectual defeat of what Yeats calls "Asiatic vague immensities," which is nothing less than the human mind's struggle to free itself from the rest of nature: "In oriental thought there is a vague conception of life everywhere, but no true appreciation of itself by the mind, no knowledge of the distinction of man's nature. . . . In Greek thought, on the other hand, the 'lordship of the soul' is recognized" (*R*, p. 164). The defeat of Asia by the Greeks stands for man's creation of himself, his emergence from the confused mass of lower nature. Man achieves the elegance of mathematics and becomes an integer at Marathon.

The battles of Salamis and Marathon represent the triumph of art over the visible world. Asia is vague because it is immense, with the immensity of number rather than size. The Persians bring their "hordes" to Marathon, the Greeks their statues. The exact political significance of the battles can be clarified by further reference to Pater. In both *Greek Studies* and *Plato and Platonism*, Pater sees the Greeks as dual, both Asiatic and European. He calls the Asiatic side of Greece the "centrifugal" (*PP*, p. 253), the wayward, the various, and local in man. In a way quite similar to Yeats in *A Vision*, Pater makes the centrifugal tendency represent both the mass, in its variety and changefulness, and the individual, in his desire not to conform. The European side of Greece, the effort symbolized for Pater by Plato, is the "centripetal tendency, which links individuals to each other, states to states, one period of organic growth to another, under the reign of a composed, rational, self-conscious order, in the universal light of the understanding" (*PP*, p. 253). The most purely Greek tendency is therefore opposed both to individualism and to the mass and represents an order in which individualism is sacrificed so that the mass may be composed.

What Pater sees as a struggle within Greek culture, Yeats dramatizes in the battle of Salamis. He does so by exaggerating one aspect of Pater's analysis of Greece. Though Yeats describes the art of Phidias as a combination of Ionic and Doric modes in *A Vision*, the drafts of "The Statues" and *On the Boiler* mention only the

Doric side. It is the "Doric studios" that make the people stare in
early drafts of the poem and the "Doric studios" whose marble
statues defeat Asia in the pamphlet. This is in line with Pater's
identification of the Ionic and the Asian, the Doric and the Euro-
pean. In fact, only the Spartans are truly European in *Plato and
Platonism,* the Spartan form as represented in athletic statues "per-
fectly responsive to the intention, to the lightest touch, of the
finger of law" (*PP,* p. 72), while the Athenians are loose, way-
ward, and changeful. Pater sees the highest achievement of Greece
in a fusion of these two tendencies, and in the days of *A Vision*
Yeats would have agreed, as he does in praising the archaic, half-
Asiatic side of Callimachus. But to make the battle of Salamis into
his central fable, he creates a situation in which the Greeks embody
only the Doric tendencies, the claims of law. There is no compro-
mise, no fusion of Asian and European, but a complete defeat of
the former, because it represents all that art must defeat in order to
endure. Thus the oddly skewed view of Salamis, in which the
Greeks defeat in the Persians elements that Pater would assign
preeminently to the Athenians themselves, the very individualism
and independence commonly associated with the city of Pericles
and Phidias.

Of course, Yeats can hardly celebrate Salamis as an achievement
of democracy, or as the emergence of Western humanism, because
he is violently opposed to democracy and individualism both. He
praises in *On the Boiler* "the caste system that has saved Indian
intellect" and dreads "the new-formed democratic parliaments"
(*OB,* p. 19). Salamis represents in his system the defeat of the
crowd, the defeat of all that is multiform or subject to change. The
odd third stanza, which carries the victory of Salamis on into Asia
on the heels of Alexander, makes it clearer what this victory means
for Yeats. Ultimately, it is the victory of solitude over the crowd,
and thus of the consciousness of the poet over the changefulness of
time:

> One image crossed the many-headed, sat
> Under the tropic shade, grew round and slow,
> No Hamlet thin from eating flies, a fat
> Dreamer of the Middle-Ages.
>
> [*P,* p. 337]

The cryptic line, "One image crossed the many-headed," is Yeats's poetic version of the progress of Greek art into Asia, as he says in a letter: "When reading the third stanza remember the influence on modern sculpture and on the great seated Buddha of the sculptors who followed Alexander."[12] Alexander is really a more convenient symbol for Yeats than the Greek navy at Salamis because he represents the true military version of the triumph of unity over multiplicity that Yeats celebrates "when the Doric studios sent out those broad-backed marble statues against the multiform, vague, expressive Asiatic sea" (OB, p. 37).

But even this image of one man bringing form to chaos is not without ambiguity. The very idea of the galleys carrying their statues is an unconsciously ironic reversal of an idea in "Art and Ideas," in which the poetry of Tennyson and Swinburne is ruined by "the conventional nobility borne hither from ancient Rome in the galley that carried academic form to vex the painters" (EI, p. 349). Yeats often pictures a dead, conventional morality in these terms, as when he complains in the Autobiography of George Russell's "too easy acceptance of those noble images of moral tradition which are so like Graeco-Roman statues" (A, p. 149). Now, however, he locates culture itself in the reproduction of such moral images in stone and particularly in the restriction of the "many-headed" art of Asia to the stereotypes of Greece.

This meaning is clearer in the early drafts than in the cramped final version of the third stanza. In the original prose draft of the poem, the figure of the third stanza is not explicitly Alexander but one "Weary of victory," who "went far from all his companions and sat so long in solitude that his body became soft and round, incapable of work or war, because his eyes were empty, more empty than skies at night."[13] This figure becomes in the final draft the "fat / Dreamer of the Middle Ages" who "grew round and slow" in the tropics. Commentators have connected this figure to a portrait of William Morris which Yeats calls "the resolute European image that yet half remembers Buddha's motionless medita-

---

12. W. B. Yeats, Letters, ed. Allan Wade (New York: Macmillan, 1954), p. 911.

13. A. N. Jeffares, A Commentary on the Collected Poems of W. B. Yeats (Stanford: Stanford University Press, 1968), p. 490. Jon Stallworthy's transcription differs from Jeffares' in minor details. See his Vision and Revision in Yeats's Last Poems (Oxford: Oxford University Press, 1969), p. 125.

tion, and has no trait in common with the wavering, lean image of hungry speculation, that cannot but because of certain famous Hamlets of our stage fill the mind's eye."[14] Thus the antithesis between the fat, slow, motionless Buddha figure and the lean, hungry Hamlet, dining off flies, which is Yeats's old opposition of the incurious, inward face and the world-considering, vital one. The eyes, the bulk, the motionlessness of this figure as it finally appears in the third stanza of the poem represent the weariness of his first incarnation in the drafts, and his gaze represents, as it always does for Yeats, the solitude of the dream. The only question is whether Alexander has not been changed out of all resemblance by his stay in Asia.

The problem, of course, is that the person who is Yeats's embodiment of authority, of law, of civilized standards, has turned into an escapist. And this raises the question of whether the whole system of the poem has more to do with the regulation of society or with an escape from it. One of the lines excised from the drafts of "The Statues" reads, "The place of passion is an empty place."[15] The emptiness is retained in the empty eyeballs of the dreamer of the third stanza, but what it indicates here is that emptiness is ideally less a condition of sight than of reality. This becomes clearer when the line is changed to read "The gods desert a crowded place."[16] The gods, and the statues that represent them, despise crowds; their natural arena is an empty one. Like the fat dreamer of the third stanza, they exist in utter solitude, and they gain all their strength from solitude. Thus the boys and girls of the first stanza come one by one to the statue, in the solitude of midnight, because it is such as to make "the people" stare. As an ideal the statues are plainly unavailable to people in the aggregate and depend for their existence on a certain distance from the crowd. The ideal is not as it is found in Winckelmann, of a society unified by art, but of a freedom from society created by art.

In several different ways the statues of this late poem retain their earlier significance for Yeats as symbols of solitude, of disdain of the earth and the crowds on it. They have never been anything other than the "dreamland marble" of his earliest poem, and the

14. Jeffares, p. 494; Ure, p. 256.
15. Stallworthy, *Vision and Revision*, p. 130.
16. Stallworthy, *Vision and Revision*, p. 131.

strain between the privacy of the ideal and the public world affects the immediate political message of the final stanza as well. George Russell said of Pearse's showdown in the Dublin Post Office in 1916 that it brought about unity of "the national being."[17] Yeats dreams that such unity might be represented by Cuchulain, a hero to Pearse and himself, and now to the Republic in the form of a statue commemorating Pearse's death:

> When Pearse summoned Cuchulain to his side,
> What stalked through the Post Office? What intellect,
> What calculation, number, measurement, replied?
> We Irish, born into that ancient sect
> But thrown upon this filthy modern tide
> And by its formless, spawning, fury wrecked,
> Climb to our proper dark, that we may trace
> The lineaments of a plummet-measured face.
>
> [P, p. 337]

Yeats says "We Irish" with such conviction in this final stanza that readers will hardly stop to notice the metaphorical trick that has made unity possible for the moment of the poem. By representing the struggle in the Post Office as something like the battle at Salamis, he has cleverly changed an internecine conflict into an exterior one. If Pearse, Yeats, and the Irish are the Greeks, just who are the Persians? In the immediate fable, the British, but the battle in the Dublin Post Office is just Yeats's last symbol of the essential conflict of modern times, the fight of art against the rising tide of abstraction, formlessness, and democracy. There are Persians in every society where there is what Yeats would call a mob, abundantly in Ireland itself, where Yeats often took the Greek mantle for Hugh Taylor, or Maud Gonne, or anyone else he felt had been poorly appreciated by the masses. The conflict of Greeks and Persians is finally that of the artist alone with the whole of society.

The final stanza of "The Statues" gives Yeats's clearest, and most mysterious, vision of the public monument and thus of the place of art in society. The monument does not unify a crowd or

17. George Russell, *The Living Torch*, ed. Mark Gibbon (New York: Macmillan, 1938), pp. 134–135.

even assemble one. Surely the "proper dark" to which Yeats sum-
mons the Irish race at the end of the poem is not a public dark but
something more like the dark of midnight, in which adolescents
elude the people who don't understand and embrace the silent
statues in privacy. For Yeats sees society as built not through
cohesion but by separation. As he sadly realizes himself, this
dream is of a civic life based on a mass desire to escape the demands
of civic life. He says of himself, Lady Gregory, and J. M. Synge,
"We three have conceived an Ireland that will remain imaginary
more powerfully than we have conceived ourselves. The indi-
vidual victory was but a separation from casual men, as a necessary
thing before we could become nationalized in that imaginary land.
. . ."[18] The Ireland of "The Statues" is an imaginary land, in
which one receives citizenship not by the normal method of join-
ing a polity, but by separating oneself from all other men. It is a
massive Island of Statues, where men consecrate themselves to
their country in privacy and silence.

The necessity of the public monument to such an ambiguous
political project should be clear. The public statue is indispensable
to Yeats not just because it has a complex critical past or an inher-
ent political ambiguity. It serves Yeats's peculiarly imagined state
in a way that any art might. For Yeats does not see political attach-
ments as acting between human beings; instead, he sees each per-
son linked singly to a center constituted by art. The lines of attach-
ment radiate from the monument and thus preempt direct connec-
tion between citizens. The allure of art as a social mechanism is
that it can allow a truly private connection between individuals and
the state, because the state is not a collective but a symbol. The
artisans of the Mausoleum collaborate in their creation of singular
and mysterious figures, the workmen of Byzantium on unearthly
shapes in mosaic. This vision of the state is Ruskin's, that dream of
a community formed by individualism, and the art work or monu-
ment is its only possible expression because, unlike laws or busi-
nesses, it does not mandate transactions between individuals but
only between an individual and itself. Whether monuments have
their own rules, their own principles of formation, that might
correspond to the laws regulating relationships between artisans is
a question Yeats leaves to his younger mentor, Ezra Pound.

18. Yeats, *Reflections*, p. 32.

PART
−II−

Ezra Pound

−4−

The Sculpture of Rhyme

Since Hugh Kenner first applied the phrase "poet-as-sculptor" to Ezra Pound, it has been clear that carving in stone is one of the best analogies for the basic activity of his poetry. Donald Davie, for example, takes Kenner's phrase as the subtitle of a full-length study that defines the place of cleanly cut stone in Pound's earthly heaven.[1] But Pound's own use of the carving metaphor reveals more than an admiration for sharp lines and solid forms. Only this metaphor combines the removal of excrescence, the abrasive cleaning so close to Pound's heart, with the act of restoration, of presenting the old anew. To preserve by elimination, to restore a tradition by cutting away unnecessary sophistications, is Pound's most basic aspiration. The metaphor ultimately concerns the capacity of space to contain, transmit, and so preserve time, and its recurrence in Pound's prose and poetry exposes one of his basic models of art: the public monument. The sacred act performed by many Poundian heroes is to repair the world's monuments, from Odysseus, who sets up Elpenor's oar, to Sigismundo, who ensconces Gemistus in the wall of the Tempio, to Apollonius, who restores the grave of Palamedes, and even to Thomas Jefferson, who resurrects a Greek temple by way of the Maison Carré for the state capitol of Virginia. Pound himself made the reerection of the

1. Hugh Kenner, *The Poetry of Ezra Pound* (Norfolk, Conn.: New Directions, 1950), p. 123. Donald Davie, *Ezra Pound: Poet as Sculptor* (New York: Oxford University Press, 1964).

temple of Venus at Terracina his one article of belief.[2] The act is so common in *The Cantos* that it must have a value in itself, apart from the nature of the god or hero commemorated.

At its most successful, Pound's poetry exploits a basic paradox of the monument, that it stands both for exclusion, because the sculptured form takes shape through the sculptor's removal of excess, and for preservation, because the statue stands against time. Where it confronts this paradox unsuccessfully, Pound's work disintegrates into competing motives, leaving in the poetry an image of a manic collector who wants to rid everyone else of excess baggage. The monument can also serve as a prototype of the poem as a preserver of culture, as a visible "tale of the tribe." On the other hand, the monument as Pound sees it is not a democratic or popular one. In "Statues of Gods," published in 1939, he calls, as always, for the reerection of temples, but says, "The cult was of the few. The evil came perhaps with the invasion of temple enclosures. Un-understanding and incapable of understanding what went on in temples, the gross apes destroyed them."[3] Monuments are, therefore, enclosures of some ambiguity in Pound's poetry. More than any other metaphor they enable *The Cantos* to contain history, as the great buildings he reveres might contain a crowd, and yet they also stand as models of the sacred as secret and unapproachable. The course of Pound's development as a poet is in large part an attempt to find a way to use, as Yeats did, these paradoxes behind the seemingly simple facade of the public monument.

I

In the earliest of his poems to concern sculpture, Pound gives his statues a thoroughly time-worn pose, one familiar from Yeats's early work and that of the Pre-Raphaelites. "Paracelsus in Excel-

---

2. Ezra Pound, *Selected Prose: 1909–1965,* ed. William Cookson (New York: New Directions, 1973), p. 53. All further references to this work appear in the text, accompanied by the abbreviation *SP.* See Leon Surette, *A Light from Eleusis* (Oxford: Oxford University Press, 1979), pp. 37 and 48, for a discussion of the Venus at Terracina.

3. Ezra Pound, "Statues of Gods," *The Townsman,* August 1939, p. 14.

sis," a continuation of the story of Browning's "Paracelsus," appeared in the Christmas anthology of the Poets' Club in 1909, and it is tempting to see it as a deliberate bid for literary-political favor. In it the forms of men "no longer human"

> seem as statues round whose high-risen base
> Some overflowing river is run mad,
> In us alone the element of calm.[4]

The description of souls as calm and peaceful statues has an uncanny similarity to Yeats's poem from *Time and the Witch Vivien*. Though it seems quite unlikely that Pound could have seen this poem, his own offering reproduces exactly the image in it of statues as removed from the hubbub of life, from what he calls in "Paracelsus" "turmoil grown visible beneath our feet," and as peaceful, calm, and aloof. In fact, Pound, like Yeats at about the same age, is simply manipulating clichés from Pater. As late as the first issue of *Blast* in 1915, Pound was still citing Pater as a model, and it is remotely possible that he offered "Paracelsus in Excelsis" to the Poets' Club as the most conventional of his verses, the most like the limp Victorian survivals to be found in their anthologies.

On the other hand, Pound seems actually to have sympathized with the romance of sepulchre and ruin that accompanies this view of sculpture. In "Piere Vidal Old," Vidal becomes the fool of all Provence for a woman who "was white then, splendid as some tomb / High wrought of marble" (*PE*, p. 31). The woman white as the tomb is, as Richard Jenkyns shows, one of the central clichés of the Victorian period, and Pound joins Yeats in homage to it.[5] Pound's early imitations of Du Bellay, Leopardi, and Heine all have to do with the poignance of monuments to "the beauty sped" (*PE*, p. 41), a poignance so appealing it seems that beauty is purposely sped along its course so as to become posthumous. In a very real and perhaps unintended sense, these poems do answer to the

4. *Personae: The Collected Shorter Poems of Ezra Pound* (1926; rpt., New York: New Directions, 1971), p. 32. All further references to this work will be in the text, accompanied by the abbreviation *PE*. See also *The Collected Early Poems of Ezra Pound*, ed. Michael John King (New York: New Directions, 1976), p. 148. The publication history of "Paracelsus in Excelsis" is given on p. 307.

5. Jenkyns, pp. 148–149, 220–221.

lines from "Die Heimkehr" translated by Pound: "Behold this book, the urn of ashes / 'Tis my true love's sepulchre" (*PE,* p. 45). Like the beloved dead, the poem achieves an unearthly purity, the absolute stillness signifying freedom from vulgar desires, through death. She is most beautiful as a monument, the book most perfect as her epitaph. Time's function here is as Kenner describes it, to give poetry a remoteness like a coat of varnish, a distance from the everyday that meant "poetry" to the belated Victorians.[6]

Such poems are interesting primarily because they show how much Pound had to overcome, in himself first of all. The distance between such sculptural references and those of Pound's maturity is shown clearly in "Apparuit," which appeared in June 1912. The woman in this poem is "carven in subtle stuff," and her body parts the "aether" as she moves. A sort of sculptural tool herself, she is also sculptured, "graven" (*PE,* p. 68). The oddity of the poem lies in its mixture of such hard imagery with clouds of "tissue" or dew, with the "goldish weft" of the woman's clothing. "Goldish" is a typical late Victorian evasion, a mark of the kind of mind that identifies poetry with indeterminacy. The woman is gone as quickly as an apparition from the grave; her frail alabaster skin is the color of the tomb, and thus the romance of the vision is essentially the same as that of the earlier poems. She is misty, remote, evanescent, and more precious for being so. That such vagueness could be mixed with the sculptural references, with the wrought gold prominent in the poem, and with sharp adjectives like "steely," shows the transitional nature of the poem. Pound is just emerging here from a period in which sculpture was more apt to connote listlessness than solidity.

Théophile Gautier was a major early influence in the direction of solidity. Brigit Patmore claimed to have introduced Pound to Gautier's work in 1912, and Pound recommended him in print in 1913.[7] In 1918, Pound traced the term "hard" to Gautier: "It is his hardness that I had first in mind. He exhorts us to cut in hard

6. Hugh Kenner, *The Pound Era* (Berkeley: University of California Press, 1971), pp. 24–25 and 30.

7. J. B. Harmer, *Victory in Limbo: Imagism, 1908–1917* (London: Secker & Warburg, 1975), pp. 76 and 121. Ezra Pound, *Literary Essays* (New York: New Directions, 1968), p. 7. All further references to this work appear in the text, accompanied by the abbreviation *LE.*

substance, the shell and the Parian" (*LE*, p. 285). This influence is certainly evident in "Albatre," printed first in March 1914, which mentions Gautier, alludes to his fierce standards of whiteness in a woman's skin, and manages to speak of alabaster in a tone of sneering urbanity completely different from that of "Apparuit." In 1915, Pound compares the verse of Lionel Johnson to "small slabs of ivory, firmly combined and contrived" (*LE*, p. 363), and, not coincidentally, imagines an influence in Gautier. "Albatre" is one of Pound's own small slabs of ivory, and though it contains no direct sculptural references beyond the title and the allusion to Gautier, it marks Pound's separation of the hard and soft in his own poetry. In 1914, Richard Aldington recalls "a hardness, as of cut stone" as the third precept of Imagism, otherwise reproducing exactly the three cardinal rules listed in Pound's "A Retrospect," which make no mention of cut stone.[8] The difference between these two sets of rules, Pound's of 1912 and Aldington's of two years later, marks the point at which "hardness" became a virtue to be publicly courted and the point at which sculpture, because of its association with that virtue, became a prototype and example for poetry. In polemic at least, sculpture is freed of the associations of softness, remoteness, romance, that cling to it in poems like "Apparuit."

Though Gautier may be Pound's chief literary influence in this respect, his acquaintance with actual sculpture during these years is at least as important. At almost the same time that he began to recommend Gautier in print, Pound announced to his mother, "Epstein is a great sculptor."[9] Three years later, he recalled having complained to Epstein at this time, "The sculpture seems to be so much more interesting. I find it much more interesting than the painting" (*L*, p. 74). Sculpture may have been more interesting to Pound because it deals more directly, more obviously, with the aesthetic question uppermost in his mind, the possibility of freeing form from representation: "So far as I am concerned, Jacob Epstein was the first person who came talking about 'form, not the *form of anything*'" (*VA*, p. 13). But perhaps another advantage

8. Harmer, p. 45.
9. *The Letters of Ezra Pound*, ed. D. D. Paige (New York: Harcourt, Brace, 1950), p. 26. All further references to this work appear in the text, accompanied by the abbreviation *L*.

enjoyed by sculpture is that it shows itself more publicly and therefore more directly confronts the same difficulties Pound faced in trying to create a new poetic tradition. Sculpture can, in cases like Epstein's monument to Oscar Wilde and his Strand figures, cause a greater stir than painting because it remains in public view.[10] Pound's first work devoted to the visual arts, "The New Sculpture," seems to respond to polemical as well as artistic issues, following as it does by only two months T. E. Hulme's defense of Epstein, "Mr. Epstein and the Critics."

Sculpture did in fact play a key role in the group of movements that were to coalesce briefly under the name of Vorticism. According to William Lipke and Bernard Rozran, Epstein's collection of primitive sculpture inspired the "primitive cubism" of the first step toward Vorticist art.[11] Both Wyndham Lewis' theories and his paintings rely on sculptural models. For one of the earliest Vorticist exhibitions, in 1913, Lewis calls for an art employing "the rigid reflections of steel and stone," and, as Richard Cork demonstrates, the language of stony solidity marks the separation of Vorticism from the influence of the Futurists.[12] Lewis' famous drawing *The Enemy of the Stars,* which illustrates the steely quality demanded in print, was, according to Kate Lechmere, executed "in direct emulation of Epstein's *Female Figure in Flenite,*" and was called in the catalogue, a "drawing for sculpture."[13] In fact, Pound and Lewis met as a result of Epstein's assurance that "Lewis' drawing has the qualities of sculpture" (*L,* p. 74).

The association of Vorticism chiefly with the vortex itself obscures the fact that all of its practitioners and apologists emphasize form in a way more appropriate to the solid, concrete medium of sculpture than to painting. The standard way of differentiating the new movement from its hated predecessor, Impressionism, was to claim that while the latter had reawakened the sense of color,

10. The attempts of the French authorities to keep the Wilde monument covered and the regular raiding parties of eminent painters and sculptors, including Brancusi, who repeatedly uncovered it, exhibit the power of sculpture's greater visibility.

11. William C. Lipke and Bernard Rozran, "Ezra Pound and Vorticism," *Contemporary Literature,* 7 (1966), 202.

12. Richard Cork, *Vorticism and Abstract Art in the First Machine Age* (Berkeley: University of California Press, 1976), p. 137.

13. Cork, p. 306, n. 25.

"Vorticism has reawakened our sense of form" (*VA*, p. 155). Or, as Pound says elsewhere, "Picasso, and Lewis, and Brancusi have made us increasingly aware of form" (*VA*, p. 248). The quality of form, as distinct from color, is most completely developed in sculpture. As Pound says, "sculpture . . . is an art of form, whose language is form and whose effects when they are lastingly impressive are by form produced" (*VA*, p. 36). So it is no surprise that Epstein led the way in speaking of form, or that it was a term of approbation to call Lewis' paintings "sculptural." And the polemicists of the movement tended to find better examples in sculpture. In Hulme's lecture on modern poetry, he compared the "new verse" to sculpture in that it molds "images, a kind of spiritual clay, into definite shapes." "Modern Art and Its Philosophy" takes as its chief modern examples "certain pieces of sculpture I saw some years ago, of Mr. Epstein's."[14]

Just as Pound followed Hulme's defense of Epstein with a defense of his own, he acquired a sculptor with whom to have a reciprocal aesthetic relationship like that of Hulme and Epstein. "The New Sculpture" declares that "Epstein is the only sculptor in England," though "more recently one has come into contact with the work of a young sculptor Gaudier-Brzeska" (*VA*, p. 181). Soon Pound was violating his own strictures on distinctions between the arts by claiming that "The Return" is "an objective reality and has a complicated sort of significance, like Mr. Epstein's 'Sun God,' or Mr. Brzeska's 'Boy with a Coney'" (*GB*, p. 85). In 1915 he published his "Affirmations" on Epstein and Gaudier-Brzeska and even planned an entire book on pre-Phidian Greek sculpture (*VA*, p. 241). In fact, Pound's definition of the vortex itself sometimes departs from the "radiant node or cluster" and the spiral to acquire some of the qualities of good stone: "condensation, concentration, hardness."[15] These are the cardinal virtues Pound discovered during his London years in a number of sources

---

14. T. E. Hulme, *Further Speculations,* ed. Samuel Hynes (Minneapolis: University of Minnesota Press, 1955), p. 75, and *Speculations,* ed. Herbert Read (London: Routledge & Kegan Paul, 1936), p. 81. Pound says in *Gaudier-Brzeska* that the new sculpture "is perhaps more moving than painting simply because there has been for centuries no sculpture that one could take very seriously." *Gaudier-Brzeska* (1916; rpt., New York: New Directions, 1970), p. 29. All further references to this work will appear in the text, accompanied by the abbreviation *GB*.

15. In a letter to F. S. Flint, 1921. Harmer, p. 171.

including Gautier, the "prose tradition" defined by Ford Madox Ford, and the methods of modern science, but sculpture, in actuality and in theory, had a major impact. At least the experience of sculpture such as Epstein's made it impossible for Pound to conceive of statues in the purely literary terms of "Paracelsus in Excelsis." No longer soft, sculpture becomes a model of the solid virtues Pound attempts to bring into poetry, "hard and concrete," as he tells Yeats, "a statue of Epstein not a musical composition by Debussy."[16]

At the same time, however, the complex of ideas surrounding Epstein and Hulme, Lewis and the other Vorticists, contains something equivocal enough to draw Pound back toward the terms of his early poem. The new sculpture may differ from the statues of "Paracelsus in Excelsis" by virtue of its hardness, but the two groups of statuary are alike in containing "the element of calm." Pound's own comments have made it common to differentiate Vorticism from Imagism by attributing greater movement to the former, but, in fact, Vorticist emphasis on clearness of form, solidity, compactness, and hardness, led naturally to stasis as a general goal. As Richard Cork points out, the curvilinear forms and representations of speed conjured up by the word "vortex" belong to Futurism and not to the art of Lewis, who proclaimed, "The Vorticist is at his maximum point of energy when stillest."[17] For all his polemicist's desire for action, Pound uses the language of stasis as consistently as Lewis. Of his own monumental bust by Gaudier-Brzeska he says, "Great art is perhaps a stasis" (GB, p. 49). Later he casts aside the equivocation: "Art is a stasis. A painter or a sculptor tries to make something which can stay still without becoming a bore. He tries to make something which will stand being looked at *for a long time*" (VA, p. 78). When Pound says of the bust by Gaudier, "There is in the final condition of the stone a great calm" (GB, p. 49), he has placed his own effigy in the world of "Paracelsus." Yet Pound's emphasis here on the static logically follows from his emphasis on hardness and sharpness. As Lewis maintains, "the battle of the *clear idea* against the *cloudy idea*" is the same as that of "the *static idea* against the *dynamic idea*."[18] The

16. Ellmann, *Yeats: The Man and the Masks*, p. 211.
17. Cork, p. 255.
18. Wyndham Lewis, *Time and Western Man* (New York: Harcourt, Brace, 1928), p. 183.

dynamic is a blur, especially in Futurist representations, and thus the goal of clear definition is necessarily stasis.

For all their polemics about modernity and all their flexing of revolutionary muscles, Lewis and Pound arrive at a value little different from Pater's "repose." Their version of the term is just as equivocal as his and contains many of the same ambiguities, though the associations it has for Lewis and Pound are almost completely different from Pater's. One major difference is the source: while Pater derives his term from Winckelmann and Hegel, the Vorticists are indebted to the much different formulation of Wilhelm Worringer. Hulme and Lewis were independently acquainted with Worringer's ideas, and both brought versions of them to London. Hulme heard Worringer lecture in 1911, and delivered his own famous lecture, "Modern Art and Its Philosophy," virtually a paraphrase of Worringer's *Abstraktion und Einfuhlung* (1908), in January 1914. Worringer's influence on Lewis is described by Geoffrey Wagner, who dates the acquaintance from the time of Lewis' studies in Munich.[19]

Worringer's value is that he makes abstraction possible by denying the old model of art history as the steady progress of technical achievement toward a representational goal. He does this not by speaking of modern art at all but by rehabilitating primitive works independently admired by Epstein as early as 1910, by Lewis, who was fascinated by the primitive sculpture in the British Museum, and by Gaudier-Brzeska, who found the primitive sculpture of the British Museum on his own.[20] More important, Worringer connects the primitive and the modern, or seemed to in Hulme's version, and thus helps to release modern artists from the restrictions of representation and to give their experiments some of the spiritual aura belonging to primitive religious objects.

Worringer is less than a source in that English art and poetry would probably have followed the same course without him, but even so, his changes in the idea of stillness or repose, coupled with

19. "Modern Art and Its Philosophy" is contained in *Speculations,* pp. 73–109. Geoffrey Wagner, "Wyndham Lewis and the Vorticist Aesthetic," *Journal of Aesthetics and Art Criticism,* 12 (1954), 1–17. For theoretical discussions of Worringer's influence on modern poetry, see Frank Kermode, *Romantic Image* (New York: Random House, Vintage, 1964), pp. 119–137, and Joseph Frank, "Spatial Form in Modern Literature," *Sewanee Review,* 53 (1945), 221–240, 433–456, 643–653.

20. See Cork, pp. 115 and 175.

the distortions of Hulme, Lewis, and Pound, help to explain how these men might simultaneously advocate a strict solidity of form and yet at the same time favor the rather misty "calm" of Pound's early poem. Worringer explains repose as part of his dichotomy of abstraction and empathy, empathy being the quality that allows true representation of natural forms, a quality lacking in primitive cultures, according to the German philosopher Theodor Lipps. Instead of explaining the abstraction of primitive art by postulating some hypothetical deficiency, Worringer assumes, with the aesthetician Alois Riegl, that primitive art simply has a different aim than that of the "best" Greek period. Abstraction reflects "the urge—in the face of the bewildering and disquieting mutations of the phenomena of the outer world—to create resting-points, opportunities for repose, necessities in the contemplation of which the spirit exhausted by the caprice of perception could halt awhile." Worringer assumes in primitive man a "space-shyness," a fear of the multiplicity and confusion of the natural world, and sees abstraction as a relief, a certainty. "In the necessity and irrefragibility of geometric abstraction he could find repose."[21] Though Worringer suspects that sculpture is by definition empathetic, since the very presence of the third dimension involves some loss of abstraction, he sees monumental geometric sculpture as offering some of the best examples of primitive consciousness. He is very much like Pater in being distressed by the capacity of sculpture to represent reality in all dimensions, while simultaneously admiring the perfect stillness of certain Egyptian and archaic Greek monuments.

The most important aspect of Worringer's work for this discussion is the shift it effects in the meaning of repose. At first, one has the feeling that all the abstract terms have remained in place from Winckelmann to Worringer, but the examples have been madly scrambled. Stillness is, of course, Winckelmann's basic characteristic of the beautiful, and as such is to be found primarily in Greek art of the "best" period. Stillness is characteristic of this period because its people were most at home in their environment, in the one moment of absolute physical and political perfection

---

21. Wilhelm Worringer, *Abstraction and Empathy,* tr. Michael Bullock (New York: International Universities Press, 1953), pp. 34–35, and 36.

granted so far to humankind. In other words, stillness for Winckelmann is identical to empathy, to the feeling that human beings are at one with their world. Very naturally then, Worringer chooses Winckelmann as his perfect example of the condition of empathy.[22] But before pushing Winckelmann across the mid-line of the dichotomy, Worringer lifts from him some of the essential ideas of neoclassical art criticism. Suppression of the amorphous and the everyday, selection of the permanent from among a welter of forms, stabilization of the type amid the idiosyncratic—there is nothing here that Winckelmann could disagree with except the attribution of all these activities to primitive humanity at odds with its environment. Stillness or repose, which once meant union with nature, the happy boyhood of the Greeks, now means fear of nature, the savage at war with what he hardly understands. The basic aim of art, to pacify form so as to render it timeless, is the same for Winckelmann's Greek and Worringer's savage, so that it seems that Worringer's work marks more a revolution in taste than a real change in basic aesthetic standards.

The suspicion quite naturally follows that Worringer sanctions in his English readers little more than a shift in taste and not the massive change in aesthetics and religious attitudes claimed by Hulme in "Modern Art and Its Philosophy." But a rule with an entirely new set of examples is still a new rule, though not perhaps in quite the way its advocates suppose. Hulme transmitted Worringer's basic distinction between geometric and vital art, as Hulme translated the terms, both in "Modern Art and Its Philosophy," given as a lecture before the Quest Society on January 22, 1914, and in an article, "Modern Art II," in the *New Age,* February 12, 1914. The idea that Hulme was a major influence on Pound has been attacked by Herbert Schneidau and Hugh Kenner, who reproduces Pound's own corrective statement about the relative importance of Hulme and Ford Madox Ford,[23] but there is no question that Pound was impressed enough with Hulme's lecture to borrow its terms. Certainly Pound wrote no articles on sculpture, or on any art, until Hulme hailed Epstein in "Modern Art and Its

22. Worringer, pp. 45 and 138.
23. Herbert Schneidau, *Ezra Pound: The Image and the Real* (Baton Rouge: Louisiana State University Press, 1969), pp. 38–73, and Kenner, *The Poetry of Ezra Pound,* pp. 307–309.

Philosophy." Suddenly after that lecture, Pound produced "The New Sculpture," (*Egoist,* February 16, 1914), "The Caressability of the Greeks" (*Egoist,* March 16, 1914), and his series of "Affirmations," including installments devoted to Epstein (*New Age,* January 21, 1915), and Gaudier-Brzeska (*New Age,* February 4, 1915). These articles reflect the basic terminology passed on by Hulme. Pound's own term, the "caressable," is essentially identical to Worringer's empathy, and Pound uses it in the same sort of historical analysis when he says that Greek sculpture "moves steadily toward the caressable" (*GB,* p. 97).[24] In "The New Sculpture," which begins as a report on Hulme's "Modern Art and Its Philosophy," Pound, in addition to giving Hulme's distinction between geometric and vital art to his readers, produces a reformulation of his own, based on a distinction between Greek sculpture, "cake-icing and plaster of Paris," and tragedy, which reminded the Greeks of "chaos and death and the then inexplicable forces of destiny and nothingness and beyond" (*VA,* p. 179). Pound thus sees in a single culture the dichotomy Worringer draws across time, with Greek tragedy expressing all the fears Worringer attaches to abstraction, while its sculpture produced "super-fashion plates." Whatever Hulme's influence on Pound's own work, the impact of Worringer's distinction on Pound's ideas of sculpture is plain, as is his respect for Hulme's ideas in this area. Years later, Pound reiterated his interest in Epstein's abstract work, "as he was when most closely in touch with Hulme and Hulme's ideas" (*VA,* p. 305).

This respect for Hulme and the consequent adoption of his ideas means that Pound participated in a general reorientation of the concept of repose that paralleled Worringer's. When Pound remarked to Laurence Binyon in 1934 that his dictum, "Slowness is beauty," "struck me as very odd in 1908 . . . and has stayed with me ever since" (*L,* p. 255), he was admitting to a change attributable partly to the London milieu. The change was wrought partly by Lewis, who identifies "the hard, cold, the mechanical and the static" as "attributes for which Vorticism had a particular partiality,"[25] and by Hulme, who calls beauty an "arrested impulse"

24. These articles are now readily available in *VA.* As further citations will show, some were later incorporated into *GB.*
25. Cork, p. 326.

in the headnote to one of the poems Pound printed along with his own in *Ripostes* (*PE*, p. 252). In fact repose survives in close to its neoclassical form, only to be applied to primitive, geometric art rather than that of the Greeks. In this way, the religious aura that surrounds primitive sculpture is transferred by Pound, Lewis, and Hulme to pure geometry, and abstract sculpture acquires many of the spiritual qualities Winckelmann attributed to the naturalistic work of the Greeks. In 1914, Pound said of Epstein's *Group of Birds* that they are "placid with an eternal placidity, existing in the permanent places. . . . Representing, as they do, the immutable, the calm thoroughness of unchanging relations, they are as the gods of the Epicureans, apart, unconcerned, unrelenting." Of Epstein's work in general, Pound says, "It has the solemnity of Egypt" (*VA*, pp. 182–183). Pound attaches to these abstract birds the mystery popularly accorded to Egypt and a permanence that has to do with the stillness of the forms. The similarity between this description and "Paracelsus in Excelsis" is evident, as is the general debt of such ideas to Pater, but Pound is also trafficking in commonplaces of his group. At about the same time, Lewis says of some German woodcuts, "This art is African, in that it is sturdy, cutting through every time to the monotonous wall of space . . . permeated by Eternity, an atmosphere in which only the black core of Life rises and is silhouetted."[26] The primitive, the abstract, and the eternal come together in such statements to define a kind of repose that is very different from Winckelmann's placid happiness and yet which remains placid all the same.

These abstract forms, because of their permanence, are monumental in more than a physical sense; they are also public monuments. Daniel Pearlman identifies the "dimension of stillness" common in *The Cantos* with the "permanent core of social order" that makes the transmission of culture possible.[27] The dimension of stillness begins to fulfill this function long before the phrase appears in Canto 49. Hulme particularly identifies the geometric, the archaic, and the still with permanent social values. "The disgust with the trivial and accidental characteristics of living shapes,

26. *Wyndham Lewis on Art,* ed. Walter Michel and C. J. Fox (New York: Funk & Wagnalls, 1969), p. 39.
27. Daniel D. Pearlman, *The Barb of Time* (New York: Oxford University Press, 1969), p. 214.

the searching after an austerity, a monumental stability and perma-
nence, a perfection and rigidity, which vital things can never have,
leads to the use of forms which can almost be called *geometrical* (Cf.
Byzantine, Egyptian, and early Greek art.)"[28] This virtual quota-
tion from Worringer appears at least twice in Hulme's papers, in
both cases associated with the creation and transmission of "certain
absolute values." The goal of all of Lewis' polemics is the restora-
tion of the "public material paradise," the external, solid, verifia-
ble world, reinforced by "all that is stable, all that is common."[29]
Since the abstract opposes the individual, the accidental, it neces-
sarily fosters the common, and, by its identification with the dim,
nearly prehistoric past, the eternal. Abstraction and culture there-
for come to be almost synonymous, and the great pre-European
civilizations, the Egyptian, the African, ultimately the Chinese for
Pound, exemplify cultures whose continuity approaches the ideal
stillness.

By a circuitous route, and in an oddly nonclassical way, such an
aesthetic comes to advocate art that is communal and public. In
1919, Pound quoted with approval a French scheme for a "Grand
Atelier in Paris to develop a communal style" (*VA*, p. 94), while at
the same time sneering at the French Academy. A communal style
is made possible, though, by abstraction, which Pound says in
conversation with Gaudier-Brzeska, "is 'abstract' in the sense of
being impersonal. Such works as the primitive art that Gaudier
admired are complete in themselves and not expressive of the art-
ist's personality."[30] The end of such art truly is the public monu-
ment, expressing the "austere permanence" Pound admired in
Gaudier and in primitive art, and so Pound describes Gaudier's
finest work as a public monument, even though it is a bust of
Pound himself. As Richard Cork says, the bust was modeled after
the monoliths of Easter Island and was designed by Gaudier as
"something larger than life, to prove that his admiration for the
'barbaric peoples' could be translated into a carving that would not

28. Hulme, *Speculations,* p. 9.
29. Lewis, *Time and Western Man,* p. 181.
30. Timothy Materer, *Vortex: Pound, Eliot, and Lewis* (Ithaca: Cornell Univer-
sity Press, 1979), p. 72. Materer is paraphrasing a translation of Sophie Brzeska's
diary account of a statement of Pound's.

Gaudier-Brzeska's Hieratic Head of Ezra Pound. Photographed at Brunnenburg by Silvie Deleu. Collection of American Literature, the Beinecke Rare Book and Manuscript Library, Yale University.

pale in comparison with its primitive predecessors."[31] It is perhaps this primitive quality that allows Pound to call it "a sort of monumento nationale," though exactly what nation his visage might serve as symbol is not clear (*VA*, p. 243). The head of this one very contentious and terribly isolated individual becomes public by becoming abstract, by borrowing some of the austere permanence of the communal images of primitive people.

Vorticism differentiates itself from its predecessor and rival, Futurism, on just these grounds. Cork sees Vorticism poised "halfway between Italian dynamism and French monumentality," but his study shows that whenever pushed to define itself, Vorticism chose the monumental to do so.[32] Hulme, though aloof from Vorticism itself, leads the way in disdaining Futurism, which is "the exact opposite of the art I am describing, being the deification of the flux, the last efflorescence of impressionism."[33] Lewis always despised Futurist attempts to import motion into sculpture because motion decreases the difference between sculpture and life, instead of increasing it, as art should. Pound tended to disparage Futurism because of its ignorance of tradition and as an offshoot of Impressionism. The whole disagreement was summed up in a shouting match between F. T. Marinetti and Lewis on the issue of speed, an argument Lewis cuts off by saying, "I am not a futurist anyway. *Je hais le mouvement qui déplace les lignes.*" As Cork points out, the quote from Baudelaire's "La beauté" had just been held up to ridicule in Umberto Boccioni's *Pittura scultura futurista,* which derides the idea that "the static concept behind all art up to the present day proves that immobility is the essential element of the masterpiece."[34] But for Lewis, especially, it is immobility that defines the masterpiece, the stasis that Cork identifies with tradition and permanent value. Futurist speed is hectic, impressionistic, and personal, while Vorticist repose is solid, public, monumental.

And yet Lewis' choice of Baudelaire's line indicates that his version of repose is bound to differ from Winckelmann's, as all versions must after so much time. Aspirations to a communal style, gestures toward tradition, admiration for the public and the

31. Cork, p. 183.
32. Cork, p. 485.
33. Hulme, *Speculations,* p. 93.
34. Cork, p. 227.

monumental, all are frustrated by the adversarial role assumed by Pound, Lewis, and Hulme, most of all by the fact that the value of repose, which seems public in its traditional context, leads to isolation if pursued in the present. After pointing out that modern man has reached primitive man's recognition of confusion and obscurity in the outer world, Worringer warns, "This recognition was fruitless, however, because man had become an individual and broken away from the mass." Abstraction in primitive societies is not the result of calculation but of "a purely instinctive creation" by "common instinct." "The individual on his own was too weak for such abstraction."[35] Thus Worringer warns his readers implicitly against applying the primitive analogy too closely to their own situation, but it was applied in this way and with distortions that exacerbated exactly the condition Worringer described. Hulme's description of primitive man, cut off from his environment and bound to fight back through the austerity of his art, is taken as a justification for the adversarial role of the modern artist. Worringer's space-shyness becomes a shyness of society, and the mess, the confusion, the threat of disorder that Worringer locates in nature, is instead found in other people. This alteration is most obvious in Pound's "The New Sculpture," which seems to show a writer experiencing the sudden release a theory gives the emotions. Pound seizes the primitive analogy for himself: "The artist recognises his life in the terms of the Tahitian savage. His chance for existence is equal to that of the bushman" (*VA,* p. 181). But what threatens the modern artist? Certainly not the same nature that threatens the poor bushman. Instead he is threatened by people in general, by nonartists. "The artist has been at peace with his oppressors for long enough. He has dabbled in democracy and he is now done with that folly" (*VA,* p. 182). Modern artists are "the heirs of the witch-doctor and the voodoo," and "the public will do well to resent" the art they are about to create. Though it is hard to take such bluster very seriously, and Pound may certainly be speaking tongue-in-cheek, the article shows a crucial distortion of Worringer's ideas, filtered through two very different minds. Abstract art, which is communal for Worringer, becomes here an individual gesture of defiance, a purposeful separation of the priv-

35. Worringer, pp. 18–19.

ileged individual. The new sculpture, which is in some cases for
Pound a "monumento nationale," is here a direct slap in the face of
the public. When Maxwell Bodenheim calls Pound himself an
"isolation of carved metal" he is worshiping at the totem erected
in "The New Sculpture."[36]

By emphasizing the isolation of the artist, his difference, the
privilege enjoyed by his perceptions, Pound returns abstract art
and the stillness behind it to the realm of the personal, toward
what the Vorticists affected to despise in Futurism. Already, Wor-
ringer's version of repose differs from Winckelmann's in turning
away from the exterior world and repudiating its most basic
forms. In a sense, this is simply an exaggeration of Winckelmann's
desire to purge the accidental from art, but in the case of Pound
and Lewis, the purge goes so far as to remove earthly material
altogether. Thus Epstein's birds are "great art" to Pound "because
they are sufficient in themselves. They exist apart, unperturbed by
the pettiness and the daily irritation of a world full of Claude
Phillipses, and Saintsburys and of the constant bickerings of un-
comprehending minds. They infuriate the denizens of this super-
ficial world because they ignore it. Its impotences and its impor-
tances do not affect them. . . . This work infuriates the superficial
mind, it takes no count of this morning's leader; of transient condi-
tions" (*VA*, p. 183). Obviously, Pound speaks for himself through
the personae of Epstein's birds, borrowing their calmness as he
does that of the statues of "Paracelsus." The element of calm or
stillness in abstract art declares here its derivation from the derisory
and isolated calm of the statues in "Paracelsus" and shows how,
for all the changes in Pound's aesthetic since 1909, he still manages
to preserve some of the fin-de-siècle pose of that period. This
world exists above and beyond the hubbub of everyday life, and is
right to do so because art distinguishes itself by shaking earthly
dust from its feet. As Lewis says, quoting with malice from
Spengler, the truly great statue "is a complex Euclidean body,
timeless and relationless, wholly self-contained. It neither speaks
nor looks. *It is quite unconscious of the spectator*."[37]

Statements like this could obviously be multiplied endlessly

36. Maxwell Bodenheim, "Isolation of Carved Metal," *The Dial*, 72 (January
1922), 91.
37. Lewis, *Time and Western Man*, p. 284.

from modern writers influenced by Symbolist aesthetics, but both
Pound and Lewis support their disdain with examples of geometric
sculpture and thus illustrate the odd paradox against which Wor-
ringer has warned them. Far from enacting a communal style, the
sculpture evoked by Lewis and Pound marks the complete isola-
tion of its creators, and the abstraction of the forms, which marked
a fear of nature in primitive people, marks here a fear and hatred of
other humans. Both Lewis and Pound paraphrase Baudelaire's "La
beauté," and the line of reasoning they follow leads inevitably to
the deathly ideal of that poem. Thus Lewis says at the end of *Tarr,*
in a passage quoted with approval in Pound's review (*LE,* p. 430),
"Deadness, then . . . is the first condition of art," just as Hulme
announces that what ordinary men "look on as dead and lifeless" is
in fact great art.[38] Like Yeats, who, beginning with different
premises, follows a very similar line of reasoning, the Vorticists
arrive at death as the ultimate aesthetic state. "Paracelsus," it will
be remembered, describes the exaltation achieved only beyond the
grave.

II

To a very great extent, these contradictions account for the
downward spiral, the inverted vortex, of Wyndham Lewis' life.
Inveighing his entire life against an age which, as he saw it, had
come to deify the personal, the interior, and the flux of experience,
he withdrew into greater and greater isolation. Lewis always con-
sidered himself a defender of public values, a foe of the Romantic
myths of interiority and privacy, and yet no one was more isolated
from the public than "The Enemy" himself. Of course, Pound's
life followed much the same course, with the same paradoxical
pleas for tradition and for public action, as Pound himself sank
further and further into mental isolation. The last poetic work of
his London years, "Hugh Selwyn Mauberley," deals with this
very problem. "Mauberley" is, of all of Pound's works of the
time, most indebted to the aesthetic ideas discussed here, and the

---

38. Wyndham Lewis, *Tarr* (1918; rpt., London: Calder & Boyars, 1968), p. 279.
Hulme, *Further Speculations,* p. 120.

difficulty of the poem is in some ways an outgrowth of the para-
doxes within those ideas. The poem makes the act of sculpture
central to a true aesthetic and yet at the same time shows how
sculpture helps that aesthetic to cancel itself.

The difficulties of "Mauberley" as a poem are quite obvious in
the simple fact that no agreement exists about such basic issues as
the number of personae. To take sides in these battles is futile, but
it might be useful to ask why such difficulties arise. Since a number
of the poem's basic terms can be understood most clearly in light
of Worringer's categories, as elaborated by the Vorticists, it might
also be possible to find one source of the trouble in his dialectic.
The second poem in the sequence seems particularly indebted to
the dichotomy, especially since it turns on the basic opposition of
stillness and movement:

> The age demanded an image
> Of its accelerated grimace,
> Something for the modern stage,
> Not, at any rate, an Attic grace;

> . . .

> The "age demanded" chiefly a mould in plaster,
> Made with no loss of time,
> A prose kinema, not, not assuredly, alabaster
> Or the "sculpture" of rhyme.
>
> [*PE*, p. 188]

The key couplet here is the first. Though representation may be
the basic demand of the age, the damning adjective is "acceler-
ated." The modern age demands a representation of its quickness,
its quirks. It favors what Pound, following Lewis, calls "the sculp-
ture of nerve-crisis" (*VA*, p. 171). In fact, the couplet very effi-
ciently identifies representation/reportage, and speed/movement,
as Hulme and Lewis invariably do. Though the age demands
faithfulness to its "march of events," the artist resolutely ignores
"the mottoes on sun-dials" and wastes his time, letting it march
past (*PE*, p. 187).

Two diametrically opposed forms of art, reflecting the opposition between the age and the poet, are the "prose kinema" and "the 'sculpture' of rhyme." Hugh Witemeyer, for one, sees this opposition as one between mimesis and imaginative art, but Pound's comments on movies make it clear that a more specific discrimination lies behind the contrast.[39] Pound makes it a habit to differentiate between the " 'art' of cinema" and the true arts, which are still: "The stasis of painting is perfectly capable of showing the feeling of violence; the cinema is only more facile, not more capable or capacious" (VA, p. 95). It is in contrast to the cinema that Pound delivers the dictum already quoted: "Art is a stasis" (VA, p. 78). Though Witemeyer traces this last comment to Joyce, the debt to Lewis and to the general Vorticist debate is obvious, especially since Pound's only mention of Joyce in this connection comes in a review of Tarr (LE, p. 430).[40] In any case, movement and mimesis are identical for Pound, because to create art that succeeds on its own terms is to slow down the merely fashionable gyrations of everyday life until they approximate the calmness of Epstein's birds or Gaudier's bust. Sculpture is, as in Pound's descriptions of Epstein and Gaudier, the art of the eternal, the lasting, and is so because it is solid and still. The inclusion of "alabaster" in the dichotomy declares the poem's debt to Gautier, and one of Pound's favorite quotes from Gautier is the famous line from "L'Art": "Le buste / Survit à la cité."[41] Sculpture simply outlasts the age.

Cinema is also the most impressionistic art, in the special opprobrious sense in which the Vorticists understood that term. As Pound says in Gaudier-Brzeska: "The logical end of impressionist art is the cinematograph" (GB, p. 89). Impressionism and the movies belong together because they both rely on motion, on "nerve-crisis," not on art. The mark of the real artist in Pound's eyes is that he does not take imprint but gives it, a very literal rendering of the words "impress" and "express" that owes something to the example of sculpture. In the same article in which he denigrates movies, Pound distinguishes between two ways of

---

39. Hugh Witemeyer, The Poetry of Ezra Pound: Forms and Renewal, 1908–1920 (Berkeley: University of California Press, 1969), p. 182.

40. Witemeyer, p. 102.

41. See John J. Espey, Ezra Pound's Mauberley (Berkeley: University of California Press, 1955), pp. 25–41.

looking at the human mind, "as that toward which perception moves, as the toy of circumstance, as the plastic substance *receiving* impressions," or as "directing a certain fluid force against circumstance, as *conceiving* instead of merely reflecting and observing" (*GB,* p. 89). The human being is obviously either sculptor or medium, clay or worker in stone. As Richard Cork points out, this distinction is a recasting of Worringer's dichotomy,[42] a recasting which first appears in Pound's report on Hulme's 1914 lecture in the mouth of a mysterious "third speaker" who says, "one might regard the body either as a sensitized receiver of sensations, or as an instrument for carrying out the decrees of the will (or expressioning the soul . . .)" (*VA,* p. 180). Whether Pound is in fact this speaker himself, or whether he simply adopts these very literal interpretations of the words "impression" and "expression," the general congruence between his terms and Worringer's dichotomy, expressed by Hulme on the same evening, is clear. Empathetic art takes on the form of the exterior world, while abstract art asserts a powerful control over that form and succeeds by subduing the world.

Thus the logical heir to the empathetic art of the past is the cinema, while modern sculpture seeks to embody all that Worringer calls abstraction. The dichotomy can also be expressed as an opposition between two different sculptural procedures, carving and modeling. When the age demands "a mould in plaster" its sin is as much to favor modeling as it is to ask for mere representation. The first procedure is a disciplined process of removal, while the second works by addition; carving is thus associated with abstraction, modeling with representation. Davie elaborates many of the differences Pound sees between carving and modeling, which are essentially those between impression and expression and, ultimately, between movement and stasis.[43] Though K. K. Ruthven derives this distinction from Michelangelo, the establishment of carving as true sculpture is a Vorticist commonplace, part of the general turn of sculptural taste away from Rodin's bronzes and toward more abstract forms in stone. R. H. Wilenski codifies the ideas of the time when he draws a major distinction between Ep-

---

42. Cork, p. 257.
43. Davie, *Poet as Sculptor,* pp. 154–159.

stein's stone figures and his bronze portraits, originally worked up in clay.[44] Gaudier also felt that "light voluptuous modelling" was "insipid" (*GB,* p. 37), and said of the sculpture he admired, "Every inch of the surface is won at the point of the chisel" (*GB,* p. 31). Modeling is dilatory, ephemeral, of the moment; carving embodies the great effort of will demanded to remove excrescence from the fundamental.

The age demands an art that is dilatory and ephemeral, that is empathetic in Worringer's terms, seeking to reproduce the form of nature, and also personal, with the Romantic emphasis on the touch of the idiosyncratic. The art opposed by the poem to these demands of the age is sculptural, which means to those schooled in the terms of Vorticism hieratic, immobile, carven, eternal, ultimately devoted to the long-lasting values that can only be called public. Part of the inherent difficulty of "Hugh Selwyn Mauberley" is the nature of this indictment: the English public is lambasted because it lives collectively the life of a Romantic individual. Though it may despise the "inward gaze" of the artist, it also wants nothing to do with "the classics" he seeks to paraphrase. The artist, isolated though he may be, stands for a more difficult and abstract art, paradoxically a more public art. Pound faces here the same dilemma Yeats does when he tries to revivify Irish culture on his own, the same dilemma any artist must face if he attempts to recreate public culture from an isolated position. "Hugh Selwyn Mauberley" is in some sense about this dilemma and the inability of art, sculptural or not, to solve it, and this is one reason why it is a farewell to London.

The paradoxical reversal of the position of the artist and that of society also accounts in part for difficulties relating to the persona or personae in the poem. The opposition between impression and expression seems very neatly to cover the dichotomy often seen between Pound himself, or E. P., and Mauberley, whom Wite-

---

44. K. K. Ruthven, *A Guide to Ezra Pound's Personae* (Berkeley: University of California Press, 1969), p. 130. Wilenski, pp. 24–25 and 92–102. Wilenski sees working in clay as conducive to "improvisation and spontaneity, to empirical recording of casual impressions and satisfactions, and to romantic recording of sudden transitory emotional reactions." See also Rudolf Wittkower, *Sculpture: Process and Principle* (New York: Harper & Row, 1977), pp. 249–256, for a history of the shift away from neoclassical emphasis on carving in stone, to Romantic preference for bronze, and then back to stone again.

meyer calls, *"the type of the impressionist."*[45] But the idea that
Mauberley can be disentangled from Pound or from a persona
called E. P. seems less tenable the more study the poem receives.
This reading, common for a number of years, takes "Medallion,"
the final poem of the sequence, as Pound's ironic example of a
washed-out aestheticism, in contrast to his own poem, "Envoi."
Jo Brantley Berryman's work on "Medallion" and "Envoi," ac-
cepted and seconded by Davie, calls into question the idea that
these are "good" and "bad" poems by "good" and "bad" poets.[46]
The denigration of Mauberley as a worker in the "second-rate" art
of intaglio also seems unwarranted.[47] If carving is to be valued
over modeling, then the cutting of the engraver can hardly be
despised. The first poem under the heading "Mauberley" presents
the work of an engraver, a worker in cameos, and it is significant
that this is one of the very few of Pound's earlier poems to be
quoted in *The Cantos*. Though the fact that Mauberley's is an "art
/ In profile" has been used to downgrade it,[48] Pound lovingly
recalls this very work in Canto 74: "le contre-jour the line of the
cameo / profile 'to carve Achaia'" (74/444).[49] He may also have
chosen to change the original line, "To forge Achaia" to make
more obvious the similarity between engraving and sculpting,
though it is repeated accurately a second time in the Canto
(74/447). In general, medallions and cameos are objects of very
high standing in Pound's poetry. If Mauberley fails "to forge
Achaia," it is not because his aspirations are too low or his art form
despicable.

Mauberley and "his" poem, "Medallion," enact the aesthetic of
sculpture as clearly as anything in the sequence. The fact that the
head of the singer, worked in "intractable amber," is compared to

45. Witemeyer, p. 176. This is, of course, one of the most common readings of
the poem. For a full demonstration, see Espey, especially p. 82.

46. Jo Brantley Berryman, "Medallion: Pound's Poem," *Paideuma*, 2 (1973),
391–398, and "The Art of the Image: Allusions in Pound's 'Medallion,'"
Paideuma, 6 (1977), 295–308. Donald Davie, *Ezra Pound* (New York: Viking,
1975), pp. 50–54.

47. Witemeyer, pp. 185–186. Espey, pp. 100–101.

48. Ruthven, p. 142.

49. *The Cantos of Ezra Pound* (New York: New Directions, 1972), p. 444.
Citations from *The Cantos* will be followed in the text by the Canto number and
the page number in this edition.

a Venus in Salomon Reinach's *Apollo* has been used to belittle the poem.[50] But, in fact, Pound cites Reinach's *Manual of Classical Philology* on several occasions as a model of literary study (*GB*, p. 115). His commendation in "Patria Mia" leaves open the possibility that *Apollo* also presents "detailed knowledge in such a way that anyone can approach it" (*SP*, p. 138). Witemeyer argues that Pound's inclusion of Reinach in *Gaudier-Brzeska* is meant as a contrast between the sculptor and the scholar.[51] "Medallion," however, does not contrast but instead combines the two. The "face-oval" of the last stanza of the poem does come from *Apollo*, as does the adjective "suave," but in describing the "bounding-line" of the hair Pound repeats a phrase he himself applies to Gaudier-Brzeska in *The Chinese Written Character:* "He was . . . used to consider all life and nature in the terms of planes and of bounding lines."[52] Reinach himself is very far from considering bounding-lines of importance. He emphasizes, in the very passage identified by Berryman as the source for this poem, *sfumato*, "a vaporous gradation of tones."[53] Pound ignores this nineteenth-century feel for the vaporous and misty, modernizing it and updating Reinach to bring him closer to Gaudier-Brzeska. The insertion of the term "bounding-line" shows Pound moving his source away from the impressionistic and toward the modern as defined by the carving of his time. If carving is to be opposed to modeling and if "Medallion" is to be considered Mauberley's own poem, then it is very difficult to see how it can be used to show him as anything other than a conscientious artist.

50. Witemeyer, p. 193. Espey, p. 78. The idea that Mauberley is condemned for comparing his lady to a work of art is a very odd one considering the number of works of art by Botticelli, Jacopo del Sellaio, Bellini, and many other artists that Pound uses to worship as incarnations of women in *The Cantos*. Furthermore, Reinach is not at all the kind of book an "aesthete" like Hugh Selwyn Mauberley would read. *Apollo* is extremely conservative in its artistic discriminations, and in it Reinach decries "the prejudices of an intolerant aestheticism," which have devalued the great classical masterpieces. Hardly what Pound would have chosen to brand his engraver as an aesthete of the 1890s. See Salomon Reinach, *Apollo* (New York: Scribner, 1924), p. 71.

51. Witemeyer, p. 193. See *GB*, p. 105, where Gaudier is described as a person who has digested all that *Apollo* has to offer.

52. Ezra Pound, *Instigations* (1920; rpt. Freeport, N.Y.: Books for Libraries Press, 1967), p. 385. The comment comes in a note to Fenollosa's essay, included in this collection of Pound's own work.

53. Reinach, p. 59.

Yet establishing the fact that Mauberley participates in the general activity of sculpture and partakes of its value does not remove the very real criticisms leveled in the poem against him. Instead, it makes it possible to see how such criticisms might be extended to the figure of E. P., or rather to show that there is but one situation in the poem, and that a very complex one, and not two very simple and contrasting ones. For, in addition to their practice in the arts of sculpture and intaglio, the personae share certain failings as well. Mauberley's topaz, the color of his medallion, reappears in Canto 5 as a kind of clue: "Topaz I manage, and three sorts of blue; / but on the barb of time" (5/17). "On the barb of time" contrasts very painfully to the wish of the poet of "Envoi," who would have his lover's graces live forever, "Braving time" (*PE*, p. 197). In all the episodes of the poem, the poet's imputed failure is the failure to brave time, to give something out of the past a living air, or to preserve something of the present from decay. The poet who faces down the age in the second poem of the sequence offers the "classics in paraphrase," and yet his case presents "No adjunct to the Muse's diadem." We can be leery of the shifting tone here and still see the similarity between this admission and the charge against Mauberley, "lacking the skill / To forge Achaia." The poet's craft approaches sculpture but it does not succeed in creating monuments. All the technical achievements of the sculpture of rhyme are insufficient, it seems, against the depredations of time. What the poet-sculptors aspire to and what they achieve are two different things, but whose is the fault? This is perhaps the central ambiguity that complicates the polemical surface of the poem: are the poets weak in themselves or are they betrayed by a foolish age?

Actually, Mauberley and the persona delimited by criticism in the first thirteen poems of the sequence share certain traits with the age that despises them. In the second poem, the age is described as sick of "the obscure reveries / Of the inward gaze" (*PE*, p. 188). Though the age demands something very like reverie, it derides that mood in its outcasts. M. Verog, for example, is detached and "out of step with the decade" because of his "reveries," just as Mauberley drifts through "porcelain revery." The use of the same word in accusation against the poet of the second poem, M. Verog, and Mauberley makes it very difficult to draw strict lines between the various "characters" of the sequence, but it also makes it difficult to construct the binary opposition between poet and age that the poem's satirical tone seems to demand. And yet these difficulties are themselves the clue, because the sequence actually shows that even the most severe and classical art can only negate its own aspirations when the fundamental dogma of the age is a personal one. To oppose the age is to become a pedant like M. Verog or an aesthete like Mauberley, and yet to accede to its wishes is to serve an impressionism even more thorough than theirs. Furthermore, to take up the adversarial role the poet seems to assume at the beginning of the sequence is, no matter how vigorous one's opposition, to end up in the same cul-de-sac as Mauberley, a copyist at the very best. The satire of the poem is finally disturbed by its thorough irony. Even though it seems to set up a situation of stark contrasts, there are no real alternatives because every course of action leads away from the ideal presented in the second poem, the public virtues of true sculpture. "Mauberley" illustrates the danger Worringer warns against, that abstraction in a nonprimitive society, without the cohesion of the primitive, cannot produce the timeless, monumental forms of the Egyptians or archaic Greeks. As Pound senses himself, the adversarial role cancels its intended effect and imprisons the poet both in space and time.

Pound sees this very situation in the art and poetry of his age. In 1918, he defined the art of stasis as against that of the cinema by saying, "It is only by selection and emphasis that any work of art becomes sufficiently interesting to bear long scrutiny" (*VA*, p. 79). Selection and emphasis mark the art of expression, as opposed to the passive receptivity of cinema, the mimesis of the mold in plaster. But in "Hugh Selwyn Mauberley," a life of "selected perceptions" leads straight to the ennui of the aesthete. Mauberley's selection "By constant elimination" gives him "an armour," a thick shell of difference and indifference. This is not a simple contradiction, because Pound's usage shows how the very virtues defined in the second poem of the sequence lead to their own defeat. Pound describes here the way that taste can cripple itself, as he does in 1920 when he says, "The taste that enables us to find the choice bit in the second-hand shop is utterly incapable of *getting anything done* . . . it is incapable of translating itself into action" (*VA*, p. 160). The curse is, Pound says, "psychological; we can

absorb, acquire, to any extent; but we can get nothing made."
This inability is what Pound would later call "part of the disease
that gives us museums instead of temples, curiosity shops instead
of such rooms as the hall of the Palazzo Pubblico in Siena" (*VA*, p.
173). The dichotomy is the old one: the age can absorb but it
cannot make; it is impressionistic, lacking the will and strength for
expression. But if a single person follows the rule of "selection and
emphasis" on his own, he ends up in Mauberley's situation, en-
closed in reverie. Poem X shows the end of such effort in the rural
isolation wherein "the Stylist has taken shelter" (*PE*, p. 195). The
real, terrible apprehension behind "Mauberley" is that expression
and impression, sculpture and cinema, are false alternatives, that
both the age and its adversary tend to repeat the same mistakes
because the public and the individual artist have, in historical con-
fusion, switched roles.

"Hugh Selwyn Mauberley" is such a difficult poem because it
relies on a series of stark, and yet false, dichotomies. The eventual
defeat of "Mauberley" is prepared when Worringer takes the pub-
lic virtues of neoclassical art criticism and identifies them with
terror and isolation, not the kind of community of man and nature
envisioned by Winckelmann. And Worringer's aesthetic standards
appeal to Pound, Lewis, and Hulme for precisely the wrong rea-
sons, because they can be used as part of a polemic against the
weakness of the age. Worringer's opposition between abstraction
and empathy entirely loses its meaning when it is used to describe
an opposition between individual and society instead of one be-
tween a society and the nature it faces as a whole. Similarly, the
dichotomy of expression and impression, which owes so much to
Worringer, dissolves when expression, cut off from public power,
becomes connoisseurship and turns into impressionism. The satir-
ical opposition between Pound and his age is a false one, because
Pound is terribly of his age, as unable to create the Palazzo Pub-
blico alone as the age is to do so collectively. In short, the virtues
of sculpture, so central to "Mauberley" and to the aesthetics of the
time, fail to add up to those of the public monument, and the all-
encompassing irony of the sequence signifies Pound's despair that
they ever will.

If there is a monument in "Hugh Selwyn Mauberley" it is a

mocking one, Mauberley's oar, relic of many drifting voyages among islands, inscribed,

> I was
> And I no more exist;
> Here drifted
> An hedonist.
>
> [*PE*, p. 203]

But the oar reappears in the most important passage of the early Cantos, begun even before "Mauberley," when Elpenor, reappearing to his shipmates, asks,

> Heap up mine arms, be tomb by sea-board, and inscribed:
> *A man of no fortune, and with a name to come.*
> And set my oar up, that I swung mid fellows.
>
> [1/4]

Elpenor, who dies because he falls into a drunken sleep in Circe's ingle, is no less a hedonist than Mauberley. Yet the lines of his monument echo throughout *The Cantos* and finally come to be applied to Pound himself. The whole of Pound's long poem is in some sense an attempt to erect this monument, to make Mauberley's ridiculous oar into a true memorial, and to make the name of the lost sailor eternal.

−5−

The Architecture of Memory:
The Tempio Malatestiano

In beginning his new poem of some length, Pound proposes to "Give up th'intaglio method" and perhaps to replace it with the "rag-bag" appropriate to the modern world: "A rag-bag to stuff all its thought in."[1] The two different methods represent two entirely different, in fact opposed, ways of arriving at poetic truth. Where one relies on selection, on the carefully incised lines of the intaglio, the other amounts to collection. The two methods are parallel to the two contrasting processes of sculpture, carving and modeling, and the way Pound toys with the idea of the latter may seem odd in view of Vorticist prejudices against it. The rag-bag is an appealing model, however, because of its capacity to store and thus to preserve whatever heterogeneous materials the poet may discover. These advantages are more apparent in the comparison made between it and a third poetic model: the public building.

The rag-bag ultimately becomes the "showman's booth" of "Bob Browning," which is "turned at my will into the Agora, / Or into the old theatre at Arles." Such public fora contain crowds, as they contain the past, and thus function as symbols of cultural continuity both across time and within particular ages. But even though these early, experimental Cantos take place in open, public

---

1. Ezra Pound, "Three Cantos," *Poetry*, 10 (1917), 113–114. Pound's first three installments of his unnamed long poem appeared in *Poetry*, June-August 1917. These ur-Cantos are usefully reprinted, discussed, and annotated in Ronald Bush, *The Genesis of Ezra Pound's Cantos* (Princeton: Princeton University Press, 1976).

spaces like the Agora, such public places seem formed as much by individual whim as general necessity. The plan of the first building introduced in the poem "Follows the builder's whim" just as the showman's booth is a "hodge-podge" changed "whenever it suits your fancy." Clearly, Pound sees a connection between the rag-bag method and that resembling a public square or building. Both seem infinitely expandable, retentive, and thus more able to contain history than a small medallion. Yet the activity of collection, associated as it is with the quirks of the individual mind, seems an inappropriate analogue for the spacious and severe public arenas Pound favors. Obviously struggling to find a model for poetic amplitude and length, a prototype for a poem to contain history, Pound tries to combine in one metaphor models of exclusion and inclusion, the public and the private, in a way characteristic of some major episodes in his finished work. The switch from a single statue to a massive public building would seem to solve many of the problems inherent in the art of "Mauberley." Yet the way that, even in this early experimental Canto, public buildings seem more responsive to private caprice than to collective need indicates that architecture contains within it ambiguities as deep as those of sculpture. These differing imperatives come together most sharply in the public building that dominates much of *The Cantos,* the Tempio Malatestiano of Rimini.

I

The Cantos begin in Pound's mind as a "cryselephantine poem of immeasurable length."[2] The word "chryselephantine," which recalls the "small slabs of ivory" he compares to the poems of Lionel Johnson, includes most of the qualities Pound reaches for in the ur-Cantos. It implies a mixed form, the ivory and gold of the ancients, and a monumental one, since the greatest and most public work of Phidias, the Athena of the Parthenon, is thought to have been executed in this mode. That Pound may have had such

2. Noel Stock, *The Life of Ezra Pound* (New York: Pantheon, 1970), p. 184. Stock quotes an otherwise unpublished letter to Milton Bronner, September 21, 1915.

large associations in mind is suggested by his comparison, in 1913, of "the epic to a temple, the *Commedia* to a cathedral, and collected short poems to picture galleries," calling these "the highest symbols of national desire and of our own present civilization."3 Pound makes such comparisons actual when he stages so much of his first three Cantos in temples and cathedrals. Like Pater and Ruskin before him, he situates himself in public places so as to make possible a connection between himself and the civilizations he admires and between these civilizations and his readers. On the other hand, he does not set out in the ur-Cantos to produce a temple, a cathedral, or a picture gallery, but all three at once, and the resulting conglomeration resembles most nearly the last of the three as a rather miscellaneous collection. Kenner asserts that "collections are *arranged*," and perhaps most are, but Pound, at this stage, proposes to turn his rag-bag inside out on the cobblestones, and to see the building ruled by "whim," not purpose.4 In Canto 5, the city of Ecbatan is called "Great bulk, huge mass, thesaurus" (5/17). The city is a storehouse, a treasury, a form of memory akin to language yet architectural and spacious, inhabited by crowds. *The Cantos* themselves might accurately receive all three designations as a memory system designed to preserve whole civilizations, which degenerates at times to undifferentiated bulk. The tension between thesaurus and collection, which is in part the tension between civilization and individual whim, informs the whole poem and is most visible when Pound talks about his work under the metaphor of public buildings.

Since Joseph Frank's essay "Spatial Form in Modern Literature" appeared, it has become common to think of poems like *The Cantos* as temporal arts attempting to achieve spatial construction.5 But Pound's analogies actually resemble certain ancient systems that use space to contain time, that see space as the basis of memo-

3. Kenner, *Pound Era*, p. 355.
4. Kenner, *Pound Era*, p. 355.
5. See Frank, "Spatial Form in Modern Literature." The debate on spatial form, with its attendant extensions and defenses of Frank's original essay, is too vast to summarize here. A good bibliography of studies on the subject appears in *Spatial Form in Narrative,* ed. Jeffrey R. Smitten and Ann Daghistany (Ithaca: Cornell University Press, 1981), pp. 245–263. In the same volume, pp. 202–244, Frank summarizes and answers criticisms of his article that have accumulated over thirty years.

ry. As Kenner says, "any object in space is a memory system."[6] A
number of writers, including Gaston Bachelard and Rudolf Arn-
heim, see memory as utterly dependent on spatial imagery: "In its
countless alveoli space contains compressed time," writes Bach-
elard. "That is what space is for."[7] Though time is compressed in
such formulations, it need not be suppressed, and the dichotomy
between the spatial and the temporal can be bridged without major
sacrifices. As E. H. Gombrich has shown, the realities of vision
dictate that any spatial investigation take place in time and that the
simultaneity seemingly offered by perspective painting is an illu-
sion, a convention.[8] By inventing the single point of observation,
theories of perspective gave the impression that the scene wit-
nessed from one spot is witnessed all at once, but this is obviously
untrue to the way people see. Space can contain time precisely
because it is not reducible to a single point, because its extension
mirrors that of time.

This capacity of space to offer itself sequentially and yet solidly
is the key to its use in the most ancient memory systems. Frances
Yates' *The Art of Memory* shows the invention and growth of an
ancient mnemonic system based on imaginary buildings, "fields
and spacious palaces of memory," to quote Augustine, which are
constructed, packed with detail, and then "walked through" to
initiate recall. Yates shows how this tradition passes through the
ages to find its most complex expression in the "memory theater"
of Giulio Camillo, a "memory monument" containing all human
knowledge in an imaginary Roman amphitheater.[9] This theater is
the most complex example of architecture acting as encyclopedia,
as thesaurus, and is also a kind of poetry machine, with a different
piece of rhetoric at every stop. By this device, Camillo attempts to

6. Kenner, *Pound Era,* p. 31.
7. Gaston Bachelard, *The Poetics of Space,* tr. Marie Jolas (Boston: Beacon,
1969), p. 8. Rudolf Arnheim, "Space as an Image of Time," in *Images of Roman-
ticism,* ed. Karl Kroeber and William Walling (New Haven: Yale University Press,
1978), p. 2. See also W. J. T. Mitchell, "Spatial Form in Literature: Toward a
General Theory," in *The Language of Images,* ed. W. J. T. Mitchell (Chicago:
University of Chicago Press, 1980), pp. 270–299.
8. E. H. Gombrich, "Standards of Truth: The Arrested Image and the Moving
Eye," in *The Image and the Eye* (Ithaca: Cornell/Phaidon, 1982), pp. 244–277.
9. Frances Yates, *The Art of Memory* (Chicago: University of Chicago Press,
1966), pp. 46 and 160. See also Ellen Eve Frank.

contain the world, or at least all its civilization, and yet at the same time the theater is a work of manic idiosyncrasy, resembling such private museums as that of Des Esseintes, Huysmans' paragon of decadence. Its organization is rigorously repetitive and symmetrical, yet symmetry in such profusion negates itself. The very bulk of the thesaurus overwhelms its sensible arrangement.

The consciousness behind this grotesque monument is not so different from that behind *The Cantos,* and the tensions within the two are very similar. Sacred places do tend to function for Pound as memory triggers, as do the "lists of beautiful objects" he calls the core of his poem.[10] Davie calls these "gists and piths" "mnemonics," and points out how each item from Pound's list tends to be matched to a single idea in the canon of Poundian knowledge: "The mnemonic for St. Ambrose, for example, from this time forward in Pound's writing is 'captans annonam,' or 'hoggers of harvest'; there is no intimation that we need to know more than this single phrase."[11] Thus Wörgl means a certain kind of proto-Douglasite scrip, St. Hilaire the room of perfect proportions, San Zeno the signed column, until the late Cantos resemble Des Esseintes at his organ, pulling out stop after stop to revive and remix the same literary sensations in new combinations.

The comparison to Des Esseintes is meant to suggest that such encyclopedias, designed to contain and preserve a civilization, have a tendency to turn into private museums. They do so when space is overwhelmed by detail so that it can no longer perform its function as scaffold for individual items. The impetus behind this transformation is much stronger for Pound than for Camillo partly because Romantic traditions of spatial memory intervene between them. In the third Duddon sonnet Wordsworth calls his poem a "speaking monument," and he does tend to describe important memories in monumental terms.[12] The very phrase "spots of

---

10. Ezra Pound, *Guide to Kulchur* (1938; rpt., Norfolk, Conn.: New Directions, 1952), p. 109. All further references to this work appear in the text, accompanied by the abbreviation *GK*.

11. Davie, *Poet as Sculptor,* pp. 144–145.

12. William Wordsworth, "The River Duddon," in *The Poems,* ed. John O. Hayden (New Haven: Yale University Press, 1977), II, 383. Interest in Wordsworth's "Essay upon Epitaphs" has led some critics to assert that the monument is the prototype for the Wordsworthian lyric. See Ernest Bernhardt-Kabisch, "Wordsworth: The Monumental Poet," *Philological Quarterly,* 44 (1965), 503–518;

time" implies that experience becomes memory by being lo-
calized, by acquiring a place like a roadside shrine. There are really
two different processes at work here, which complement one an-
other partly because of Wordsworth's faith in their congruence.
The act of a moment becomes a monument, a "shrine" or "me-
morial," as he says in *The Prelude,* but the poem also makes "uni-
versally received truths" seem "revelations of the moment." Poet-
ry eternalizes the moment, but it also, as Ernest Bernhardt-
Kabisch says, makes "the monumental momentary."[13] Rossetti
seems to repeat Wordsworth when he says, in his prefatory sonnet
to *The House of Life,* "A sonnet is a moment's monument," but, in
fact, he introduces an important reversal of terms.[14] Rossetti de-
sires to fix the moment, as Pater does, because it is fleeting, and
because there is no stable truth beyond such brief moments of
intensity. Whereas Wordsworth wants to bring the eternal down
to earth, to make it local and familiar, Rossetti wants to make the
local stand in for the vanished monument of eternal truth.

The resulting "aesthetic of glimpses" has an odd effect on Vic-
torian ideas about public buildings and their capacity to contain
time.[15] One of Ruskin's seven lamps of architecture is the lamp of
memory, of which he says, "there are but two strong conquerors
of the forgetfulness of men, Poetry and Architecture, and the latter
in some sort includes the former, and is mightier in its reality."
Architecture becomes here the great conservator of tradition, the
model for a poem of memory, but Ruskin disliked the classical
architecture so often associated with such conservation and pre-
ferred Gothic partly because it is a concretion of individual mo-
ments: "It admits of a richness of record altogether unlimited. Its
minute and multitudinous sculptural decorations afford means of
expressing, either symbolically or literally, all that need be known

---

D. D. Devlin, *Wordsworth and the Poetry of Epitaphs* (Totowa, N.J.: Barnes &
Noble, 1980); and Geoffrey Hartman, "Wordsworth: Inscriptions and Romantic
Nature Poetry," in *Beyond Formalism* (New Haven: Yale University Press, 1970),
pp. 206–230.
    13. William Wordsworth, "Essay upon Epitaphs, III," *Prose Works of William
Wordsworth,* ed. W. J. B. Owen and Jane Worthington Smyser (Oxford: Oxford
University Press, 1974), II, 83. Bernhardt-Kabisch, p. 509. The citation from *The
Prelude* is XII, 208–210.
    14. Rossetti, p. 59.
    15. The term is Kenner's.

of national feeling or achievement."[16] Ruskin's Gothic cathedral seems very much the kind of memory system fancied by the ancient mnemonic system, all the more useful because it has more niches into which to tuck specific memories. The peculiarly Victorian aspect of this conception is that national memory need be multitudinous and minute instead of large and simple. Gothic is a collection, an amalgamation, and achieves largeness by addition, not expansion. The difference between the public and the private in such a system is simply that of number: if Wordsworth's memories require a single spot, a national tradition must require a myriad of spots.

Pound betrays much the same consciousness when he compares his sacred buildings and his rag-bag, seeing each as a rather shapeless container out of which will spill a pile of shiny objects. The comparison violates any concept of buildings as rather rigid in plan, but it answers to the Victorian idea of monuments as simple collections of moments. What is missing is the matrix, the ground that gives space its shape by existing around and between objects. As Georges Poulet says of Proust, there is no sense of space as prior to specific places, no route from the Guermantes to the Méséglise way.[17] The lack of such a coordinating matrix causes architectural constructions to collapse, to succumb to their own complexity as does Camillo's theater. Robert Harbison makes the same point in connection with Francesco Colonna's *Hypnerotomachia Poliphili,* which Frances Yates identifies as a mnemonic system gone mad. Poliphilo's villa is so intense in each of its individual follies and yet so obscure as to the pathways between, that space ceases to be an exterior medium altogether. The motive is, as Harbison asserts, a "fear of loss or forgetting" so intense that nothing can be left out or even dimmed in the slightest. But the result is a journey so totally "without coordinates" that it seems to be taking place only within the mind.[18] The capacity of such mon-

16. John Ruskin, *Seven Lamps of Architecture* (1849; rpt., London: Dent, 1907), p. I and p. 187.

17. Georges Poulet, *Proustian Space,* tr. Elliott Coleman (Baltimore: Johns Hopkins University Press, 1977), pp. 41–42.

18. Robert Harbison, *Eccentric Spaces* (New York: Knopf, 1977), pp. 74–81. Yates, p. 123. Harbison also discusses the intense clutter of Ruskin's bedroom at Brantwood, "tomb of utter self-absorption, space with no height and no breadth" (p. 37).

uments to contain and preserve time simply collapses in a rubble of individual decorations. Part of the advantage of the ancient mnemonic system was the way it made the interior exterior, objectifying the knowledge of the mind. Losing the space that makes this possible creates a kind of vacuum, shrinking memory until it is again interior and private, reducible almost to a single point.

II

Such is the situation of the Tempio Malatestiano, which takes the place of the Agora and the temple at Arles in the final version of *The Cantos,* and is, like them, both rag-bag and monument. The Tempio is one of Pound's most intriguing metaphors for his poem and one that clearly exposes the complicated relationship in *The Cantos* between architecture and poetry, space and memory. The Tempio embodies a much more complex relationship between poetry and spatial form than Frank's theory suggests and at the same time shows some of the difficulties Pound faces in matching poetic method and public aspiration. The early Renaissance structure itself was conceived as a complex memory system, one which would both immortalize and codify the court of Sigismundo Malatesta. Under construction as of 1447, the building was to have given the court a triumphal setting, as a "pantheon of heroes."[19] Seven arches along each side of the structure were to have held the sarcophagi of the *uomo illustri* of Rimini, including the poet Basinio, and at least one philosopher who never served that court, Gemistus Plethon, whose ashes Sigismundo brought back from Constantinople after a campaign against the Turks. Thus Sigismundo becomes one of Pound's heroes through an act of near-resurrection, the first to follow Odysseus in raising a true monu-

---

19. Rudolf Wittkower, *Architectural Principles in the Age of Humanism* (London: Warburg Institute, University of London, 1949), p. 33. Unless otherwise specified, descriptions of the Tempio are based on Wittkower's discussion. For a general overview of the history behind the Malatesta Cantos, see John Drummond, "The Italian Background to *The Cantos,*" in *An Examination of Ezra Pound,* ed. Peter Russell (New York: Gordian Press, 1973), pp. 100–118. The most compete discussion of the relationship between the Malatesta Cantos and the Tempio is in Davie, *Poet as Sculptor,* pp. 120–134.

ment. Much of Pound's respect for Sigismundo depends on the act of preserving Gemistus' name and ideas, and thus furthering the introduction of neo-Platonic ideas into Renaissance Italy. The pantheon is thus a great deal more than a glorified graveyard. Because the court and the interests of Sigismundo seem, at least to Pound, to encompass so much of what is valuable in his time, the Tempio becomes a compendium of civilization, preserving, through Gemistus, the classical past as well as the life of the Renaissance.

The Tempio was also designed to immortalize Sigismundo himself and his wife, Isotta, whose sarcophagi were to occupy two great arches at the very front of the structure. The arches are modeled after the triumphal arch of Augustus in Rimini, and so their very shape indicates the conquest of time that is the building's purpose. As a letter from one of his stewards, included in Canto 9, indicates, Sigismundo had work begun on Isotta's sarcophagus before any other feature of the building. This rather macabre act is evidence of Sigismundo's desire, above every other motive, to immortalize Isotta. Pound certainly interprets it thus, taking one of his favorite lines from Landor, "Past ruined Ilion Helen lives," and altering it to fit the situation: "Past ruin'd Latium" (9/41). In fact, the Tempio might be thought of as essentially identical to Isotta, bearing as it does her initial intertwined with Sigismundo's as its chief device, and containing a number of arcane references to her in its decorations.

These acts of memorialization have for Pound a rather broad public significance. Isotta is much more than the consort of Sigismundo; she is a goddess to the people of Rimini and thus a kind of *genius loci*. At the end of Canto 9, Pound quotes the phrase "populo grata (*Italiaeque decus*)" from the medal of Isotta cast by Matteo de' Pasti in 1446. That Isotta is pleasing to the people and the ornament of Italy as well as of Sigismundo's eye gives her a certain civic significance. Pound seems to take this as sanction to see the whole building, and the whole commemorative project behind it, as a public act. In Canto 89, he says, "POPULUM AEDIFICAV-IT / which might end this canto, and rhyme with / Sigismundo" (89/596). The variation of "templum aedificavit," applied throughout *The Cantos* to Sigismundo, contains the "rhyme," the assertion that his building and the people are identical. Sigismundo's popularity with his people, so great it threatens his enemies at the end of Canto 11, is associated with Galla Placidia through a repetition of one of Pound's favorite phrases: "In the gloom, the gold gathers the light against it" (11/51). In Canto 11, the phrase seems to describe the bonfires of Sigismundo's subjects, lit to welcome him back from Sparta, but in fact the line is Pound's shorthand for introducing the subject of Galla Placidia, as for example in Canto 21 (21/98). The glow of these bonfires and the glow of the roof of the mausoleum of Galla Placidia can be compared because both are expressions of the will of an entire people: "every self-respecting Ravennese is procreated, or at least receives spirit or breath of life, in the Mausoleum of Galla Placidia" (*SP,* p. 322). Like the mausoleum, the Tempio is a shrine to an empress from whom, in her interred state, a whole people is to gather sustenance. It shares this distinction with other monuments, institutions like the Florentine bank, the Monte dei Paschi, of which it is said in Canto 43, "there was the whole will of the people," (43/218), and the Duomo of Ferrara:

> Sed et universus quoque ecclesie populus,
> All rushed out and built the duomo,
> Went as one man without leaders
> And the perfect measure took form. . . .
>
> [27/130]

The greatest public function, finally, is to refine and transmit tradition, as these workers on the Duomo do, "refining the criterion." And this is how Sigismundo's Tempio serves the public, "a precise definition transmitted thus Sigismundo" (74/425). To transmit is to memorialize, and to give memory to a people is to give coherence and strength to their civilization.

Yet Pound signifies one of the problems with this tradition in a very ambiguous statement about the Tempio in *Guide to Kulchur:* "It is perhaps the apex of what one man has embodied in the last 1000 years of the occident" (*GK,* p. 159). The sense of the sentence is very difficult because it could mean that the Tempio is the highest reach of a thousand years of culture, as embodied in one man, or that Sigismundo has managed to embody more than any one man of the last thousand years. The suggestion behind the word "apex" is that the whole millennium has been struggling toward this point, but the suggestion behind "one man" is that Sigismundo has managed it alone. The ambiguity of this sentence reveals an unwillingness on Pound's part to decide whether the Tempio represents the high-water mark of a cohesive culture or the work of one man, alone and removed from the culture of his own time. Pound says, as if to clarify the sentence, "A cultural 'high' is marked." And yet he can never shake the appeal of that phrase "one man," which returns later in *Guide to Kulchur* when Pound says the Malatesta Cantos, and by implication the Tempio, express "the effect of the factive personality, Sigismundo, an entire man" (*GK*, p. 194). In fact, Pound asserts in the same book that Sigismundo accomplishes everything "*against* the current of power" (*GK*, p. 159). The very spatial confusion of Pound's terminology indicates the conflict. How can an apex of culture be achieved if the current is against it? The nineteenth-century language of cultural rise and fall conflicts with Pound's Romantic notions of the hero as outcast. This side of Sigismundo, the singular man, accounts for a different aspect of the Tempio, one which intrigues Pound for very different reasons.

The memory system embodied by the Tempio Malatestiano is in fact a private and secretive one. The Tempio is actually more of a major remodeling job than a new building, based as it is on an existing Gothic church dedicated to San Francesco. The church becomes the Tempio by being encased inside a new facade. Unwilling and unable to tear down the old church, Sigismundo gives it a new skin that purposely suppresses many of the features of the old building. The classically inspired side arches run athwart but do not replace the original window openings, thus causing an odd disjunction of exterior and interior. In most photographs of the building taken from the front, the peak of the church can be seen just barely protruding from the unfinished facade, as if looking out from behind a disguise.[20] Pound seems to have been fascinated by hybrid buildings of this kind. The church of San Pietro in Marino, which is the "splay, barn-like church" of the first ur-Canto, is one example, enclosing within its Renaissance incarnation a pagan temple. An even more curious example is the Parisian house of

20. One such photograph is included in Adrian Stokes's *The Stones of Rimini* (1934; rpt., New York: Schocken, 1969), Plate 25. Stokes's book is the best available pictorial record of the Tempio.

The Tempio Malatestiano. Alinari/Art Resource, Inc.

Canto 7, whose "walls of a sham Mycenian, / 'Toc' sphinxes, sham-Memphis columns," hide "a cortex . . . Shell of the older house" (7/26). There are layers of history in such buildings, and this must be the aspect of them that fascinates Pound, but the latest layer is rarely the most effective in his eyes. The Renaissance never gets the pagan temple as "trim" as it once was, and the modern surface of the room in Canto 7 is utterly sham.

Perhaps Sigismundo's rebuilding of the church of San Francesco could be thought of as a restoration because his changes essentially obliterate the Christian character of the building and give it a pagan and somewhat neo-Platonic one. Pound quotes the words of Pius II against Sigismundo in Canto 9: "and built a temple so full of pagan works" (9/41). "Pagan" is hardly a term of opprobrium for Pound, who sees Sigismundo as having reached back to a world nearly lost to modern man. But the disapproval of the pope does account for much that is hermetic and cryptic inside the Tempio. Neo-Platonism is a hermetic religion in the root sense of the word, in any case, but the decorations of the Tempio have often been considered a kind of arcane code known only to Sigismundo. Roberto Valturio, Sigismundo's engineer, ascribes the decorations to Sigismundo's "researches," and seems subtly to advertise their hermetic nature by saying they will appeal more to the learned than to the rabble.[21] Some aspects of the decoration were certainly meant to remain mysterious, including the initial letter of the inscription on Isotta's tomb: "D ISOTTAE ARIMIN-ENSI B M SACRUM." The D could stand either for "Dominae," wife, or "Divae," goddess, and the ambiguity slightly shields Sigismundo's deification of his consort. But under this inscription, hidden on a second plaque apparently undiscovered until 1912, is another inscription bearing a date that commemorates the year in which Sigismundo first possessed Isotta as his mistress. Other devices decorating the interior and exterior of the building, such as the intertwined initials and the date 1450, which apparently commemorates the legitimation of two of Sigismundo's children by Isotta, increase the sense of secret significance.[22] Their full mean-

21. Stokes, pp. 241–244. Some of these arcane interpretations are considered and dismissed in Jean Seznec, *The Survival of the Pagan Gods* (New York: Harper/Bollingen, 1953), pp. 132–137.
22. Stokes, pp. 194, 202–204. Isotta's tomb is pictured in Stokes's Plate 37. See

ing was known only to one man, and they were entirely personal to him. Therefore it is impossible to pretend that the Tempio was constructed by a people or even a culture. Sigismundo takes a church and consumes it with a building of his own, replacing the cross with his own initials, the decorations with his own devices, the Virgin with his mistress. What was once an exterior is now an interior, bearing a private system of symbolism where it once bore a public one. The enclosure of the old church within the new temple is symbolic of the alienation of the space from public view.

The change and the hybrid nature of the resulting structure are reflected in Pound's own ambivalence about the role of the public in erecting it. On the frontispiece of *Guide to Kulchur,* he says, "There is no other single man's effort equally registered," and every reader must feel in Pound some thrill of approval at what a single man can do. The process by which he does it is perfectly described in a passage from Erwin Panofsky quoted by Davie: "The great man of the Renaissance asserted his personality centripetally, so to speak: he swallowed up the world that surrounded him until his whole environment had been absorbed by his own self."[23] Thus Sigismundo swallows San Francesco to make it the Tempio Malatestiano. Pound can call his Cantos "the tale of the tribe" and then in the next breath celebrate Sigismundo as "an entire man" because he thinks the tribe has nothing to fear and everything to gain from being swallowed by such men (*GK,* p. 194).

Pound's desire to have it both ways, to see the Tempio as a public expression and as an entirely personal one, is also revealed in his ambivalence about the architecture itself. The Tempio is not just a Renaissance sheath fitted over a Gothic plan; it also bears inside Byzantine marble purloined from the church of San Apollinaire in Ravenna. A report of the "theft" and a bill of sale are both included in Canto 9. In fact, Sigismundo was so hard pressed for stone that he raided the local graveyard, so that, as Adrian Stokes reports, the facade even now bears faint inscriptions to

---

also P. J. Jones, *The Malatesta of Rimini and the Papal State* (London: Cambridge University Press, 1974), p. 213.

23. Davie, *Poet as Sculptor,* p. 130. Francis Haskell comments in *Patrons and Painters* that it was two hundred years before another Italian religious structure so glorified a man instead of the divine (p. 249).

bygone Riminese.[24] Though the main architect, Leon Battista Alberti, is often praised for the skill with which he adapted his own style of architecture to the existing structure, the whole cannot help but be a bit miscellaneous. The structure is a magnificent hybrid, such as Pound might well admire as a forerunner of his poem, but each of the three main elements compromises the other two, so that even Alberti's design is "a mixture of classical and late Gothic elements."[25] The interior bears little or no relationship to the exterior, so that, as Wittkower says, "one enters the building but only to find with amazement that one is inside a Gothic church."[26] The Gothic interior is not clearly intelligible, however, because the decorations, using in many cases Byzantine marbles, are "so massed as positively to compromise the recognizability of the structure."[27] Even Stokes, an ardent partisan of the Tempio reliefs, admits that the design of the interior "cannot fill anyone with particular satisfaction."[28]

In descriptions like these, the Tempio begins to resemble the "Toc" interior of Canto 7, an ancient shell with an extra helping of ornament on top. Pound is certainly conscious of this aspect of the building, since at the end of Canto 9 he describes the "filigree hiding the gothic" (9/41). Filigree can hardly be a word of Poundian approbation, and Pound does call the Tempio a "jumble and a junk shop" (*GK,* frontispiece) and a "medley" (*VA,* p. 167). Yet if it is in these terms, as Pound admits, "a failure," it "nevertheless registers a concept" (*GK,* frontispiece). Pound suggests research into Gemistus' manuscripts to divine this concept, which he identifies in Canto 83 with water, but he also offers one explicit architectural concept unifying the design, the sphere expressed as a circle, "there always as principle and as cause of a solidity, a satisfaction which no other base-form could have attained." This concept is revealed in the number of circles scattered throughout the design, and by "Pasti's medal of intention" (*VA,* p. 168). The

24. Stokes, p. 177.
25. Wittkower, p. 34. By and large, Wittkower considers Alberti's compromise a success.
26. Wittkower, p. 33.
27. Leonardo Benevolo, *The Architecture of the Renaissance* (Boulder, Colo.: Westview Press, 1978), I, 110.
28. Stokes, p. 184.

The interior of the Tempio. Isotta's tomb is visible at the right. Alinari/Art Resource, Inc.

medal referred to, by Matteo de' Pasti, shows the Tempio as it would have looked if Sigismundo had been granted the money and the peace to complete it. The chief feature of the proposed building, dominating what is now thought of as the Tempio itself, is a huge dome, and Pound is correct is identifying this dome as the unifying feature of the Tempio's design. As Joan Gadol reports in her work on Alberti, the altar of the renovated church was to have gone in the center of a round chapel, surmounted by the dome, whose cupola would have answered exactly in position and size to the altar area below.[29] This strong concentricity derives from Alberti's belief in the circle as the most appropriate shape for a church, as most nearly reflecting the infinity of God.[30] Pound was interested enough in Alberti to read his *Trattato della pittura,* to which he refers in an article written in 1922, while he was working on the Malatesta Cantos, and may therefore have found this "principle of intention" in Alberti himself (*VA,* p. 173). At any rate, he is absolutely right in referring to the dome as both the mystical and the architectural principle within the Tempio's confusion.

Unfortunately, the dome was never built and the circle never managed to assert its cohesive effect over the rectangle of the original plan. The focus of the Tempio is therefore not on a single, central altar, from which everything radiates in semi-divine fashion, but on numerous, variously decorated, side chapels, spaced one next to the other along the side walls. And Pound, despite his comments on the circle, seems happy with this situation. He says in his review of Stokes's book that the Tempio "would have been a far less daring synthesis had all its details been fully digested and reduced to a unity of style, à la Palladio" (*VA,* p. 168). The miscellaneous effect is precisely what Pound likes about the building, and he admires it for the same reason he admires the hodge-podge of the showman's booth, because both manage to register an individual fancy: "As a human record, as a record of courage, nothing can touch it." The Tempio can, in Pound's mind, serve as record, as memory, because it is multitudinous, minute, full of anecdote.

29. Joan Gadol, *Leon Battista Alberti: Universal Man of the Early Renaissance* (Chicago: University of Chicago Press, 1969), p. 120. A photograph of the medal showing Alberti's plan for the dome appears on p. 98. See also Peter Murray, *Architecture of the Renaissance* (New York: Abrams, 1971), p. 60.
30. Wittkower, pp. 3–4.

The individual moment reigns in a conglomeration of similar moments, just as it does in Ruskin's version of Gothic.

III

Pound's various comments about the Tempio reveal a deep conflict between the claims of form and those of anecdote, between the unity of an impersonal design and the unity arbitrarily imposed by the human personality, which is finally a conflict between two uses of the Tempio, as public monument and private shrine. Since the Tempio is one of Pound's metaphors for his own work, the conflict also reveals itself in the structure of *The Cantos,* especially that of the Malatesta Cantos, 8–11. One side of this conflict can be represented by Alberti, who would seem, as artist and polymath, to be a perfect hero for *The Cantos.* He would also seem to be a man after Pound's heart, a foe of ornament so rigorous he was once reprimanded for trying to paint the choir of SS. Annunziata white, removing all its decorations.[31] Alberti corresponds to that side of Pound that always hammers away at the idea of form, of formal purity as an immutable and clear principle untouched by individuals. This is a side of Pound developed by the example of Epstein and Gaudier-Brzeska, that found in sculpture a kind of form independent of representation as well as free of personality. Piero della Francesca, whose work also decorates the Tempio, is Pound's most common Renaissance example of this kind of form, which he identifies with Vorticism: "an attempt to revive the sense of form—the form you had in Piero della Francesca's *De Prospettive Pingendi,* his treatise on the proportions and composition" (*VA,* p. 153). Though Pound may not have known it, Francesca owes much of his treatise to Alberti, as do all Renaissance writers on perspective.[32] But Pound commonly uses Francesca as his representative of the sense of form reawakened by Vorticism (*VA,* p. 177) and of "Proportion, laws of proportion" (*VA,* p. 247), even of proportion in architecture.

Pound holds very strong ideas on this subject, ideas which may

31. Wittkower, p. 9.
32. Gadol, p. 62.

have been inspired by and which certainly parallel those of Alberti. Particularly in the early 1920s, he harped in article after article on the necessity for the proportional arrangement of architectural details, especially of windows and doors: "Architects seem to have forgotten that the ordinary house façade is an oblong pierced by several small oblongs beside and above an oblong or arched door. The proportion of these oblongs can attain 'the qualities of music,' it does in any number of palazzi in Verona" (*VA*, p. 174). Since this statement appears in the same article in which Pound commends Alberti, it is possible that his idea of musical proportion in buildings begins with Alberti, who, as Wittkower shows, codified musical intervals as architectural proportions. It is Alberti who makes one of the more famous statements of this idea, in a letter to Pasti about some proposed changes in the Tempio: "You can see where the sizes and proportions of the pilasters come from: if you alter something, all that harmony is destroyed [si discorda tutta quella musica]."[33] Thus Alberti's idea of the Tempio answers exactly to Pound's demands for respect of form and proportion in building. For both men, the ability to hold a number of elements in proportional relationship in the mind marks the sense of form.

Unfortunately, Pound did not possess this sense himself. The stories of his ineptitude as a sculptor are only one indication.[34] Even more revealing is the way his architectural criticism clings to the surface of the building. Though he takes care to warn that his article "Parallelograms" concerns only the "façade of a city house set in a block," Pound in fact sees even detached buildings as "fronts": "the city house-front, the small city house-front, and the suburban house-front" (*VA*, p. 82). His next article on the subject is called "Super-fronts" (*VA*, p. 83). Pound sees himself at work

33. D. S. Chambers, *Patrons and Artists in the Italian Renaissance* (London: Macmillan, 1970), p. 182. For the original, untranslated text, see Wittkower, p. 103. It is also possible that Pound's phrase is a poorly remembered version of Pater's famous statement about the arts approaching the condition of music. As Hugh Honour shows, the comparison between architecture and music was very common in the nineteenth century. See *Romanticism* (New York: Harper & Row, 1979), p. 158. But the very nature of this equation, which compares the two arts not in structure but in emotional expressiveness, shows the difference between Pater and Alberti, who saw the two as enjoying the same kind of abstract, eternal rules of proportion.

34. Kenner, *Pound Era*, p. 390. See also Charles Norman, *Ezra Pound* (New York: Macmillan, 1960), p. 248.

on a theory of proportion and composition, but the proportions under consideration work in two dimensions, not three. Pound realizes this, and contends that the facade "is simply the part of architectural art which comes first into the scope of this criticism and, being in the street, most concerns the man in the street" (*VA*, p. 84). But the simple fact is that Pound, like Ruskin before him,[35] prefers to see in terms of surfaces, not solids, and that for all his talk about the dimensionality of sculpture he does not see buildings as spatial arrangements of solid mass but as signboards bearing a legend of windows and doors.

This preference affects Pound's reading of the Tempio and the poetry he bases on it. For Pound, as for Adrian Stokes, the Tempio means the bas-reliefs inside, not the architectural structure of Alberti. But for a brief mention of "a few arches" in Canto 9, the design of the building is not mentioned in the poem itself, nor is Alberti one of the artists whose name comes to be a shorthand for great art because of his relationship to the Tempio. Pound is not concerned with the overall architectural design of the temple, nor is he bothered particularly by its hybrid nature, because for him the Tempio is not a building but a gallery, a container for the reliefs. If Pound were truly interested in proportion or composition his natural shrine would be Alberti's Sant' Andrea in Mantua, which successfully reflects its architect's desire that nothing in a building be "unequal, incongruous, out of proportion, or not conducive to the general Beauty of the whole."[36]

But Pound is not really serious about his ideas of proportion, or rather he sacrifices these ideas to another, stronger imperative. For Pound, the author of the Tempio is not Alberti at all, but Sigismundo. And Sigismundo's genius is not the genius that brings all details into a harmonic relation, that composes and dissolves incongruity in design, but the genius that sees beauty in the incomplete: "The Tempio was stopped by a fluke? or Sigismundo had the flair when to stop it?" (*GK*, p. 159). Rather than a strong architectonic sense, Sigismundo has a flair for details: a bit of Bellini, a bit of Piero della Francesca, a bit of the old Byzantine from Ravenna. Sigismundo is, above all, a collector, and Pound

---

35. See Mario Praz, *Mnemosyne: The Parallel between Literature and the Visual Arts* (Princeton: Princeton University Press, 1970), pp. 38–39.

36. Quoted in Gadol, p. 140.

betrays, in a very revealing statement, his admiration for the collector's avarice: "Federigo Urbino was his Amy Lowell, Federigo with more wealth got the seconds" (*GK,* p. 159). Of all the possible aspects of Sigismundo's personality, Pound seems to choose the collector to identify with and thus to cast himself as a collector and quasi-patron. Though Pound proclaims that Sigismundo "cut his notch," the collector differs markedly in kind from the other hero of the Tempio, Agostino di Duccio, the sculptor. Whereas the sculptor's talent is to demark form with finely cut lines, essentially to pare away excess, the collector conglomerates. The two actions are diametrically opposed and represent opposed ambitions never quite reconciled in Pound's art: the desire to remove excrescence, to reveal the essential, precise definition through an abrasive cleaning, and the preservationist's desire to bring everything into the ark of the poem that it might be saved. The Tempio stands where these two desires, that of form and that of anecdote, cross, and Pound's statements about it are so problematical because it seems impossible to decide between them. The original opposition between intaglio and rag-bag is not resolved but simply obscured.

Pound seems actually to rejoice that the Tempio does not succeed in fulfilling the ideas of form he shares with Alberti. He prefers that it be miscellaneous, that it contain designs of great beauty "down to simple botch, and physical figures so defective that they wouldn't get by a simple Atlantic City or Ziegfeld judging committee. And thank heaven, there is nothing, utterly and completely nothing that theory can now do to it; or about it" (*VA,* p. 169). The collection is always incomplete simply because its variety imposes no necessary limit. Thus Sigismundo's talent is "flair," the connoisseur's eye for the choice bit, the savoir faire that knows when not to push things too far. The only principle that does unify the collection inside the Tempio is Sigismundo's personality. It is a private monument most of all because the details exist in relation to one another simply by virtue of the appeal they hold for one man. Pound specifically disdains the unity of proportion or design, even though he seems at times to admire it, in favor of the unity of personality. His ideas about these architectural matters directly parallel his dilemma about the public status of the building. Though he would like to see it as the apex of a culture, as the act of a people, it continually resolves itself back into a hermetic jewel box. The strong sense of form and proportion that represents fidelity to eternal and suprapersonal measure is sacrificed to a taste for the hybrid, the intricate, the various, and the private.

IV

Sigismundo's "flair" recalls the very first building to appear in *The Cantos,* one formed "by the builder's whim." The terminological similarity reveals the Tempio's lineage from that building and also shows that, despite many poetic advances over the ur-Cantos, those concerning Sigismundo still take the rag-bag as their model. Pound's admiration for the studied incompletion of the Tempio betrays his intention to retain the hodge-podge method of those early experiments. Harbison compares the Tempio, on similar grounds, to Colonna's *Hypnerotomachia,* pointing out that when the architectural aesthetic of such constructions is carried over into literature, what results is a maddening episodic maze, "the pure *and then and then* structure."[37] The same equation Harbison observes between the Tempio and the *Hypnerotomachia* exists between the Tempio and the post-bag whose fragments take up much of the Malatesta Cantos. Even when not giving notes from the bag, Pound strings together nonsequential bits of Sigismundo's life with a deadening list of ands: nineteen on pages 42 and 43 of Canto 10 alone. Pound's insistence on this conjunction is obviously purposeful. These are the "fragments you have shelved (shored)," and Truth and Calliope slug it out over the contents of a wastebasket. But nothing is further from Kenner's spirited concept of syntax in *The Cantos* as an active transfer of energy, and, in fact, nothing is further from truly spatial form. The conjunction produces, as Harbison asserts, a kind of pure succession that signifies the utter collapse of space. The advantages that caused the ancient mnemonic system to use spatial form are thereby sacrificed. Pure succession easily gives the impression that each moment is the same moment, so that reiteration replaces history and memory is lost.

37. Harbison, pp. 81–82.

To be fair to Pound, *any* account of Sigismundo's life gives this feeling. The discontinuous, fragmented method of the Malatesta Cantos may more closely approximate historical accuracy than that of any other section of the poem simply because Sigismundo's life seems to have had no continuity. A modern scholarly history such as P. J. Jones's *The Malatesta of Rimini and the Papal State,* just by virtue of its rigor and completeness, gives the same impression of a single action almost endlessly repeated without variation: Sigismundo changing sides. Trapped between Florence, Milan, Venice, and the pope, with a cloud of other princelings and condottieri swarming around him, biting seemingly at will, Sigismundo survived by sacrificing continuity. This is the story Pound gives in the Malatesta Cantos, and for once chronology truly would be a violation of historical truth. Such temporal disorder reflects Sigismundo's status as outcast, as a small man kept hopping by the forces around him, and this seems to be precisely the aspect of Sigismundo that holds Pound's interest.

Almost the whole of Canto 10 is taken up with feuds, betrayals, and slanders. Pound's personal relish for this sort of thing is reflected in his comparison of Sigismundo's nemesis, Federigo d'Urbino, to his own, Amy Lowell. And there seems to be an exact congruence between the status of outcast, the lack of continuity in Sigismundo's life, and the style Pound chooses to represent it:

> With the church against him,
> With the Medici bank for itself,
> With wattle Sforza against him
> Sforza Francesco, wattle-nose,
> Who married him (Sigismundo) his (Francesco's)
> Daughter in September,
> Who stole Pèsaro in October (as Broglio says "*bestialmente*"),
> Who stood with the Venetians in November,
> With the Milanese in December,
> Sold Milan in November, stole Milan in December
> Or something of that sort,
> Commanded the Milanese in the spring,
> the Venetians at midsummer,
> The Milanese in the autumn,
> And was Naples' ally in October. . . .
>
> $\qquad\qquad\qquad\qquad\qquad\qquad$ [8/32]

The beastliness is Francesco Sforza's, as is the inconstancy, but Sforza's shifts become Sigismundo's because of the realities of power: "And he's lost his job with the Venetians . . . And Wattle never paid up on the nail / Though we signed on with Milan and Florence" (9/37). The life of the outcast is the life of anecdote, the pure "and then and then," because he lacks the power to forge a true story line. Davie asserts that this "shabby diplomacy" is redeemed by "the work of art that was coming out of it, the Tempio."[38] But the life of the condottiere and the design of the Tempio are one, each is essentially anecdotal and capricious. Or rather, the Tempio presents to Pound two aspects, the classical form of Alberti's shell and the mercurial decorations inside, and though Pound feels strongly the demands of form, he chooses anecdote because it more nearly approximates the mercurial quality of Sigismundo's personality. The Tempio embodies the art of the outcast, not the unity of a public design, but the miscellaneous baggage of the man on the run, faithful to no formal imperative but representation of an individual psyche.

In Pound's case, spatial form is not a critic's metaphor but a primary ambition of the poet. Statue and monument function as poetic models for Pound because they achieve a status he envies for his poem. Their stability over time, their role in tradition, the aid they offer to personal memory, all are aspects he might borrow for *The Cantos*. The monument also offers a model for generalization, for bridging the gap between intaglio and epic so painful in the ur-Cantos. The public building is one of Pound's earliest metaphors for his own poem, attractive because it contains history by housing a collection of beautiful objects. His comparison of temple and rag-bag, however, betrays an allegiance to a theory of building that is not truly spatial at all, that sees a building simply as a collection of individual caprices. His admiration for the multitudinousness of the Tempio interior could be Ruskin's admiration for Gothic, an admiration that declares a public ambition but that very easily becomes an entirely personal one. Pound is of the nineteenth century enough to feel the charm of anecdote and to sacrifice his desire for design and proportion to it. A parallel sacrifice is that of the public ambition behind his poem to the person-

38. Davie, *Poet as Sculptor*, p. 126.

ality of Sigismundo. A man who put the words *res publica* on his notepaper, Pound still admired the Romantic outcast, the man whose glamor is based on his opposition to the public. The unscrupulous patron, general of the arts, is only the positive side of this myth. All these questions, the architectural arrangement of the poem, its relationship to a public, to tradition, and to memory, are intimately connected and are worked out in the various public buildings that decorate *The Cantos*.

—6—

A Trace in the Manifest

I

In *Guide to Kulchur,* Pound says of the Tempio, "You can contrast it with St. Hilaire. You can contrast it with ANY great summit done WITH the current of power" (*GK,* pp. 159–160). The builders of St. Hilaire, free of the kind of opposition that dogged Sigismundo, produced an entirely different kind of monument, expressive of pure form where the Tempio expressed a thousand anecdotes. This contrast between two holy places epitomizes one of the basic tensions within Pound's aesthetic. The claims of selection and the claims of retention clash in Pound's comments on the Tempio, and he seems at times to become the kind of collector he derides in "Hugh Selwyn Mauberley," simply because memory has no alternative but collection. In St. Hilaire, however, he finds a monument that preserves by selection and thus harmonizes one of the most basic dichotomies in his work. The action of carving and the clean lines of the sculptor are put to the service of a public tradition, thus forming a monument that does not collapse or fold inward on itself.

The shorthand for St. Hilaire in *The Cantos* is "St. Hilaire its proportion" (51/250), a perfection of form best illustrated in the room "wherein, at one point, [there] is no shadow" (87/573). Thus it stands as an example of that side of Pound's architectural ideas that is sacrificed in the Tempio to the lure of the personal and anecdotal. In the tower room, perfect form brings a perfect clean-

liness, a shape free of all the bric-a-brac of the world outside. At
that single point in the tower room of St. Hilaire, one wins free-
dom from "ÀGALMA," from false monuments and images:

> haberdashery, clocks, ormolu, brocatelli,
> tapestries, unreadable volumes bound in tree-calf,
> half-morocco, morocco, tooled edges, green ribbons,
> flaps, farthingales, fichus, cuties, shorties, pinkies,
> et cetera
> Out of which things seeking an exit

$$[40/199]$$

In Canto 40, Hanno's voyage is a break-out, a flight from such
things to the fundamental:

> Out of which things seeking an exit
> To the high air, to the stratosphere, to the imperial
> calm, to the empyrean, to the baily of the four towers. . . .

$$[40/201]$$

Hanno seeks the pure calm above the world that Pound describes
in "Paracelsus," and like Pound at St. Hilaire, he finds it in a tower
room whose bareness resembles "the ineffable crystal." This mon-
ument, so different from the "jumble" and "junk shop" of the
Tempio, becomes Pound's most perfect version of the combina-
tion of sculptural virtues and public memory.

  The equation between the sculptor's carving and the art of
memory developed in Pound's mind partly because of his acquain-
tance with another sculptor, Constantin Brancusi. Pound's articles
on Brancusi testify to the impact that artist had on him in the early
Paris years, an impact based in part on the way Brancusi had
effected his exit from bric-a-brac and confusion: "When all France
(after the war) was teething and tittering, and busy, oh BUSY,
there was ONE temple of QUIET. There was one refuge of the
eternal calm that is no longer in the Christian religion. There was
one place where you cd. take your mind and have it sluiced clean"
(*VA*, p. 307). This temple was Brancusi's studio, which Pound
wanted desperately to convert into a public monument in actu-
ality. In a letter to William Bird in 1926, he says that if he had had

any money, "Brancusi's temple" would have been built (*L,* p.
201). In fact, Pound's mind teemed with temples in the early
1920s. Noel Stock reports that Pound visited Brancusi's studio
with Bride Scratton, in whose divorce Pound apparently played an
important part, and that the two planned together "a temple to the
true religion" like Brancusi's projected Temple of Love.[1] The real
nature of the true religion seems a bit transparent in this anecdote,
which bears a humorous resemblance to Yeats's project with
Maud Gonne. But a column based on Brancusi's *The Kiss,*
which Scratton and Pound saw in Brancusi's studio, was ultimate-
ly erected as a public monument in Rumania.[2] It seems very odd
that a column depicting such a private embrace could become the
main structural member of a gate commemorating resistance to
the Germans in 1917, but in fact, Brancusi's style is valuable as a
model for Pound precisely because it makes such transformations
possible.

Sculpture of the kind Pound witnessed in Brancusi's studio is
fundamentally monumental because its forms are the basic constit-
uents of memory itself, the pure geometric solids Plato calls beau-
tiful in and of themselves.[3] Such forms underlie all appearance and
serve to knit together the otherwise chaotic world; as eternal con-
stants they function as nature's memory. In Brancusi's work the
"triangle and the circle" are "master-keys to the world of form,"
not Brancusi's world of form, "but as much as he has found of
'the' world of form" (*LE,* p. 443). Pound also maintains that
Brancusi's sculpture effects an "approach to the infinite *by form*"
(*LE,* p. 444). Since Pound was introduced to such ideas by Ep-
stein, the first to speak of "form, not the form *of anything,*" it is

1. Stock, p. 244.
2. Stock, p. 244. For a description of the projected Temple for Indore and the
monument at Jargu, see Sidney Geist, *Brancusi: A Study of the Sculpture* (New
York: Grossman, 1968), pp. 111–113, 119–125. There is a rather different descrip-
tion of the Temple in *VA,* p. 283.
3. Plato's description is as follows: "a straight line or a circle and resultant
planes and solids produced on a lathe or with a rule and square. . . . these things
are not, as other things are, beautiful in a relative way, but are always beautiful in
themselves." *Philebus,* tr. J. C. B. Gosling (Oxford: Oxford University Press,
1975), p. 51. It was rather common in these years to cite this passage in defense of
abstract form. See Reyner Banham, *Theory and Design in the First Machine Age*
(Cambridge: MIT Press, 1960), p. 205. Pound first mentions the "circle absolute"
in 1912 (*SP,* p. 362).

natural for him to find them preeminently in sculpture and to refer to statues repeatedly as if they represented Platonic essences. Thus Gaudier-Brzeska's sculpture exhibits "some realm of 'Ideas,' of Platonic patterns" (*VA*, p. 183), while Brancusi's produces "the form which is the sort of Platonic quintessence" (*VA*, p. 172). Brancusi's studio, therefore, is not just an atelier, but "a Platonic heaven full of pure and essential forms" (*VA*, p. 172). The sculptor does not copy appearance, but looks beyond the world as we imperfectly see it, to represent directly Plato's heaven of pure idea.

Being eternal, such forms inhabit the dimension of stillness that is the very essence of memory. Brancusi, "surrounded by the calm of his own creations" (*LE*, p. 444), amid his own "serene sculpture" (*VA*, p. 171), inhabits "a temple of peace, of stillness" (*VA*, p. 172), a serene and eternal Platonic heaven. Previously, Pound had followed Lewis in identifying art with stasis, but by this time stillness has acquired an almost sacred quality quite different from the purely ethical import it had for Lewis. It is this kind of stillness, derived more from Brancusi than from anything in London, that pervades certain episodes in *The Cantos*. Stillness is one of the primary qualities of the Valhalla Pound constructs for his "men of craft" in Canto 17:

> Marble trunks out of stillness,
> On past the palazzi,
>   in the stillness
>   [17/76]

Davie has effectively tied this passage to the reverence for Istrian marble celebrated in *The Stones of Rimini*,[4] but the "white forest of marble" is as much Brancusi's as it is Sigismundo's. In an unpublished and undated article, Pound seems to paraphrase this Canto in describing the heaven he found in Brancusi's studio: "The white stillness of marble. The rough eternity of the tree trunks" (*VA*, p. 307). Pound's observation here of the marble column based on *The Kiss* and the wooden *Endless Column* is combined, it seems, in one forest of marble tree trunks for Canto 17.

The eternity of sculpture and the world of memory are therefore

4. Davie, *Poet as Sculptor*, pp. 127–131.

identical if sculpture acts to cut forms down to their basic enduring elements. That Pound sees the act of memory itself as such an abrasive carving is shown in his final version of "Donna mi prega," Canto 36. A metaphysical definition of love, Canto 36 locates love's place in the mind, identifying it with memory: "Where memory liveth / it takes its state . . ." (36/177). The earlier version of "Donna mi prega" that appears in *Personae* makes the spatial nature of memory a bit clearer by placing love "in memory's locus" (*PE*, p. 248). A more important change moves the poem in the opposite direction. The line once translated as "And wills man look into unformed space" appears in Canto 36 as "Willing man look into that forméd trace in his mind" (36/178). The second version is apparently a misreading, a replacement of "non formato" or "non fermato" by "un formato." Pound attempts, as James Wilhelm says, to tie this line back to the earlier passage on "memory's locus,"[5] and he does so by borrowing from Remy de Gourmont a line that is perhaps more central than any other to the definition of the monument that appears in *The Cantos*.

The evolution of this line itself is indicative of the role sculpture plays in Pound's aesthetic. Pound first quotes this boast of Remy de Gourmont's in 1915: "Je sculpte une hypothèse dans le marbre de la logique éternelle" (*SP*, p. 419). He later translates the line without identifying its source in a letter nagging the Nobel Prize committee for its failure to recognize true merit: "The carving a thesis in eternal beauty or in lasting verity! ! !" (*L*, p. 26) In 1921, he takes it as the informal epigraph of his essay on Brancusi, and glosses it by saying, "A man hurls himself toward the infinite and the works of art are his vestiges, his trace in the manifest" (*LE*, p. 441). To carve a trace in the manifest, to cut something tangible and lasting in human memory is to succeed as an artist.

When Pound needs a metaphor for memory in Canto 36, he reaches for his own adaptation of Gourmont's carving metaphor. In this version of the Cavalcanti translation, memory seems even more actively sculptural, since the trace is "formed." Instead of

5. James Wilhelm, *Dante and Pound* (Orono: University of Maine Press, 1974), p. 83. For a definitive text, translation, and commentary on the poem, see J. E. Shaw, *Guido Cavalcanti's Theory of Love* (Toronto: University of Toronto Press, 1949).

saying "None can imagine love / that knows not love" as he does in the earlier version, Pound says in Canto 36, "Unskilled cannot form his image." The act of memory becomes an active one, dependent on skill, and conceiving of love comes to resemble conceiving a work of art. Another change suggests that such skill is very much like Brancusi's. What once read as "Love does not move, but draweth all to him" is changed to "He himself moveth not, drawing all to his stillness" (36/178). Memory becomes that realm of stillness described in Canto 49, and a loved person or thing endures when the lover can form a place to receive it in that dimension. Thus Borso, Carmagnola, and Sigismundo live in the pure marble temple of memory in Canto 17, as the nymph Ileuthyeria of Canto 2 lives forever in ivory stillness.

Pound's mistranscription, mistranslation, and misunderstanding of "Donna mi prega" requires extraordinary erudition to unravel, and the difference between his last two versions of the poem cannot be accounted for in any simple way. But the resemblance between the added language and the language of his Brancusi essays, including notes for a book on Brancusi contemplated in the early 1930s, between the two versions of "Donna mi prega," suggests that Pound's concept of memory moves closer to the kind of temple inspired in him by the sculptor. Later paraphrases of Canto 36 in the Pisan Cantos make this affinity even clearer. The phrase "formato locho" reappears in Canto 74, and is translated again in Canto 76:

> nothing matters but the quality
> of the affection—
> in the end—that has carved the trace in the mind
> dove sta memoria
>
> [76/457]

This final version of Cavalcanti's phrase is almost purely Pound's, adapted more from Gourmont than anything in the original poem, and it makes quite plain that the act of memory and the act of sculpture are one and the same. The *formato locho,* or prepared place, is in fact a kind of carved resemblance, a perfect niche, worked by the sharpness of intellect or affection.

Most discussions of the carving metaphor, including Kenner's and Davie's, consider it primarily as a way of treating individual objects, individual works of art. Both see carving as one of the criteria Pound uses to discriminate between honest and dishonest art, and this is certainly one of its major functions.[6] But such discussions leave out the element of time, the connection between carving and memory, and thus tend to see carving more as a question of statues than of monuments. As the evolution of Cavalcanti's "formato locho" suggests, however, the carving metaphor comes into closer and closer association with the idea of memory as *The Cantos* progress. This development may be explained partly by Pound's long association of carven forms with Platonic essences, and thus, rather indirectly, with anamnesis, or memory of a purer state. That world of forms is very often associated in Pound's mind with sculpture, as the best expression of Platonic essences on earth, and so it is natural for him to reverse the equation and to imagine a Platonic heaven as populated by sculptured forms. He has, in fact, already done so in "Paracelsus in Excelsis," and very little he will ever say about sculpture will contradict the essential feeling of that poem. Associating the act of carving specifically with memory does, however, represent an important extension of such ideas. It equates the act of cutting with the act of preserving, the clear definition with the clear memory. As memory comes more and more to concern Pound, especially at Pisa, this equation comes to the fore, and all statues and sculptured forms, in addition to most buildings, become monuments. One of the comforts Pound derives for himself while imprisoned at Pisa is that time itself can act as a sculptor, preserving the valuable by whittling away the dross. In fact he begins to see memory as an active principle in nature, more than a willful act of an individual mind, so that time has a way of annulling itself, preserving as much as it destroys.

Pound thus defines, with the help of Cavalcanti, Gourmont, and Brancusi, a kind of monument dependent on the immutable laws of proportion, on the reductive cleaning, that can be associated with one side of the Tempio, that presided over by Alberti. This definition of the carven memory comes into its final form at pre-

6. See Kenner's list of discriminative criteria, *The Poetry of Ezra Pound*, p. 315. Concerning the *formato locho* itself, however, Kenner does say that it invokes "memory hypostasized as part of an extramental world of forms" (p. 284).

cisely the same time that Pound is exalting a quite different monument in *Guide to Kulchur,* praising there the variety, the *lack* of composition in Sigismundo's method. Pound never resolves this basic ambiguity in his thought, even though Brancusi and the Parisian milieu to which he belongs offer him a possible model of memory that harmonizes the competing claims of selection and retention that lie at the bottom of the difficulty. But it is clear from Pound's writing on Brancusi that the new sculpture he discovers in the Paris studio advances ideas first discovered in London, and that certain ideas current in Paris at the time help to solve contradictions left over from the Vorticist years. The model of memory thus composed survives into the very latest Cantos, even though it never completely displaces a competing idea of sculpture still rooted in the nineteenth century.

II

Brancusi is but a single individual, and Canto 36 is an image of memory as a personal faculty. But the carving that preserves a loved object in human memory can be seen as a dynamic of history, with aesthetic progress as the sculptor instead of any person, and this particular aspect of the modernist idea enters *The Cantos* more and more as they concern the monument. When Pound used, in one of his "Paris Letters" to *The Dial,* the phrase "the freshness of the classic," he said something he might have said at almost any time in his life, but which had a special significance in the Paris of 1921.[7] The quarrel between Futurism and Vorticism continued in Paris in these years, though Vorticism as a movement was dead, over precisely this issue. Whereas a Futurist such as the visionary architect Sant' Elia could speak of the "tremendous antithesis between the modern and the ancient world," a whole host of groups and subgroups advocated a modernism based on certain principles from antiquity.[8] A single example typifies this conflict.

7. Ezra Pound, "Paris Letter," *The Dial,* 71 (September 1921), 457.
8. Antonio Sant' Elia, "Futurist Architecture," in *Programs and Manifestos of 20th Century Architecture,* ed. Ulrich Conrads (Cambridge: MIT Press, 1970), p. 34.

Marinetti proclaimed that the automobile meant the demise of the Winged Victory as a thing of beauty, whereas Le Corbusier's *Towards a New Architecture* juxtaposes pictures of automobiles with those of the Parthenon to argue that the same design laws obtain in each case.[9]

These attitudes toward monuments and the monumental reflect a basic disagreement about the nature of aesthetic progress, a process both sets of groups insist they are advancing. Whereas Marinetti and Sant' Elia object to the "embalming, reconstruction, and reproduction of monuments and ancient palaces" as a betrayal of the modern, Corbusier and other architects, artists, and designers associated with his movement of the 1920s, called Purism, or with the Dutch group De Stijl, insist that modernism advances toward a style reflecting classical monuments, in what Theo van Doesburg called the "original-monumental."[10] They escape contradiction by arguing that the monuments of antiquity reflect most perfectly the pure geometric forms the *Philebus* identifies as beautiful in and of themselves. Classical monuments such as the Parthenon thus become examples of nonrepresentational, nonreferential art, an art independent of taste and association, intrinsically beautiful. Corbusier and Amédée Ozenfant maintain that the "great works of the past are those based on primary elements, and this is the only reason why they endure."[11] A commonplace of the time became the comparison of machine parts and ancient monuments, such as Corbusier's illustrations of the Delage brake placed next to closeups of the Parthenon. As Frederick Etchells, former Vorto-Futurist and Corbusier's English translator, says, the Parthenon has much in common with "a first-rate modern concrete structure or a Rolls Royce."[12]

This peculiarly modern monumentalism closely resembles

9. F. T. Marinetti, "Futurist Manifesto, 1909," *Futurist Manifestos,* ed. Umbro Apollonio (New York: Viking, 1973), p. 21. Le Corbusier, *Towards a New Architecture,* especially pp. 4, 15, 29, and 109.

10. Sant' Elia, p. 36. Theo van Doesburg, "Evolution of Modern Architecture in Holland," *Little Review,* 11 (Spring 1925), 48–49. Van Doesburg is against the *imitation* of ancient monuments, but in favor of a monumentalism based on simplicity and scale.

11. Le Corbusier and Amédée Ozenfant, "Purism," in *Form and Function,* ed. Tim and Charlotte Benton (London: Crosby, Lockwood, Staples, 1975), p. 90.

12. Frederick Etchells, Intro. to Le Corbusier, *Towards a New Architecture,* p. x.

Pound's own use of the geometric forms of the *Philebus* to sanctify the sculpture of Brancusi and Gaudier-Brzeska. The correspondence extends as well to the theory of artistic progress advanced by Corbusier. Progress, for Corbusier, is a process of refinement of certain *objet-types:* "objects tend toward a type that is determined by the evolution of forms between the ideal of maximum utility, and the satisfaction of the necessities of economical manufacture, which conform inevitably to the laws of nature."[13] This evolution, governed by mechanical necessity, produces perfected forms, which resemble the forms already discovered by great sculptors and architects of the past. Thus Corbusier can say of the Delage brake: "This precision, this cleanness in execution goes further back than our re-born mechanical sense. Phidias felt in this way: the entablature of the Parthenon is a witness."[14] Progress, in this analysis, works backward, and not by addition but by subtraction. "Selection" is one of Corbusier's favorite words, and selection in any mechanical process will inevitably result, he suggests, in pure aesthetic form, as already revealed by Greece.

Pound, of course, always denounced Futurism for its ignorance of the past, and he always revered ancient buildings. But his association in the early 1920s with Brancusi, Léger, Picabia, Cocteau, and other Parisian artists places him in a welter of groups influenced by "monumental" definitions of aesthetic progress like Corbusier's. As Reyner Banham has established, the various elements of the Purist aesthetic, "the object, the type, the platonic, mechanistic and geometric preferences," had been current as far back as 1913, and the language of Vorticism included most of them. The idea of the *objet-type* and that of the pure Platonic solid are obviously identical to ideas Pound applies to the sculpture of Epstein

13. Quoted in Banham, p. 211.
14. Le Corbusier, *Towards a New Architecture,* p. 129. The idea of mechanical selection as an evolutionary process leading to beauty is, in fact, quite an old one. In *Pioneers of Modern Design,* Nikolaus Pevsner discovers it even in Wilde (p. 27) and Gautier (p. 135). The oldest example was probably the ship, as noted by Robert MacLeod, *Style and Society: Architectural Ideology in Britain, 1835–1914* (London: RIBA Publications, 1971), p. 74. As the next chapter will show, this metaphor was available to Americans such as Greenough in the early nineteenth century. The major difference in Corbusier's version, besides an appreciation of the standardization simply unavailable to the nineteenth century, is the Platonic idea of the *objet-type,* with its almost mystical perfection far beyond mere efficiency. See Banham, pp. 212–213.

and Gaudier-Brzeska. But, as Banham says, the elements do not coalesce into a "coherent aesthetic philosphy" like that described above until Corbusier and the early 1920s.[15] Of Pound's closest associates in Paris, Brancusi and George Antheil were inducted into De Stijl, Fernand Léger wrote for *L'Effort Moderne*, prototype of Corbusier's journal *L'Esprit Nouveau*, and Cocteau gave that journal its name.[16] Pound's enthusiasm for such men endured even the sourness of the late 1930s, and he could admit then that " 'We' London 1914 were subsequent to a great deal of Paris" (*SP*, p. 457), that is, Paris more completely handled the aesthetic problems posed by Vorticism. Just as Brancusi's example helps to move the Cavalcanti translation closer to an artistic definition of sculpture as memory, the Parisian experience in general moves Pound to an idea of aesthetic memory in time that affects the later Cantos.

The language of the Brancusi essays themselves reflects many of these assumptions. The habitual reference to Brancusi's studio as a temple of quiet is hardly startling until one reflects that the forms inside that studio were likely to be of highly polished metal or in shapes very little suggestive of traditional temples. But Pound reflects the Purist aesthetic in other works, odd enterprises obviously the result of enthusiasms engendered in these years. A book on Brancusi was planned and partially executed, as was a book to be entitled *Art and Machines*.[17] This project seems to have been inspired partly by Léger, whose essay "The Esthetics of the Machine" in the *Little Review* of Spring 1923, was dedicated to Pound. As early as 1922, Pound commented about Léger in *The*

15. Banham, p. 212. Andrew Clearfield, "Pound, Paris, and Dada," *Paideuma*, 7 (1978), 113–140, is a good example of the way that Pound's years in Paris are seen primarily in relationship to Dada. Clearfield ultimately finds that Dada made little impact on Pound, despite his relationship with Dadaists such as Picabia.

16. Banham, p. 196 and p. 206. It might also be mentioned that while Pound was on the editorial board of the *Little Review* it published articles by van Doesburg, Hans Richter, El Lissitsky, Laszlo Moholy-Nagy, Adolf Loos, André Lurcat, who was a French disciple of Loos, Enrico Prampolini, a Futurist turned Constructivist, and Frank Lloyd Wright. This gave the *Little Review* a pool of contributors overlapping that of *De Stijl* as well as *L'Esprit Nouveau* and *L'Effort Moderne* (see Banham, pp. 186–188).

17. Notes for the projected Brancusi book appear in *VA*, pp. 306–309, along with some correspondence between Pound and his parents, who were to send him photographs of machines from Philadelphia. See also the letter to the editor of the *New Review*, *VA*, pp. 215–217.

Dial: "one knows of the time he stopped painting and for some years puzzled over the problem of ideal machines, three-dimensional constructions having all the properties of machines save the ability to move or do work."[18] *Art and Machines* was not begun until June, 1925, when Pound first wrote to his parents with a request for photographs of machinery and spare parts. The question was so much a part of aesthetic discussion in Paris in 1924–1925 that Jane Heap, co-editor of the *Little Review,* was inspired by a trip there to plan a Machine-Age Exposition to be sponsored by the *Review* and a supplement to the *Review* that would reprint many articles it had published on the subject in the past.[19]

Machinery, of course, had a similar vogue before the war, when Hulme used it as a prototype of geometric art, of a "new geometrical and monumental art." *Blast* had advertised itself under such headlines as "THE TURBINE."[20] But the very energy emanating from such references shows how far they are from celebrations like Corbusier's, which retain none of the Futurist fascination with speed. Moreover, Pound was not inspired to write a study of art and machines until after having lived in Paris, and the assumptions made by that study show its derivation from common aesthetic discussions of the 1920s. As early as 1918, Pound had exclaimed, "All the brains have gone into devising new and luxurious lines for bathroom fittings and for the bodies of automobiles. *Line* in automobiles has been for years magnificent and expressive" (*VA,* p. 82). But he did not make the connection he made in 1927 between the "formal beauty of machines" and the "proportions of architecture and sculpture" (*VA,* p. 216). This commonplace occurs as well in Léger's article of 1923: "a machine or manufactured object can be beautiful when the relationship of the lines which inscribe the volumes is balanced in an order equivalent to that of earlier architecture." Léger continues, "I have to introduce you to a new order—the architecture of machinery," and compares machines "to the Roman style which balances vertical lines by the

18. Ezra Pound, "Paris Letter," *The Dial,* 74 (December 1922), 88. See also *VA,* p. 217.

19. Anderson, *The Little Review Anthology,* p. 341. The supplement was XII.1 (Spring-Summer 1926).

20. Hulme, *Further Speculations,* p. 130. *VA,* p. 151.

round arches of the windows."[21] Pound extends the analogy by referring to ugly machinery as "gothic . . . having the defects of the gothic" (*VA*, p. 217).

Pound thus follows a fashion of the 1920s by comparing machines and monuments. However, he is not primarily interested in the architectural qualities of machinery. He disdains the static, structured components as obeying "the same laws as other architecture" (*VA*, p. 302). Instead, his interest centers on the moving parts, because only they illustrate the principle of perfection in art typified by machines. The stable, structural components of a machine can be designed according to any principle, according to any taste, but the moving parts are designed by necessity, where form is "imposed by necessities and efficiencies of the machine" (*VA*, p. 217). Necessity is a kind of force, like the speed of the machine itself, milling away excrescence and superfluity: "The good forms are in the parts of the machine where the energy is concentrated. . . . The beauty comes from the efficiency at one point (vortex)" (*VA*, p. 301). On the other hand, Pound is as interested in "the sockets in which the moving parts move" because the important factor is not motion itself, not speed at all, but the effect that motion has on form, cleaning it, giving it "the clear hard edge" (*VA*, p. 300). For the same reason Léger found that ideal machines failed to express the beauty of actual machines: actual machines were *already* ideal, having been idealized by the necessities of work, "forced by necessity" (*VA*, p. 301). Thus Léger says, "The more the motor perfects its function of utility the more beautiful it has become."[22]

Obviously, Pound has imbibed, through Léger perhaps, one of the basic ideas of Purism, as the ideology of Corbusier and Ozenfant came to be known, the evolutionary beauty of mechanical efficiency. The appeal of the idea, for Pound as well as the Purists, is that the human designer, with all his propensity for flash, fashion, and ornamental taste, is replaced by an impersonal force, designing objects according to immutable and ancient laws of beauty. Grain elevators or telephones come to resemble Greek

21. Fernand Léger, "The Esthetics of the Machine," *Little Review*, 9 (Spring 1923), 46.
22. Léger, p. 46.

temples because they follow the same physical laws, known to the genius of the Greeks and revealed to the modern world by the genius of its machines. This idea lifts modern design out of the ebb and flow of style and makes it utterly different from all earlier changes in human taste, in the eyes of its proponents in any case, by its derivation from empirical formal laws instead of human caprice.

Part of the seductive power of this idea comes from the social implications of the new style. Machines are not designed by individuals, according to this analysis. Pound speaks of "the inventor's thought," and then corrects himself: "or, better, the thought of the series of inventors" (*VA,* p. 303). The path to perfect design is an evolutionary one, governed by what Corbusier called "the law of Mechanical Selection."[23] Inefficient design destroys itself through inefficiency, simply by dying out. The resulting beauty is quite impersonal. Pound believed that "machines are in a 'healthy state' because one can still think about the machine without dragging in the private life and personality of the inventor" (*VA,* p. 303). The individual whims responsible for so much bad art in the past, especially that of Impressionism, are negated by mechanical necessity, resulting in a kind of collective art. In the same way the first De Stijl manifesto declared that the use of machine-made materials "removes the personal character from a building and thus tends towards a group art."[24] Thus machines and the pyramids are brought together by Corbusier, and Pound can see machinery as the product of an impersonal tradition, like a monument from the past.

Machinery, in this analysis, is the perfect public monument, enduring through time by expressing a suprapersonal will and imperative. The language Pound applies to machinery resembles very closely that which he applies to Brancusi, and together the two subjects illustrate a definite trend in his thinking of the 1920s. By excluding the muss and fuss of the contemporary world, really by carving it away from the interior of his studio as he would carve excess from around a shape in marble, Brancusi isolates certain

23. Banham, p. 211.
24. Banham, p. 152.

enduring, eternal forms. In the case of machinery, time itself accomplishes the same thing, sculpting by the law of necessity. The correspondence between the two cases is clearly illustrated in notes remaining for the projected but unfinished book on Brancusi, which also show the mystical aura such ideas acquire from Pound's neo-Platonic interests. The notes suggest that Brancusi succeeds by turning himself into an impersonal natural principle. There is in his studio "no Freud, no Viennese complex" and thus "I have seen people sick with worry and nerves pretty well cured by a visit." They are cured, apparently, by having all that Viennese twaddle removed from their systems, by art that is *"not like the work of a human being, it's like something created by nature"* (*VA*, p. 308). Brancusi's sculpture seems to Pound to have been created not by art but by evolution, and Brancusi himself becomes a force, an impersonal, almost godlike power. The notes degenerate into a list, but some of the elements of this fairly gnomic list can be read in light of the published Brancusi essay and the writing on machines. Point 2 covers "the world of forms," about which nothing more is said, but the Brancusi essay makes it plain that Pound means the Platonic forms of the sculpture. Points 4 and 5 were apparently to declare at some greater length that "Brancusi's only living rivals [are] Bliss and Company or other realizers of form." Bliss and Company made presses, several examples of which appeared in photographs Pound had collected for his book on machines. Thus the two great sculptors of the modern world are Constantin Brancusi and a maker of heavy machinery, obviously because the necessities of machine manufacture tend to create the same sort of Platonic forms incarnated in Brancusi's studio. In fact, Point 4 is also entitled "The Great Form, united," as if it were to concern the very apotheosis of form. This steady advance from Bliss and Company to the empyrean ends with Point 6: "Optional. Singing light" (*VA*, p. 309).

This approach, by way of Bliss and Company, to the pure neo-Platonic light shows the advantage of an art created by forces, not by individuals. The simple necessity to do work, to achieve efficiency, operates on the forms of Bliss and Company until they reach such a perfection as to radiate pure light. Forms radiate this pure Plotinian light when they most nearly resemble the true heavenly forms,[25] and they are apt to do so when shaped by some agency other than defective human will. The idea that a statue is achieved by the removal of excess, a process akin to purification, is a neo-Platonic one, which receives its best-known expression in Michelangelo's poem "Si come per levar." The important aspect of the machine is that the agent of removal, and thus of purification, is not an individual artist, but the force of time. What might be seen as the destructive aspect of time is in fact converted into that which preserves by purging and purifying. Corbusier says, "Culture is the flowering of the effort to select. Selection means rejection, pruning, cleansing: the clear and naked emergence of the Essential."[26] Humans must struggle in their art to reach the essential, but they reach it every day in their machines, where necessity takes the effort out of selection. The process exactly mirrors that in Canto 40, when Hanno breaks away from "ÀGALMA," from bric-a-brac and decoration, to "the imperial / calm, to the empyrean . . . the NOUS, the ineffable crystal" (40/201). The beauty of the machine idea is that it sees such break-outs as occurring as the result of collective will. That is, Hanno achieves a kind of privacy by rejecting the excrescences of pseudo-civilized life, but Pound sees humanity as making such rejections collectively in certain aspects of its culture. In fact, this is what tradition is for Pound, selection, not retention, and the act of preservation and that of rejection are not antithetical any longer but complementary.

Herbert Schneidau has noticed a basic resemblance between Pound's idea of tradition and the metaphor of sculpture: "when he talks about his research into 'what has been done, once for all,' and into 'what remains for us to do,' his words evoke an image of gradual emergence, like that of the form in a late Michelangelo statue."[27] As Schneidau suggests, this idea makes culture a process of gradual removal, like the model offered by Corbusier. The process defined as culture is one of removal and destruction such that tradition resembles Michelangelo's statue "that grows the

25. Panofsky, *Idea*, p. 27.

26. Le Corbusier, *Towards a New Architecture*, p. 139.

27. Schneidau, p. 155. For another discussion of selection in Pound's idea of culture, see Christine Brooke-Rose, *A ZBC of Ezra Pound* (Berkeley: University of California Press, 1971), p. 18.

more, the more the stone diminishes."[28] Pound pursues this para-
dox throughout *The Cantos*. The Rimini bas-reliefs are called "a
clean-up" in Canto 92 as if they took away from rather than added
to the world's store of decoration. The best example is perhaps the
city of Wagadu, which is created by a process of cleansing.[29] In
extremity, mankind saves itself by casting off ballast, as Odysseus
on his raft is commanded in Canto 91 to "get rid of parapernalia"
and Ouan Jin is silenced for "making clutter" and threatening his
clan.

The sculptor's art is therefore a very basic metaphor for the
work a culture does to maintain tradition. A statue that represents
tradition is by definition a monument, and the example of Bran-
cusi's sculpture is so central to *The Cantos* because it shows how
the technical virtues of sculpture can act to sustain and preserve
culture. Such monuments begin to escape the fate of the Tempio
and do so by reflecting a different set of aesthetic assumptions. Or,
rather, Pound's decision in favor of form over anecdote, of selec-
tion over accretion, corresponds to a theory that makes the art
produced general and collective, not private. The Tempio pre-
serves because of its capacity; it can contain everything amid its
jumble. Like the rag-bag to which it corresponds and the post-bag
on which the Malatesta Cantos are modeled, it is a symbol of
shapeless retention. Brancusi's forms, on the other hand, like an-
other Pound monument, St. Hilaire, preserve by reduction, exclu-
sion, and their bareness serves a stronger, wider memory than the
Tempio's profusion. The tower room of St. Hilaire "wherein, at
one point, [there] is no shadow," represents, like the tower of
Canto 40, the triumph of selection.

Elements of a different aesthetic remain in Pound's mind, how-
ever, until the very end of his life, perhaps because he never de-
sanctifies any example of art once it has been placed in the personal
pantheon, but also because the appeal of impersonal design is only
one of a number of imperatives. The famous fly-tying passage of
Canto 51 emphasizes handwork, just as the usury passage empha-
sizes individual craftsmanship: "That hath the light of the doer"

28. Quoted by Panofsky, *Idea,* p. 116.
29. See Massimo Bacigalupo, *The Forméd Trace: The Later Poetry of Ezra Pound*
(New York: Columbia University Press, 1980), p. 377.

(51/251). Recognizable in such passages is a pure Ruskinism utterly foreign to the praise of impersonality Pound voices in Brancusi's studio and certainly to the emphasis on machinery in his proposed book. As always, Pound's aesthetic seems to look two ways, one direction, that toward Ruskin, epitomized by the column at San Zeno, signed by and equivalent to its maker, the other by St. Hilaire, formed by the eternal, impersonal laws of proportion that were anathema to Ruskin.[30] The two examples are simply incompatible because, as Ruskin realized, respect for "principles" negates the free expression of craftsmen like the one who signs his column.[31] Pound himself is so far from realizing this incompatibility that in the very same essay in which he commends Léger's experiments with machines he cites the San Zeno column with a complaint against mass production (*VA*, p. 172–173). The tower room at St. Hilaire is the more fruitful example, finally, because of the kind of tradition it implies, the kind of public monument it is. For Ruskin's model to work, a large group of individuals, all acting on their own personal impulses, must come together to build a large, collective, but not impersonal, project. But for St. Hilaire's model, community is realized over time, in a process of transmission made possible by impersonal principles. Community exists cumulatively through history, not simultaneously in a single instant of time.

The almost Darwinian model of history offered by Corbusier is valuable to an understanding of Pound because it resolves one of the most basic tensions in his work. The act of memory, crucial to art and to culture, seems essentially retentive, and thus the museum or thesaurus seems its purest image. But collection is anathema to some of Pound's deepest principles, no matter how much of a collector he may have fancied himself, because collection tends to deny the claims of structure, to defeat significant arrangement of itself. It is akin to modeling or building up, not to carving and whittling down. Brancusi, on the other hand, like Michelangelo or Bliss and Company, builds by whittling down. Selection *is* retention if it proceeds toward certain Platonic solids first discovered in

30. Kenner observes that Pound's love of the motto of the San Zeno column, "Adamo me fecit," is pure Ruskinism (*Pound Era*, p. 323).

31. See John Ruskin, *The Stones of Venice* (London: Smith, Elder, 1853), III, 95–100.

the great monuments of antiquity. The selector, the carver, escapes the isolation of Mauberley not by achieving immediate community with his fellows, which he is likely to avoid, but by touching a mystical community linked by the pure geometric forms. Pound can therefore retain his Ruskinian sense of the "doer" and still pay homage to impersonal formal principles, harmonizing the worlds of Alberti and Sigismundo.

III

The best definition of this kind of monument comes, appropriately, in *Rock-Drill,* a book named after an early, industrially inspired sculpture by Epstein, perhaps one of the few works of sculpture to incorporate an actual working machine.[32] The essential passage, in Canto 87, begins with the idea of a very small force breaking a huge mass: "pine seed splitting cliff's edge." A fragment from the Machiavelli quotation that begins *Gaudier-Brzeska* connects this process of natural quarrying to the activity of sculpture. But the sculpture here is the force within the seed, the slow, cumulative energies of nature. Like the forces behind the machinery of Bliss and Company, these evolutionary forces produce beauty because ugliness is momentary, and the age-long time scheme of nature effaces it, producing the beautiful:

> Only sequoias are slow enough.
> Bin Bin "is beauty".
> "Slowness is beauty."
> [87/572]

Gaudier-Brzeska's rival is the sequoia, as Brancusi's rival was Bliss and Company, because natural physical forces, given time, will produce forms cut as cleanly as any sculptor's. This is the slow

---

32. For a discussion of Epstein's sculpture and photographs of it in its various incarnations, see Cork, pp. 466–482. The piece was constructed between 1913 and 1915 and shown at the London Group Exhibition in 1915. It is possible that Pound's title was suggested to him by Lewis' review of Pound's letters, "The Rock Drill," *New Statesman,* April 7, 1951, but in *Poet as Sculptor* Davie says the title comes from the sculpture itself (p. 55).

chisel the pine seed applies to the cliff, which seems to give this section of *The Cantos* its name. The relationship between the seed and Epstein's sculpture, which features a carved anthropoid atop a commercial pneumatic rock-drill actually purchased from the company, is an important one, not just because it connects the activity of the pine seed to that of a sculptor Pound admired. Epstein's sculpture is a forerunner of the machine vogue of the 1920s, all the more significant because it chooses a machine that bears an implicit resemblance to the artist/sculptor himself. The industrial drill, the sculptor, and the pine seed are equivalent in the way they work on hard substance to create beauty. All three wear away excrescence to reveal fundamental forms, man very quickly, machines and nature as part of a slow process. All three carve a trace in the manifest.

Nature thus produces its own tradition, its line of succession "from the / San / Ku / to Poictiers." Perhaps only a sequoia could survive the two thousand years from the ministry of the San Ku to the building of St. Hilaire at Poitiers, but between the two there does exist a root system; or rather the conditions of life on earth are such that buildings like St. Hilaire will be brought into being at intervals whenever men are wise enough to let these laws prevail. The tower room at Poitiers is in one sense a creation of the pine seed, the slow sculpting of nature, and therefore is more a monument to nature than to man. The precise description of such monuments is unraveled slowly over the next several lines:

> The tower wherein, at one point, is no shadow,
> > and Jacques de Molay, is where?
> and the "Section", the proportions,
> > lending, perhaps, not at interest, but resisting.
> Then false fronts, barocco.
> > "We have", said Mencius, "but phenomena."
> monumenta. In nature are signatures
> > needing no verbal tradition,
> oak leaf never plane leaf. John Heydon.
>
> > > > [87/573]

In one sense, St. Hilaire is the monument lauded in this passage, but behind it lie the forces in nature that make all phenomena into monumenta. Here St. Hilaire, with its pure proportions, stands as a clear rival to the Tempio, but the real focus of the sacred is not the building at all but the sculptural principle of which it is only an example.

The essential opposition in the passage is between "barocco" and the tower room. The word "barocco" stands for all that is cleaned away, the paraphernalia created by Ouan Jin, the bric-a-brac of Canto 40. The phrase "false fronts" recalls Pound's own articles on architecture of 1918–1919, so concerned with "fronts," and thus Pound's own confused ideas about proportion and decoration. There is, in fact, a kind of double movement in the passage, that of human history, which moves from San Ku to Poitiers in seeming perfection, "then" to be adulterated with false fronts, and that of nature, which begins with the pine seed and ends with the same pure faithfulness to type: "oak leaf never plane leaf." Nature never produces barocco, and so it is the constant against which human styles can be measured and reformed.

Representative of this constant in architecture is the golden section, the the unchanging pattern of relationships that ensures perfect proportion in building. Pound mentions the section many times in his prose and often uses proportion as a shorthand for architectural beauty. His reverence for Piero della Francesca, for example, is based largely on the artist's researches into proportion. Proportion is a side of Pound's architectural interest that is finally slighted in his work on the Tempio, but here it comes to be identical to the process of memorialization, the very essence of the monument. This taste is shared with Corbusier, whose house at Garches takes its form from the *section d'or,* and whose interest in proportion ultimately leads to the Modulor.[33] The concept comes up so much because it has a very basic usefulness for both Pound and Corbusier. As Erwin Panofsky says of artists of the Renaissance, the theory of proportion satisfies both an empirical, Aristotelian mind, and a mystical, neo-Platonic one.[34] Based on exact observation and empirical fact, the laws of proportion arrived at in the Renaissance offer at the same time a connection to the mystical cosmology based on harmonic relationships. Pound too has a

33. See Rowe's article on Garches, pp. 1–27, and *Towards a New Architecture,* p. 72.

34. Panofsky, *Meaning in the Visual Arts,* p. 90.

very empirical definition of form as what works well, but he breaks out, time and again, into neo-Platonic raptures, as in the notes for the Brancusi book. The movement is the same here, from the golden section to John Heydon, and the basic idealism behind laws of proportion seems to make the equation possible. Formulas like the golden section bridge the gap between a rigorously empirical method and a mystical result, allowing Pound and Corbusier to claim neutrality for their method and at the same time enjoy the authority of pseudo-religious results.

Certainly, the tower room at St. Hilaire receives a mystical beauty by achieving perfect architectural form. The room contains the "singing light" mentioned as the last subject to be treated in the book on Brancusi, released by the perfection of its shape. Clean itself, it performs a cleansing action on man, removing his shadow. Though Pound praises the proportions of St. Hilaire in *Spirit of Romance,* published in 1910, it is hard not to associate this tower room with Brancusi's temple or with the studio inside which one was "sluiced clean." St. Hilaire is Pound's example in "Medievalism" of "clean architecture," embodying a cleanliness that is seen when "the body of air [is] clothed in the body of fire" and not "carnal tissue" (*LE,* 153). In Canto 80 as well, "brown meat . . . leather and bones" stand between man and "luz" (80/511–512). The magic of the proportions seems almost to release the observer from his body altogether, as if the room were his body, the body of fire.[35]

Phenomena become monumenta when they are stripped of brown meat and bric-a-brac because only the clean, still form can live in the memory. Stillness is contained within movement just as the light is contained within flesh, and such stillness is the basis of memory. Of Confucius in Canto 80 it is said "in his moving was stillness" (80/512), as if stillness were a quality existing somehow

35. The phrase "brown meat" can in fact be traced directly to Brancusi. Epstein reports that Brancusi liked to dismiss Michelangelo by pinching the flesh on the back of his hand and saying "beef steak." See *An Autobiography* (New York: Dutton, 1955), p. 49. Pound quotes this aphorism, saying, "sculpture has NOTHING to do with beefsteaks," in an unpublished article on Brancusi (*VA,* p. 306). He also adopts Brancusi's disdain of "beefy statues" in the *Little Review* article on the sculptor (*LE,* p. 442). Thus the complaint in "Medievalism" that in Baroque art "there is a great deal of meat" (*LE,* p. 153) begins with Brancusi and ends, ultimately, in Canto 80.

at the core of motion. Here Confucius resembles the image of love in Canto 36: "He himself moveth not, drawing all to his stillness" (36/178).

The representative of such perfect stillness in nature is the sequoia, a kind of Confucian plant, whose slowness is equal to the depredations of time. But all plants contain a stillness like the sequoia's, a consistency not to be perverted by time, and thus all plants are natural monuments. Not only does the pine seed mimic the sculptor in working on stone; it mimics the monument itself by carrying within it the memory of form. In nature, form is the "germinal perfect," (*VA*, p. 190), the intelligence in the seed that ensures an "oak leaf never plane leaf." The seed is the storehouse of form as well as of food, the memory of a perfect germinal tradition, and so all the phenomena it produces are "monumenta." The tradition of San Ku and Poitiers and the tradition of the pine seed are really one, since both preserve a perfect form, working as a sculptor does, by hacking away the inessential and using solid stone to enclose the pure light renewed from year to year.

Pound's final monument is therefore scientific, in a way, and neo-Platonic. The "signatures / needing no verbal tradition" represent an instinctive natural affinity described by John Heydon. The lines in Canto 92—"so will the weasel eat rue, / and the swallows nip celandine" (92/618)—are, as Walter Baumann says, examples of the way that animals make use of the doctrine of signatures, as Heydon describes it, thus creating a kind of nonverbal tradition.[36] Human beings have a similar kind of memory, as Massimo Bacigalupo points out, quoting Pound's belief in "a tradition that runs from Mencius, through Dante, to Agassiz, needing no particular theories to keep it alive."[37] A tradition that needs no verbal tradition, and a monument without a structure, this kind of memory is governed by necessity alone. The same beliefs, the same ideas, endure among intelligent people for the same reason that the weasel eats rue, or that the golden section continues to be used for building: because they work. The implicit Darwinism shines through the neo-Platonic examples, since the consistency,

36. Walter Baumann, "Secretary of Nature, J. Heydon," in *New Approaches to Ezra Pound,* ed. Eva Hesse (Berkeley: University of California Press, 1969), p. 312.

37. Bacigalupo, p. 191.

like that of "oak leaf never plane leaf," is organic and not really mystical. Or it might better be said that the passage demonstrates again Pound's habitual elevation of the empirical standard, that which works, to the level of a Platonic essence. Nature, with its instinctive hatred for "barocco," spontaneously creates enduring monuments just as machines do, by eliminating the dross. Pound does not, however, abandon the actual architecture of monuments. A page or two later he typifies tradition as "Chiefs' names on a monument" (87/575). Instead, he gives the most complete definition of a monument, as a spatial arrangement that contains and preserves time. From the carving of the pine seed to the biological memory of the oak leaf is a single step, incorporating most of the important strands of Pound's thinking on the subject.

Therefore, in Canto 90 the whole constellation of references recurs in a much more explicit reference to actual monuments of stone. The movement is still "from the San Ku / to the room in Poitiers where one can stand / casting no shadow" (90/605), but with the added pronouncement "That is Sagetrieb, / that is tradition." "Sagetrieb" is Pound's synthetic word for the talk of the tribe, the "oral tradition" (89/597), which becomes the tale of the tribe in epic poetry. This oral tradition is explicitly paralleled to the tradition of building that accounts for the continuity of culture from San Ku to Poitiers: "Builders had kept the proportion. . . ." In this citation, proportion seems little more than a workshop convention, but the Canto begins to stir this convention together with other references into a mystical mixture. The very laws of proportion cited owe something directly to Alberti, who is quoted a page later: "The architect from the painter . . ." (90/607). In one of his early architectural articles Pound quotes Alberti's statement to the effect that the architect learns from the painter and, coincidentally or not, talks much about the need for proper proportions in building (VA, p. 173). In this Canto, Alberti's spirit seems to act upon nature so as to give it the form of a temple, "the stone under the elm / Taking form now . . . the stone taking form in the air" (90/607–608). At last the "Grove hath its altar," answering the plea that echoes throughout The Cantos: "aram vult nemus." The temple is "not yet marble" at the beginning of the Canto, but as it progresses the stone and water gather together to make an altar. Appropriately, the spirit of Alberti presides over this altar, which is in fact the monument Elpenor pleads for at the outset of the poem:

> "and with a name to come"
> εσσομένοισι
> aram vult nemus
>
> [74/446]

This tradition of proper proportions, this attention to form, gives the sort of temple that will immortalize Elpenor, and, not incidentally, establish a tradition composed of public materials. Only in passages like this does the poem succeed in telling its readers the way in which it can be read as the tale of the tribe, not by passing on wisdom, but by showing how wisdom is passed on.

In Canto 34 John Quincy Adams deplores the "Plain modern and tasteless monuments to George Clinton / and Elbridge Gerry," and laments, "we have neither forefathers nor posterity, / a few years will efface them" (34/168). The memory Adams despairs of is the public one that changes a loose collection of immigrants into a tribe. The actual stone monuments are incidental, mere examples of a country so amnesic that it lives in a bubble of the pure present. Almost from the first, Pound tries to define poetry in such a way that it could link forefathers and posterity so that tradition might live and the new escape mere novelty. His very last authorized publication is a translation of the Horatian Ode whose boast is the same as that of Gautier and Gourmont, but the eternity of art is not often for Pound their kind of haughty triumph over life. The eternity of art is in his poetry identical to the continuity of the race, giving it integrity as memory gives integrity to individuals. In trying to create this memory he turned himself into that oddly modern figure, the public recluse. It is that role, finally, that tells the most about Pound and about one of his dearest projects: the modern monument.

The American Monument:
Stevens, Berryman, and Lowell

CHAPTER

−7−

The American Sublime

I

The equestrian statue is one of Wallace Stevens' most poignant figures, standing at the exact intersection of mockery and reverence, irony and hope. The iconoclastic desires of the poet who says "bare earth is best" topple the statue over and over again, while the worshiper of the imagination reerects it. "The American Sublime" is poised between these two extremes, in the balance of utter bafflement. The poet contemplating the sublime unwillingly assumes the stance of General Jackson, posing for a statue, and so becomes the butt of a kind of mockery he has indulged in himself. The vulnerability of the statue to "the mockers, / The mickey mockers" is total, and yet how can the sublime exist if it must "go barefoot / Blinking and blank?"[1] Stevens reduces the sublime to "The empty spirit / In vacant space," but how can one worship emptiness? His questions, "What wine does one drink? / What bread does one eat?" have to do with the symbolism of worship. One knows that the sublime is nothing more than spirit, but the mind is used to having help in its contemplation of spirit, and these symbols are in fact the basis of poetry. Without some sort of physical symbolism, an icon, some bread and wine, the body of

1. Wallace Stevens, *Collected Poems* (New York: Knopf, 1977), pp. 130–131. All further references to this work will be made in the text, accompanied by the abbreviation *CP*.

the sublime evaporates, never to be resurrected, and worship and poetry both come to a standstill. The statue is therefore both terribly vulnerable and absolutely necessary, a martyr to the mind's own need for realism and a means for the mind to touch the real.

As Stevens' title suggests, the balance between these two needs is more precarious in America, where even General Jackson shares the poet's fidgety embarrassment with the idea of the sublime. And Stevens tended to feel this embarrassment most particularly in the late 1930s and early 1940s, when the Depression and the Second World War made the statue seem more ludicrous than ever. "The Noble Rider and the Sound of Words" is his attempt to answer the questions posed by "The American Sublime," and it naturally uses the equestrian statue to do so. Stevens feels true admiration for Verrocchio's statue of Bartolommeo Colleoni, "a form of such nobility that it has never ceased to magnify us in our own eyes." He makes the ruthless condottiere sound like Marcus Aurelius but only to show how powerful "the noble style" can be, how it is possible for an artist like Verrocchio to lift his subject quite free of reality. On the other hand, he cites a picture, a comic reduction of the equestrian theme to the level of the merry-go-round, called *Wooden Horses,* which is "not without imagination," but whose interest comes purely from a "ribald and hilarious reality."[2]

The American genius is to combine the two halves of this dichotomy in a figure that is untrue to the requirements of both. Stevens' example is Clark Mills's equestrian statue of Andrew Jackson in Washington, one which deserves all the mockery of "The American Sublime." In comparison to the Colleoni, Mills's statue seems virtually two-dimensional, a tin soldier on a toy horse. Not only had Mills not executed any figure of such a size before, he had not even *seen* a full-size equestrian statue before completing his own.[3] Having seen both horses and men in abundance was apparently no help, for all that Mills conveys is the utter falsehood of the noble pose, the pure calculation behind the grand gesture, as if a child were acting Colleoni in a play. As Stevens

2. Wallace Stevens, *The Necessary Angel* (New York: Random House, Vintage, 1951), pp. 8 and 12.

3. Tom Armstrong et al., *200 Years of American Sculpture* (New York: Godine, Whitney Museum, 1976), p. 292.

says, it is "neither of the imagination nor of reality."[4] It is not of the imagination because Mills circumvents Jackson entirely in the interests of achieving a stereotypical pose, and for the same reason it avoids reality. The American sublime is in this case a false one, a desire for idealization without the means to satisfy itself.

For Stevens the failure is especially discouraging because it seems to display an essential weakness in the American imagination, a resistance in American materials to the idealization of poetry. Behind the equestrian statue stands Plato's noble rider, the soul in his chariot, and thus "the idea of nobility," which has ceased, for Stevens and for his audience, to have much appeal. Stevens is concerned with "the fortunes of the idea of nobility as a characteristic of the imagination, and even as its symbol or alter ego." The idea of nobility "exists in art today only in degenerate forms or in a much diminished state" because of "the pressure of reality." Stevens chooses for the imagination a trope that is decidedly un-American, primarily because he wants to confront the suspicion of elitism and anachronism excited by the word "nobility." "It is hard to think of a thing more out of time than nobility." The Depression and American ideals in general combine to make it seem obscene and dead. Stevens is perfectly in character in wanting to defend poetry from its strongest opponents and in being one of those opponents himself. "For the sensitive poet, conscious of negations, nothing is more difficult than the affirmations of nobility and yet there is nothing that he requires of himself more persistently, since in them and in their kind, alone . . . are the reasons for his being. . . ."[5]

In "The Noble Rider and the Sound of Words," Stevens questions the place of poetry in a time of economic and political difficulties, and its place in America at any time. The word "nobility" challenges the very resistance to idealization, to the claims of the sublime, that Stevens himself expresses. It violates that respect for the ordinary that underlies so much of his poetry. What he imagines is "an interdependence of the imagination and reality as equals,"[6] but what he describes is the stand-off resulting from their equally compelling arguments. Thus "The American Sublime"

4. Stevens, *Necessary Angel*, p. 11.
5. Stevens, *Necessary Angel*, pp. 5, 7, 12–13, and 35.
6. Stevens, *Necessary Angel*, p. 27.

An early view of Clark Mills's equestrian statue of Andrew Jackson in Lafayette Park, Washington, D.C. Courtesy of the Library of Congress.

ends with a question and "The Noble Rider" with a hope, and the equestrian statue continues to find a place in Stevens' work as the symbol of a difficult, nearly impossible, compromise. The public monument symbolizes the relationship between poetry and politics, between the poet and his readers, and between the poetic and its material. It is part of the nature of American poetry and of Stevens' imagination that the public square should never enjoy its statue for very long.

II

The history of American ideas about the monument suggests that Stevens' pessimism is well founded. Before any native monuments had been constructed in the United States, Tocqueville observed: "In democratic communities the imagination is compressed when men consider themselves; it expands indefinitely when they think of the state. Hence it is that the same men who live on a small scale in cramped dwellings frequently aspire to gigantic splendour in the erection of their public monuments."[7] Between the vast number of small dwellings and the very few colossal projects, Tocqueville found "a blank," which is essentially the same blank Stevens confronts in "The American Sublime," the blank where a compromise between realism and idealism might exist. But Tocqueville was wrong when he suggested that the dichotomy between the leveling of each citizen's pretensions and the expansion of the country's can be expressed as a contrast between private structures and public ones. The conflict exists within American monuments themselves.

The conflict is comically vivid in the controversy over the first important public monument to be created by an American, Horatio Greenough's seated figure of Washington, commissioned by Congress in 1832. The unhappiness caused by this statue shows the essential contradiction that tends to vitiate American monuments, as well as the aesthetic difficulties faced by sculptors and poets alike. It might seem that the public monument should be a quintessentially American form of art. James Fenimore Cooper thought

7. Tocqueville, II, 56.

so when he encouraged Greenough and lobbied on behalf of his career: "Of all the arts, that of statuary is perhaps the one we most want, since it is more openly and visually connected with the tastes of the people, through monuments and architecture, than any other."[8] Sculpture, in this analysis, is the populist art, the most civic art, and the one most needed by the educational interests of a young country. In both the United States and France during the Third Republic, democratic sentiments caused an explosion in the number of commissions for sculpture, both public and private.

Greenough's *Washington* was the first of these monuments in the United States, and it is crucial to understand why it was such a failure with the public. The statue did inspire tremendous revulsion almost from the first, and after Greenough requested that it be removed from its original place in the Capitol, because of inadequate lighting, it became the butt of crude jokes and the object of vandalism, a veritable orphan in Washington until it was lodged finally at the Smithsonian, a building Greenough loathed. Greenough's basic miscalculation was certainly to have dressed Washington in a Greek costume in imitation of Phidias' Zeus. Faithfulness to prototype left Washington's chest bare, and there was a great deal of knuckleheaded criticism of this impropriety, not the least from Hawthorne, who declared, "Did anyone ever see Washington naked! It is inconceivable. He had no nakedness, but, I imagine, was born with his clothes on and his hair powdered."[9]

Hawthorne tried to carry off his own discomfort with a joke, but the question of dress and undress was a serious one. The real controversy, among intelligent people of good will, was not over Washington's bare chest, but over the Greek drapery itself. Even such close friends of Greenough's as Washington Allston and the Danas were uncomfortable with the idealization of the dress. Greenough was particularly perturbed because he had received

8. Sylvia E. Crane, *White Silence: Greenough, Powers, and Crawford, American Sculptors in Nineteenth Century Italy* (Coral Gables, Fla.: University of Miami Press, 1972), p. 44.

9. Nathaniel Hawthorne, *The French and Italian Notebooks,* ed. Thomas Woodson (Columbus: Ohio State University Press, 1980), p. 281. The most complete description of the *Washington* fiasco is in Nathalia Wright, *Horatio Greenough: The First American Sculptor* (Philadelphia: University of Pennsylvania Press, 1963), pp. 117–159. Emerson was not of Hawthorne's opinion and in fact helped Greenough in an attempt to light the statue.

conflicting advice during his work. These conflicts reveal a basic ambivalence about the whole project. Cooper advised Greenough at one point to keep the statue "as servant and simple as possible . . . Aim rather at the natural than the classical." Two years later, however, Cooper advised in favor of "elysian" dress, "to prevent us from thinking of tailors and breeches." Edward Everett, another close friend, was similarly torn, changing his mind at least three times between a prejudice against "the old contemporary uniform, his weary boots and clubbed hair" and another against classical dress. A similar indecision paralyzed Greenough's advisers on the question of size. At first, Everett declared the statue should be "as near colossal as modern taste permits. . . . I want a colossal figure." Yet almost in the same breath, he reminded Greenough, "Your Washington must after all be a statue of a man and in dimension." Though Greenough's brother Richard warned him "that a horse by Phidias of twice the size of life would not be appreciated by 10 men in America," Greenough's own tastes ran to the colossal, and he made the seated Washington about ten feet tall.[10]

The contradictions in the advice given Greenough reveal a basic indecision about the extent to which Washington should be idealized and an ambivalence about the very nature of the project. How to portray Washington is obviously the first question faced by American monumental art, and the inability of such men as Cooper, Hawthorne, Allston, Everett, the Danas, and Greenough to decide between conflicting impulses makes the failure of the monument a national one no less than the failure of Clark Mills's statue of Jackson. It is, as Stevens says, "a thing that at least makes us conscious of ourselves as we were, if not as we are."[11] Greenough comes in for such abuse because he violated the American desire to celebrate only plain men, and because he could not solve the conundrum of how to celebrate plainness without transfiguring it. The sculptor Henry Kirke Brown later complained of the statue that "there is no trace of Washington's humanity, or that he

10. Wright, p. 129. Crane, pp. 69, 75, 74, and 127. The question of dress in monuments to contemporary men was also a controversial one in England. See Benedict Read, *Victorian Sculpture* (New Haven: Yale University Press, 1982), pp. 164–167.

11. Stevens, *Necessary Angel*, p. 11.

Horatio Greenough's *Washington* after its banishment from the Capitol.
Courtesy of the Library of Congress.

was a being who lived and moved among us and acted for us." "It is not *our* Washington," according to Leonard Jarvis.[12] The problem would not exist later with Lincoln, because Lincoln's plainness and pain perfectly exemplified the nation's myth of its own crisis. But Washington represents the nation at its most abstract, when only its principles exist, and thus the clash between his idealized figure and his personality as a man is almost inevitable. The conflict is over the idea of nobility, and Greenough faced it as painfully as Stevens did, in a very different time.

His failure to resolve the conflict, however, is somewhat puzzling, and, since Greenough was possibly the most sophisticated American aesthetician of the time, ominous for American monuments. His difficulty is the more relevant to the questions Stevens confronts because Greenough's aesthetics are so thoroughly modern. Greenough himself warned against the "adoption of admired forms and models for purposes not contemplated in their invention," an absurdity he found as ridiculous as "a fellow-citizen in the garb of Greece."[13] This mysterious, seemingly unconscious negation of his own practice in the Washington statue points up the extremely problematic relationship between Greenough's ideas and his practice. The basic principle behind all of his architectural ideas is the "unflinching adaptation of forms to functions."[14] Beauty exists where efficiency has been served, as in many machines, where "the straggling and cumbersome machine becomes the compact, effective and beautiful engine."[15] In fact, Greenough's ideas remarkably anticipate Pound's. They agree in their hatred of excess, in their emphasis on efficiency of form, in the need to throw off the purely conventional, even in the example of machine design as prototype of aesthetic purity. Greenough attracted the notice of F. O. Matthiessen four decades ago because of the modernity of his thought and for the uncanny similarity between his ideas and those of Thoreau. There is also an obvious

12. Wayne Craven, "Henry Kirke Browne: His Search for an American Art in the 1840s," *American Art Journal,* 4 (November 1972), 56. Wright, p. 129.

13. Horatio Greenough, *The Travels, Observations, and Experiences of a Yankee Stonecutter* (New York, 1852; rpt. Gainesville, Fla.: Scholars Facsimiles, 1958), pp. 134–135.

14. Greenough, p. 162.

15. Greenough, p. 139.

community of mind between Emerson and Greenough, especially given Greenough's emphasis on the organic. In fact, Greenough draws a basic distinction in his architectural writings between the organic, buildings "formed to meet the wants of their occupants," and the monumental, a term which covers all that is incidental to function.[16] In architecture, Greenough repudiates the monumental, and the ideas he shares with Emerson and Thoreau, as well as the different ideas he shares with Pound, reflect a sophisticated, progressive distrust of conventional monuments totally unlike the squeamishness that greeted Washington's bare chest.

The actual statue remains, however, as a colossal embarrassment to Greenough's reputation as modernist before his time. Despite his disapproval of extraneous, nonfunctional detail, Greenough habitually encrusted his works with allegorical gewgaws, cumbersome in concept and execution. The original design for *Washington* was to have surrounded him with figures including Columbus, a stealthy Indian, King Philip, and a settler, but this scheme changed to accommodate a chorus of abstract figures: Oppression, Independence, Remonstrance, Resistance. Moreover, this is not a youthful taste outgrown in later years. Greenough's later projected monument to Cooper is just as festooned, with pedestals for subsidiary statues of Cooper's characters, allegorical figures "embodying national traits described by the poet," and a colossal bronze of Cooper himself, at least this time in modern dress.[17] Even Nathalia Wright, Greenough's most convinced partisan, admits that Greenough's sculptured works are essentially ornamental, and that "he was too deeply convinced of the vitality of tradition to be a genuine organicist and of the essentially ideal nature of art to be a complete functionalist."[18]

Therefore, what might seem a rather straightforward conflict between the public and an artist dissolves when it becomes clear that the artist compromises his own principles, as well as violating public taste. It is not possible, furthermore, to blame neoclassical training, as Sylvia Crane does.[19] As Wright points out, Greenough's first master was Lorenzo Bartolini, whose work repudiated

16. Greenough, pp. 144–145.
17. Greenough, p. 174.
18. Wright, p. 190.
19. Crane, p. 148.

neoclassicism and who exhorted Greenough not to copy from the antique. Moreover, the functionalist aesthetic was just as active in Italy as was the widespread practice of eulogizing and copying the ancient, as both Crane and Charles Metzger show in their comparisons of Greenough and the art historian Francesco Milizia.[20] Greenough tried to harmonize the two aesthetic traditions by claiming that the nude is the most "functional" of sculptural types: "In nakedness I behold the majesty of the essential, instead of the trappings of pretension."[21] The nude thus becomes organic instead of monumental, but it is also obviously associated, purposely so in Greenough's work, with the classical sculpture of Greece. Any comparison between Hiram Powers' *Greek Slave* and Erastus Dow Palmer's *White Slave* makes vivid the difference between nudity that is naturalistic and nudity that is essentially copied from Greek forms, and Greenough's work obviously places itself in the second category.[22]

The failure of Greenough's monumental art comes instead from the peculiar contradictions inherent in American monuments. First of all, functionalism, Pound notwithstanding, is not a very useful principle to apply to works of art. What is the function of a national monument? Clearly, Greenough felt that the function of a monument is to inspire and instruct. This abstract ambition and not the dress is the fundamental problem with *Washington* as a piece of sculpture. The weakest element of the statue is the strained and theatrical pose of the arms, one pointing skyward, the other offering a sword, a pose necessitated by Greenough's idea of Washington as medium between God and man. Of course, the didactic intent breaks the statue on a contradiction: it cannot be informed by a function that will always be extraneous to itself. Sculpture, for Greenough, is a medium, not an end in itself, so that despite all his talk, his statues are always finally governed by ideas that are applied and not organic. Functionalism, in fact, cripples Greenough's artistic endeavor because it has no way to provide for the ideal, except by way of the supremely efficient. When Green-

20. Wright, pp. 61–62. Crane, pp. 154–158. Charles R. Metzger, *Emerson and Greenough: Transcendental Pioneers of an American Aesthetic* (Berkeley: University of California Press, 1954), pp. 143–144.

21. Greenough, p. 202.

22. See Armstrong et al., p. 48.

ough feels the need to idealize, he must necessarily turn to Greece, or to Rome, or to some other borrowed tradition, because his own is an aesthetic with a blind side in exactly that direction. Greenough called his statue of Cooper the "abstract type of the American ideal man," and then placed him foursquare in a classical temple, as if Cooper's own ideal men were Greeks and not Indians.[23] Greenough's opposition between the organic and the monumental inevitably places his own sculptural work in the second category, no matter how much he wanted to argue the contrary. In fact, the dichotomy of organic and monumental is the one expressed in all the conflicting desires of Cooper, Everett, and the others for Greenough's work. It must be realistic, sensible, indigenous, contemporary, and yet elevated, inspiring, abstract, ideal. The statue fails not because Greenough was a muddy thinker or a bad craftsman, but because two contradictory desires conspire to thwart one another in his work. The resulting product is neither organic nor monumental, or as Stevens would say, neither of the imagination nor of reality.

III

The controversy around Greenough's *Washington* thus tells a great deal about the difficulties Stevens faces in applying the artistic imagination to public materials in America. The problem is an enduring one, suggesting that the conflict is basic to America's representations of itself. One of the very next Washingtons to follow Greenough's, Thomas Crawford's equestrian statue for Richmond, was saved somewhat from absurdity by the Virginia legislature, which imposed contemporary dress on the main figure and reduced Crawford's allegorical companion-figures with a ruthless eye for expense and fol-de-rol. Like Greenough, Crawford argued that American history should not be represented by Greek forms, and like Greenough, he turned to Greek forms whenever he needed an ideal figure such as the allegorical figure of

23. Crane, p. 126. See Greenough's essay on this project in *Yankee Stonecutter,* pp. 158–177.

America on the Capitol in Washington.[24] In a later generation, John Quincy Adams Ward achieved his first portrait statue by clothing the Apollo Belvedere, and he placed no fewer than eleven prominent Americans, including Roscoe Conkling, in a relaxed stance copied from antique models. Daniel Chester French also studied the Apollo Belvedere before designing his *Minute Man*.[25] More is involved here than an inability to break away from neoclassical models. The case of the American Indian is a revealing one, because it offers an indigenous myth, a home-grown ideal celebrated since Cooper. It would also seem to be a subject running directly against the grain of neoclassical presumptions and aesthetics, and yet, time after time, the Indian becomes the Greek. Thomas Crawford's mourning chief on the Capitol pediment is the earliest example.[26] Henry Kirke Brown tried sculpting his first Indian in Rome, found that instead he had produced an Appolino, and then went ahead and changed the name. Even after much minute study of Indians out west, Brown made *The Choosing of the Arrow* entirely classical, so that a contemporary could call it, without falsehood, "as beautiful as Apollo." This is the same Brown who disapproved of Greenough's *Washington*.[27] Even Augustus Saint-Gaudens produced an Indian in Rome by studying ancient statues, a procedure that resulted in a piece true to its models.[28]

These examples indicate a basic distrust of American materials on the part of the very artists who are supposed to idealize them and a distrust of actual models on the part of men who profess to be celebrating American actuality. What it seems to show is that insistence on the real simply prevents American sculptors from finding their own method of idealization, so that the statues are not realistic but slavishly derivative. The complicated situation of American taste in this respect is most completely expressed in Hawthorne's *French and Italian Notebooks*. Hawthorne's record of his trips to the various galleries and museums of Rome and Flor-

24. Crane, pp. 350–351, 360.

25. Lewis I. Sharp, "John Quincy Adams Ward: Historical and Contemporary Influences," *American Art Journal,* 4 (November 1972), 74–75. Armstrong et al., p. 50.

26. Crane, p. 362.

27. Craven, pp. 45 and 51.

28. Louise Hall Tharp, *Saint-Gaudens and the Gilded Era* (Boston: Little, Brown, 1969), p. 48.

ence is fascinating for its vacillation between worship and ennui, and his relationship with the American sculptors then resident in Rome is similarly ambivalent. His rapturous praise of William Wetmore Story's *Cleopatra* in *The Marble Faun* made the reputation of that very unsatisfactory statue.[29] And yet Hawthorne was frequently stone-cold to the whole idea of sculpture, especially as practiced by Americans. He is pained by the idea that Joseph Mozier's inept productions "will be as indestructible as the Laocoon; an idea at once awful and ludicrous," and is, in fact, tempted by the idea that Americans should not have statues at all: "it is an awful thing, indeed, this endless endurance, this almost indestructibility, of a marble bust! Whether in our own case, or that of other men, it bids us sadly measure the little, little time during which our lineaments are likely to be of interest to any human being. It is especially singular that Americans should care about perpetuating themselves in this mode. The brief duration of our families, as a hereditary household, renders it next to certain that the great-grandchildren will not know their father's grandfather. . . ."[30]

Hawthorne would perhaps have been comforted by the turn-of-the-century practice of making huge monuments of staff, a mixture of plaster and straw, and then destroying them after a year or two. But the durability of sculpture is only one of the vexing questions it raises. The seemingly innocuous one of dress remained even more nettlesome. Like Cooper and Everett, Hawthorne held entirely contradictory opinions on the question. He visited Crawford's studio in Rome after the sculptor's death but before the shipment of the figures of the Washington monument to Richmond and was disconcerted by the "coat, waistcoat, breeches, and knee-and-shoe buckles of the last century—the enlargement of those unheroic matters to far more than heroic size having a very odd effect." In an argument with Hiram Powers, Hawthorne objected to modern dress, arguing that "two or three centuries hence, it would create, to the people of that day, an impossibility of seeing the real man through the absurdity of his envelopment, after it shall have gone entirely out of fashion and remembrance." In fact, Hawthorne very sensibly pointed out to Powers that

29. See Woodson's note on p. 739 of *The French and Italian Notebooks*.

30. Hawthorne, *French and Italian Notebooks*, p. 154. Nathaniel Hawthorne, *The Marble Faun* (Columbus: Ohio State University Press, 1968), pp. 118–119.

Daniel Webster, for example, might have been most himself in a dressing-gown, but later, when Powers complained of having to clothe *his* Washington, Hawthorne declared, "I wonder that so very sensible a man as Powers should not see the necessity of accepting drapery; and the very drapery of the day, if he will keep his art alive. It is his business to idealize the tailor's actual work."[31]

This last is, of course, the crux, and the source of the seeming contradiction in Hawthorne's arguments. How to idealize the American everyday? In an argument with Anna Jameson, who despised modern dress in sculpture (and these repeated arguments in Hawthorne's notebook show that the question was far from a trivial one), Hawthorne burst out "that either the art ought to be given up (which possibly would be the best course) or else should be used for idealizing the man of the day to himself." This is the source of Hawthorne's disgust with American sculpture, its inability to meet his own demand that it idealize without falsifying the contemporary. He was himself at a loss to say how this should be accomplished, and so he decided "the less we do for art the better, if our future attempts are to have no better result than such brazen troopers as the equestrian statue of General Jackson, or even such naked respectabilities as Greenough's Washington. There is something false and affected in our highest taste for art; and I suppose, furthermore, we are the only people who seek to decorate their public institutions, not by the highest taste among them, but by the average, at best."[32] Hawthorne places public monuments in an impossible double bind: the high is false and affected, the low inappropriate. He does not dream that the productions of Mills and Greenough are affected precisely because men like himself long for the ideal and despise it at the same time. In "Outlines for a Tomb," Whitman turns away from "monuments of heroes"[33] to a characteristic catalogue of household and workplace scenes, but something in Hawthorne prevents such a turn, except in utter disgust and exasperation.

Hawthorne's disgust has a deeper cause than the problem of

---

31. Hawthorne, *French and Italian Notebooks,* pp. 129, 320, 281.

32. Hawthorne, *French and Italian Notebooks,* pp. 431–432. The previous statement is on p. 209.

33. Walt Whitman, *Leaves of Grass,* ed. Harold W. Blodgett and Sculley Bradley (New York: New York University Press, 1965), p. 379.

dress. It is a symptom of a confusion in his aesthetic attitude toward sculpture that he barely senses but that prevents him both from enjoying antique sculpture as he feels he should and from describing what American monuments might do to better their condition. The famous description of Story's *Cleopatra* in *The Marble Faun* indicates two warring systems of taste. On one hand, Cleopatra is "fierce, voluptuous, passionate, tender, wicked, terrible, and full of poisonous and rapturous enchantment," a Romantic heroine of the wildly changeable sort that so often comes to no good in Hawthorne's own work. And yet, on the other hand, "A marvelous repose—that rare merit in statuary, except it be the lumpish repose native to the block of stone—was diffused throughout the figure."[34] This is, to be sure, "the repose of despair," of the fiery heroine momentarily at bay, but it is represented nonetheless as the cardinal virtue of sculpture, whose art it is, apparently, to restrict the very emotions it suggests. Repose is one of the most common terms of sculptural criticism in *The Marble Faun*, applied to *The Dying Gladiator*, to Kenyon's pearl-fisher, and of course to the *Laocoön*. In fact, Hawthorne reproduces almost exactly Winckelmann's appreciation of the group, with Winckelmann's favorite metaphor for repose: "What he most admired was the strange calmness diffused through this bitter strife; so that it resembled the rage of the sea made calm by its immensity. . . ." The handbook Hawthorne used in Rome gave appropriate references to Winckelmann in describing the *Laocoön*, so that it is not difficult to discover the source of this terminology.[35]

Nothing would be at all wrong with this kind of handbook-borrowing, except that Hawthorne does not share the aesthetic behind Winckelmann's terms. Over and over, he finds himself chilled and repelled by classical statuary, retires in disgust, and then forces himself back on another day to try desperately to be charmed. The problem is a basic antipathy to classical art: "Classic statues escape you with their slippery beauty, as if they were made of ice. Rough and ugly things can be clutched. This is nonsense, but yet it means something."[36] It has the same meaning as his

34. Hawthorne, *Marble Faun*, p. 126.
35. Hawthorne, *Marble Faun*, p. 16, 118, 391. See *French and Italian Notebooks*, p. 744, for Murray's Handbook on the Laocoön.
36. Hawthorne, *French and Italian Notebooks*, p. 404.

disappointment with Italian ruins because they are not covered with ivy and as his grateful appreciation of Giotto's campanile because its decorations are so minute and complicated. The smooth and refined lack "heart," the essential touch of the flawed human that was all the interest of things for Hawthorne. Nothing could interest him less than the human form without blemish, without the birthmark. If Hawthorne had gone to certain Paris studios he might conceivably have seen sculpture to satisfy him, but in Crawford's studio, or Powers', or in the Capitoline Museum, or the Uffizi, he saw only the classical, praised to the skies. So his judgment is uncertain and changeable: "I used to admire the Dying Gladiator exceedingly; but, in my later views of him, I find myself getting weary and annoyed that he should be such a length of time leaning on his arm, in the very act of death. . . . Flitting moments—imminent emergencies—imperceptible intervals between two breaths—ought not to be encrusted with the eternal repose of marble; there should be a moral stand-still in any sculptural subject, since there must needs be a physical one."[37] Hawthorne admires Story's statue because he can imagine in it just such a fleeting moment, as he had originally admired the *Gladiator* itself. The human interest of extreme emotions is at odds with the strict demands of repose, but Hawthorne does not follow his own taste but capitulates to the standards of the guidebooks. Schooling himself in sculpture, he schools himself in dislike, and his basic standards are so contradictory that he vacillates about individual pieces until he throws the whole subject over in despair. What Hawthorne wants is Romantic sculpture, the convoluted, warm, human surface of bronze, not cold marble and its repose, but repose means sculpture to him, and so he must be dissatisfied. The confusion in his aesthetic mirrors the confusion of his ideas about American monuments. His natural bent is toward the intimate, the everyday, the flaw in men and women, and yet his perfectly conventional ideas about the monumental mean that he demands precisely what will disappoint him.

The advent of Romantic sculpture in America might have brought a solution. Obviously, Hawthorne's actual standards favor the kind of thing Saint-Gaudens was to perfect. The kind of

---

37. Hawthorne, *French and Italian Notebooks,* p. 511.

surface offered by bronze, as distinct from the hardness and smoothness of marble, makes clothing a bit more plausible. The material offers a spontaneity lacking in marble, and the style of workmanship that it fostered emphasized the rough and unformed in a way that might have given Hawthorne some sense of heart. But nothing more clearly indicates the ambivalence behind the American sublime than Saint-Gaudens' public monuments, which, despite changes in materials and aesthetics, carry the contradictions forcibly home to Lowell and Berryman.

Ernst Scheyer points out in Saint-Gaudens' public works a characteristic disjunction.[38] In Saint-Gaudens' earliest large commission, the figure of David Farragut stands with every crease and fold in his rumpled uniform faithfully preserved, on a flowing proto-art nouveau pedestal decorated with delicately carved women swimming in curlicues of hair. In the famous relief of Colonel Robert Gould Shaw, the black regiment stumbles forward under the beneficent flight of an angel in gossamer. A similar angelic Victory leads General Sherman through Union Square, while a huge figure of Christ stands behind Phillips Brooks, lightly touching his shoulder. The hero in each case is a triumph of realistic portraiture, in contemporary dress that makes no concessions whatsoever to elevated sentiment or abstract ideals. The uniform of the Civil War, in particular, seems invented for bronze, and Saint-Gaudens manages to preserve as many wrinkles and sags as a Matthew Brady photograph. But the other figure is almost comically different. She is allegorical, ideal, serene, and clothed in the kind of stuff that exists only to show off the delicacy of the sculptor's work. Often she has wings. Scheyer has established that these figures owe a direct debt to Burne-Jones, whom Saint-Gaudens extravagantly admired. Contemporary critics linked them as well to G. F. Watts and Gustave Moreau.[39] It seems inconceivable that Moreau should have influenced a monument to the Civil War, and the combination of Moreau and General Sherman is a more violent one than even those Yeats concocts, but the woman floating above Colonel Shaw is unmistakably the sister of the frozen women of the Pre-Raphaelites and the Symbolists.

38. Ernst Scheyer, *The Circle of Henry Adams: Art and Artists* (Detroit: Wayne State University Press, 1970), pp. 220–221.
39. Scheyer, pp. 220–221.

Saint-Gaudens' largest public work was, in a manner of speaking, the Columbian Exposition of 1893 in Chicago, whose sculptural decorations he masterminded, assigning each major installation to one of his pupils. Henry Adams felt that the exposition, so largely the creation of close friends of his, among whom were Saint-Gaudens and Richard Morris Hunt, represented a basic test of American aesthetics and American ideals.[40] If the exposition does, as Adams suggests, sum up all that the nineteenth century had to offer, then it shows that the disjunction between the two figures of a Saint-Gaudens' monument is even more general than Scheyer believes. Like other huge monuments of the time, including the Dewey Arch and the Victory Arch, the sculptures of the exposition were constructed of a temporary plaster material on wooden armatures, a medium which allowed the sculptors a postively wicked license. Frederick MacMonnies' *Barge of State,* which Scheyer calls "one of the most dreadful catastrophes to befall American sculpture,"[41] combined all the worst aspects of every period of art from the frigidity of the classical to the physical bravura of Michelangelo, from the decorative excess of the Baroque to the slavish realism of the Romantics. Yet Saint-Gaudens found it "the most beautiful conception of a fountain of modern times west of the Caspian Mountains." Daniel Chester French, another Saint-Gaudens pupil, designed a figure of the Republic in gilded plaster sixty-four feet high. Rigidly neoclassical, marooned in a pool to symbolize the protectiveness of America's oceans, she had virtually nothing to do with, and none of the virtues of, French's realistic portraiture. The whole project was steeped in the desire to portray the most exalted ideas possible, and it is significant that this moral idealism should be expressed in an art so utterly indiscriminate and uncontrolled.

But it is the exposition buildings themselves that illustrate the basic dichotomy behind the project. They were essentially long train sheds, constructed so as to provide huge open interior spaces.

40. "Chicago asked in 1893 for the first time the question whether the American people knew where they were driving. . . . Chicago was the first expression of American thought as a unity." Henry Adams, *The Education of Henry Adams* (1918; rpt., Boston: Houghton Mifflin, 1961), p. 343.
41. Scheyer, p. 241. Saint-Gaudens' comment below is quoted on the same page.

As such they exhibit on the inside many elements of modern architecture, especially in their large open floor plans ruled by repetitive structural elements exposed to view. Louis Sullivan's Transportation Building is often held to be an extremely successful example of this kind of proto-modern architecture. But Sullivan complained that the exposition had wrought damage that "will last for half a century from its date."[42] This was because the exterior of the buildings never had anything to do with the interior or with the mode of construction. The architecture was, as one architect admitted, a "decorative mask." The buildings did not "express actual structure" but served as "architectural screens."[43]

There is a wild eclecticism to the exteriors of these buildings, combining Roman, Greek, Spanish, Venetian, Near Eastern, and a dozen other styles. Since the exterior facades are constructed of staff or plaster, the materials offer no impediment to the fancy of the architect and bear no relationship whatsoever to the style he chooses. On the inside, the buildings display their own functionalism as they display American products and manufacturing processes. On the outside, the staff ornaments take the shape of Beaux Arts fantasies of the wildest kind. The point is not to disparage any particular style of architecture but to see that for these artists and architects, at this critical juncture in American taste, moral idealism is expressed not in the pure usefulness of the train sheds but in the white, derivative surface of the White City. According to Adams, the exposition was evidence of a "sharp and conscious twist towards ideals," but even Adams, student of the dynamo, failed to see the exterior idealism of the staff cladding as a diversion from a different idealism expressed inside the sheds.[44]

Saint-Gaudens solves the problem faced by Greenough and Hawthorne simply by splitting his art in two. The bipartite monument allows him to represent both the real and the ideal at their most extreme and enables him to satisfy all the contradictory desires of Americans about their heroes, that can never be satisfied by compromise but only by the kind of split he effected. Rather than

42. Stanley Appelbaum, *The Chicago World's Fair of 1893: A Photographic Record* (New York: Dover, 1980), p. 7. Appelbaum's book is by far the most complete record of the exposition.
43. Henry Van Brunt, quoted in Appelbaum, p. 14.
44. Adams, p. 341.

being harmonized, the conflict is exacerbated over time. The wild
excess of the Columbian Exposition is a direct result of the kind of
realism Saint-Gaudens practiced. Idealism can be so unrestrained
only when it is assumed to have nothing whatsoever to do with
actuality, only, in fact, when ideals have ceased to have much
meaning. This is a point made by Scheyer, who sees an irreconcila-
ble "dichotomy of realism and idealism" as the basic characteristic
of the artists who, like Saint-Gaudens, were associated with Henry
Adams.[45] The dichotomy is the one described by Stevens and felt
by him, because it is characteristic of any American art attempting
to work with public ideals.

For various reasons, sculpture suffers from it whereas painting
does not. As Scheyer says, landscape and genre painting, especially
that of Jean François Millet, acquired a tremendous popularity in
nineteenth-century America because they managed to combine
scrupulous observation and high idealism. Scheyer follows Van
Wyck Brooks in suggesting that the biblical aura of Millet's pic-
tures accounts for this capacity to idealize the very ordinary.[46] The
habit of worshiping and transfiguring American landscape makes
painting in some ways a more natural monumental art than sculp-
ture. Whitman compares the landscape of the west to "all the
marble temples and sculptures from Phidias to Thorwaldsen," and
the mountains are certainly a more appropriate monument to the
virtues of Americans like Whitman than most of those carved out
of stone.[47] The grand paintings of Albert Bierstadt, Frederick E.
Church, and Thomas Cole are, as Barbara Novak suggests, public
works, monumental ones in more than size, and satisfy the desires
of minute observation and national expansiveness at the same
time. Novak shows how these painters resemble scientists such as
Louis Agassiz in their careful researches and in their faith that
careful research is a direct approach to the sublime.[48] All this is
made possible by the special American faith in the land, by the
simultaneous traditions of empiricism and transcendentalism in the
investigation of nature. Sculpture, needless to say, has nothing like

45. Scheyer, p. 249.
46. Scheyer, p. 31.
47. Quoted in Barbara Novak, *Nature and Culture* (Oxford: Oxford University
Press, 1980), p. 154.
48. See Novak, chapter 1 and p. 89.

landscape to work with, and, worse yet, it tends to contemplate society rather than nature. The large public works of Greenough and Saint-Gaudens celebrate civic virtues, not natural ones, and they are forced to find ways to amplify a single human being. The great landscapes are, significantly, nearly empty. The very smallness of the figures in them gives a sense of freedom and possibility amid all that unclaimed space. Sculpture has no technique with this capacity to exalt except the magnification of the figure, but magnification violates all the virtues for which the American hero is celebrated in the first place.

The history of American monuments is therefore one of compromises and contradictions. The opposed impulses are perfectly represented in the two figures of a Saint-Gaudens monument, the drab and anti-heroic human and the ephemeral angel. When contemporary American poets choose Saint-Gaudens as a subject, they do so partly because his work epitomizes their own difficulties in conceiving of a public poetry. For both John Berryman and Robert Lowell, in their poems on the monument to Colonel Shaw, the basic dichotomy is that between angel and man. The irony of the disproportion is one of their basic points, but there is also a longing, and a concerted attempt, to blend them. Saint-Gaudens' inability to do so becomes their own, and his failure prefigures the failure of poetry to assimilate, use, and transform the materials of the contemporary world.

Stevens' exploration of the dichotomy, and his hopes for its solution, are contained in "The Noble Rider." His sense that American monuments cannot be of the imagination or of reality is founded on the same apprehensions described here in earlier writers and artists. In many ways, Stevens belongs with the group described by Scheyer as gathered around Henry Adams, skeptical and idealistic, without faith yet concerned with the religious idea. Moreover, their symbols of the ideal share a common background. The women in Saint-Gaudens' monuments have the same prototypes as Stevens' celestial paramours. In *Owl's Clover* he will pit these women at their weakest against the realities of the Depression, just as Saint-Gaudens perches them amid the carnage of the Civil War. The difference is that Saint-Gaudens ignores the contradiction, while Stevens worries it to an unhappy end. Despite his failure, there is no other metaphor he could have chosen than the American monument.

—8—

The Noble Rider

I

It is common to see Stevens' concern with the monument as an episode of the 1930s, a brief spasm of guilt issuing only the failure of *Owl's Clover*. Though *Owl's Clover* is his most complete and convoluted approach to the problems of the monument, it is really just a slightly politicized version of a search carried on throughout his work, because the public monument is a particularly apt example of a figure longed for by the imagination. "Lions in Sweden," for example, dismisses "Fides, the sculptor's prize," along with "galled Justitia" and all the other allegories of the savings banks, and yet concedes that "the whole of the soul . . . Still hankers after sovereign images" (*CP*, p. 125). The stone souvenirs represent a failed aspiration like that which created the gods, "companions, a little colossal . . . assumed to be full of the secret of things," who witness to the "peculiar majesty of mankind's sense of worth."[1] The noble rider is this kind of colossal companion, not a falsification of mankind, but a fiction faithful to the imagination and representing the imagination's answer to the irresolvable practical problems of living. Stevens keeps this idea, as he does all ideas, on a very short leash. The idea of nobility has the propensity

1. Wallace Stevens, *Opus Posthumous,* ed. Samuel French Morse (New York: Knopf, 1957), p. 208. All further references to this work will be made in the text with the abbreviation *OP*.

to rise out of sight, and then Stevens mocks it as everyone else does, but it nevertheless represents a very ordinary aspiration, one that is close to reality because it is felt as an exigency in every life. "In the Element of Antagonisms" celebrates a "chevalier of chevaliers," another noble rider in "burnished solitude," around whom birds twitter with the same mockery found in "The American Sublime." This statue is whisked away by the mighty wind, since it is weak and somewhat silly, and yet the poem ends on an "alas" that is only part mockery. The rider is, after all, "greater than" the "genii" so lately banished. He is our own nobility, and not some alien presence, and his diminishment is a defeat for the imagination.

There is a special irony, then, in the mockery of "The American Sublime." To turn on such symbols our withering powers of deflation is only to defeat ourselves, to use the mind to check its own powers. An antipathy between monument and people means a war between the imagination and its source, between reality and its possibilities for freedom, and this accounts, more than political conviction, for Stevens' heat on the subject. A truly unpleasant poem like "Dance of the Macabre Mice" acquires its creepy tone from Stevens' pure identification, for once, with the side of the statue. The mice hunger more for debasement than for food because they represent a perversion of the heroic idea, a power that mice achieve by debunking and destroying the colossal. They are more powerful than the Founder only in their power to spoil whatever he can found: "Whoever founded / A state that was free, in the dead of winter, from mice?" (CP, p. 123) Racing over the statue they efface "the lordly language of the inscription," and poetry is trivialized and debunked as well. The mice are identical to the mockers of General Jackson, and in both cases the hunger for deflation is ultimately self-consuming, self-deflating. The mice devour their only chance to become other than mice.

The statue also has its antipathies, and Stevens is also concerned to describe the ways a monument can fail the people beneath it. In "Parochial Theme," the poor become "those for whom a square room is a fire . . . those whom the statues torture and keep down" (CP, p. 191). Here the statue is a purely political tool, symbol of oppression and of a hatred of change exactly opposite to the manic change of the mice. The fear at the bottom of such poems is of a deadly hatred between people and monument, an exaggeration of their natural and necessary tension into antipathy. Stevens tended to feel this fear especially strongly during the Depression, when it seemed that the idea of nobility depended on a cruel ignorance of the ordinary. Throughout his life he vacillated between the iconoclasm of the mice and fear of what the mice stand for. The monument is such a necessary subject for him because it represents the point at which these conflicting fears meet. The vision of "colossal companions," of the people comforted by "sovereign images" of their own making, remains a goal the poetry constantly aspires to.

In trying to fashion a poetic monument, Stevens confronts some of the same conflicts that so confounded Greenough, Hawthorne, and Saint-Gaudens. *Owl's Clover* is such a strongly dialectical poem partly because the contradictory impulses behind American monuments persisted into the 1930s, for Stevens to compromise as neither Greenough nor Saint-Gaudens could. The extremes of the dialectic are more strictly separated in Stevens' time because of the poetic materials he has to work with. Besides trying to postulate a place for the imagination in the Depression, *Owl's Clover* attempts to apply the poetic ideas of modernism to the American situation. Saint-Gaudens found it possible simply to hang a Pre-Raphaelite angel above a realistic relief, but for Stevens the whole question is to find some meeting point for the two. *Owl's Clover* is an important poem because the incompatibilities it attempts to blend, the imagination and reality, American realism and idealism, contemporary life and the high poetic of modernism, continued to demand Stevens' attention to the end of his life.

II

Owl's Clover proceeds by negation, beginning with the fall of a traditional monument and then offering one by one the alternatives posed by poetry. It is in this sense a part of the tradition begun by Yeats in "Meditations in Time of Civil War" and "Nineteen Hundred and Nineteen." It is a rather Yeatsian poem in any case, a poem that proceeds by picking and choosing through a trunkful of potential images, many of which seem derived directly from Yeats. Because the poem has an unhappy issue, however, Stevens' attempt seems to dramatize a difficulty even deeper than Yeats's.

Owl's Clover was begun in social concern, in the concern that the gaudy poetry of *Harmonium* sorted rather poorly with the Depression and that any poetry would seem frivolous and self-indulgent if it ignored the political and economic problems of the world.[2] "The Old Woman and the Statue" is the first product of that concern. Stevens explained to Hi Simons in a letter, "Although this deals specifically with the status of art in a period of depression, it is, when generalized, one more confrontation of reality (the depression) and the imagination (art)."[3] As he explained in "The Irrational Element in Poetry," "The old woman is a symbol of those who suffered during the depression and the statue is a symbol of art" (*OP*, p. 219).

In this poem, art is abashed by reality. The statue, "a group of marble horses," is flourished over with wings, flowing manes, and bunched muscles, but "The mass of stone collapsed to marble hulk" when confronted by the old woman. What was meant to fly is suddenly earthbound, tied down by "that tortured one, / So destitute that nothing but herself / Remained." The marble horses could achieve flight only if the old woman were removed, as if they could fly only in a sky "Untroubled by suffering." Their sudden heaviness is linked to the thwarted motions of the old woman's mind. She is on a "search for clearness," a clearness in the atmosphere that might allow her to rise up and forget her troubles. Instead, she finds "this atmosphere in which her musty mind / Lay black and full of black misshapen." Clearness is a term Stevens uses to mean a freedom for the mind, an expansion of it in space like that suddenly enjoyed by Emerson in *Nature* when he feels himself become a single transparent organ of sight. But even if the old woman were to have such an experience, the blackness of

2. *Owl's Clover* was originally published in a limited edition by Alcestis Press in 1936. In a shortened form it appeared in *The Man with the Blue Guitar* (New York: Knopf, 1945), pp. 39–72. The longer, original version appears in *Opus Posthumous*, pp. 43–71. I have used this text but have not given individual page numbers, since it is fairly obvious which section of the poem each quotation comes from.

3. *Letters of Wallace Stevens*, ed. Holly Stevens (New York: Knopf, 1966), p. 368. All further references to this work will appear in the text, with the abbreviation *LS*.

her mind is such that it would simply paint the night blacker, making it "a place in which each thing was motionless." It is, as Helen Vendler says, a hellish version of the desire to be one with nature, where the old woman and nature are one, but "in an expunging blackness, not in ecstasy."[4] Thus the imagination is utterly defeated by reality, and both woman and statue are motionless. In the same letter to Simons, Stevens speaks of art and reality as having a "universal intercourse, a coexistence as a man and woman find in each other's company." Here the coexistence does not occur and birth does not take place. The statue is simply monstrous and immobile, like the statue of Jackson, neither of the imagination nor of reality.

Having written this condemnation of uninvolved art, Stevens was especially annoyed by an attack Stanley Burnshaw published in *New Masses*. Burnshaw scorned Stevens for writing poetry having nothing to do with "the murderous world collapse."[5] The second part of *Owl's Clover* therefore became a response: "Mr. Burnshaw and the Statue." Stevens chooses to assume the voice of a Burnshaw revolutionary and to present art in its feeblest light. The statue becomes the plaything of a dead society, "a thing from Schwarz's," a concoction of "sugar or paste or citron-skin," which can never satisfy the appetites of serious people. As Stevens told Simons in another letter, the imagination itself is seen as a function of a past society, while the coming revolutionary order monopolizes reality, "hot and huge with fact."

This revolutionary rhetoric is assumed ironically, and Stevens offers his first alternative ironically in the invocation to "all celestial paramours," who are asked to "Chant sibilant requiems for this effigy," the statue. The paramours suggest that the sexual conjunction of imagination and reality is still in Stevens' mind, but they are also comic versions of the mysterious women of Symbolist poetry. They are festooned with the clichés of decadence,

---

4. Helen Vendler, *On Extended Wings: Wallace Stevens' Longer Poems* (Cambridge: Harvard University Press, 1969), p. 104. Besides Vendler's, the most substantial discussion of *Owl's Clover* is by A. Walton Litz, *Introspective Voyager: The Poetic Development of Wallace Stevens* (New York: Oxford University Press, 1972), pp. 202–228.

5. Quoted in Samuel French Morse, *Wallace Stevens: Poetry as Life* (New York: Pegasus, 1970), p. 148. Morse covers the general circumstances of the writing of *Owl's Clover* on pp. 147–159.

"frigid / And crisply musical," bringing "down from nowhere nothing's wax-like blooms," like the deadly women common also in Yeats's poems on statues or the angels in Saint-Gaudens' monuments. Here they are completely ineffectual. Their waxy pallor, their "pittering sounds," will have no effect at all on reality.

It seems, though, that Stevens is trying to reform certain tendencies of his own poetry, since he completely deflates these paramours and then attempts to rehabilitate them. The fact remains that even the masses demand statues: *The Mass / Appoints These Marbles Of Itself To Be / Itself.*" They demand an ideal, yet the simple bombastic "appointment" of a monument does not give it a relationship to reality. Stevens sets out to show that his paramours are preferable to any monument, because they can reflect the chief feature of reality, which is change.

To do so, he describes "A trash can at the end of the world," where statues come to rubble, but where the paramours, like "younger bodies, because they are younger, rise." They, and not the marbles, are the imaginative expression of the new order, because only they have the capacity to become new. As they do, they begin to dance, not in the "awkward steps" they used before, but "ring in radiant ring." This dance is like the one that became a symbol of perfect art for French and English poets at the turn of the century. Frank Kermode says of Arthur Symons' "The World as Ballet," "It is the dancer's movement (contrasted with the immobility of sculpture), and the fact that this movement is passionate, controlled not by intellect but by rhythm and the demands of plastic form, that make her an emblem of joy . . . and give her a fantastic reality."[6] Even the details of Stevens' dancers recall the dancers of Yeats, sharing the "great whirl of shining draperies" that became, according to Kermode, a symbol of art to Mallarmé and Yeats. The whirling drapery and the dance represent an art that is supple, a symbol that changes as reality changes, that results from the conjunction of imagination and reality. They are, incidentally, what Lewis Mumford calls for instead of monuments: "self-renewing organisms."[7] In dancing, the paramours turn their backs on the statue and are "captured by the sky, / Seized by that

6. Kermode, *Romantic Image*, p. 73.
7. Mumford, pp. 439–440.

possible blue." They achieve flight as the statue never can, as the marble horses failed to in "The Old Woman and the Statue."

"Mr. Burnshaw and the Statue" is an attempt to reconcile the poetry of *Harmonium* to the Depression by reworking an earlier Symbolist inheritance, the "One of Fictive Music." Stevens changes the emphasis from the deadly women of Baudelaire ("Your eyes / Were solemn and your gowns were blown and grief / Was under every temple-tone") to the dancer of Yeats's "Among School Children." Like Yeats, he attempts to replace the obsolete civic symbols with mysterious women whose antecedents in French and English poetry are decidedly noncivic. Apparently, Stevens was not satisfied with this solution, because the last section of "Mr. Burnshaw," which contained the dance, was not included in any reprintings of the poem. "The Statue at the World's End," the version of "Mr. Burnshaw" that was reprinted, leaves the paramours' adaptability to change an open question. They may escape the rigidity of the statue and achieve flight, but the very metaphor of flight suggests an escape from the real into the celestial. And the basic contention of the third section of *Owl's Clover,* "The Greenest Continent," is that all celestial metaphors are passé. The blue sky becomes an empty European heaven, stripped of the comforts and illusions of civilized European life by war. The sky also represents a bygone Romantic heaven. Stevens says, "There was a heaven once" where each individual walked

> Noble within a perfecting solitude,
> Like a solitude of the sun, in which the mind
> Acquired transparence and beheld itself
> And beheld the source from which transparence came. . . .

This is the Emersonian vision again, transparency become transcendence, but in "The Greenest Continent" that heaven, that "upper dome," is part of the past, as useless as a thing from Schwarz's. In the modern world bareness is not clarity, as it was for Emerson. Modern life

> bares an earth that has no gods, and bares
> The gods like marble figures fallen, left
> In the streets.

As in "The Old Woman and the Statue," bareness, the bleakness of reality, defeats the statue, crumpling it like paper.

Bereft of heaven, celestial figures are simply ludicrous:

> Angels tiptoe upon the snowy cones
> Of palmy peaks sighting machine-guns? . . .
> Angels returning after war with belts
> And beads and bangles of gold and trumpets raised. . . .

This is simply "bosh." What Stevens opposes in "The Greenest Continent" to the fallen statue and the dead heaven full of ludicrous angels is Ananke, "the common god." Ananke is the god of necessity, "unmerciful pontifex, / Lord without any deviation." This god is an attempt to save something of the Romantic inheritance as the dancing paramours were an attempt to save the Symbolist one. Making a god of necessity is what Emerson does when time and circumstance prove the vision of *Nature* to be somewhat unreal. He says in *Fate,* "Let us build altars to the Beautiful Necessity, which secures that all is made of one piece; that plaintiff and defendant, friend and enemy, animal and plant, food and eater are of one kind."[8] Or, as Stevens says, "He is that obdurate ruler who ordains / For races, not for men." The unity that was once sought in direct communion with nature, that was once provided by reference to some transcendent heaven, is now provided by necessity, which forcibly unifies all. Necessity "caused the statue to be made / And he shall fix the place where it will stand." The problem of the relation of reality and the imagination is thus solved by necessity, which is almost a parody of the transcendent force Romantic poets felt behind their poems. But the crown Ananke wears is a "starless" and a joyless one.

Obviously, Stevens could not be satisfied with this. To achieve community only through necessity, to connect the imagination of the poet to the whole of society only insofar as they are both prodded forward by a blind force, is not much of a victory. It is less an interdependence of imagination and reality than a complete subjugation of the imagination to the force of the real. The poem

8. Ralph Waldo Emerson, *The Conduct of Life* (Boston: Houghton Mifflin, 1904), p. 49.

has veered in the direction opposite to that of the celestial paramours but has found an extreme no more satisfying. Yet Stevens' mind turns more and more to community in *Owl's Clover,* as he tries to find a way to give the poet a crown greater than Ananke's.

The Bulgar or Socialist who speaks in the next section of the poem, "A Duck for Dinner," holds up the specter of collectivism as if it were inimical to art: "Is each man thinking his separate thoughts, or, for once, / Are all men thinking together as one . . . thinking a single thought?" This kind of collectivism "was not contrived for parks" and has nothing to do with "the statue, white and high." The Bulgar describes a kind of public life too vibrant and too turbulent to be contained in "the sheep-like falling-in of distances" in a park, where every line converges on a single monument. Even the socialist vision is one of "concentric mobs" converging on some orator or an artist like the Basilewsky Stevens mocks as the "newest Soviet reclame." Thus collectivism can become the basis of the poet's triumph in a "metropolitan of mind." It does so when the poet, through his own artistic aspirations, senses the future that the group aspires to and thus becomes himself the statue, "inscribed on walls . . . Complete in bronze on enormous pedestals." This statue, as "white and high" as the one rejected by the Bulgar, nevertheless helps the "sprawlers on the grass" to "see and feel themselves, seeing / And feeling the world in which they live." It can do so because "The statue is the sculptor not the stone." When "he carved himself, he carved his age, / He carved the feathery walkers standing by." This is the poet as central man, hero, and acknowledged legislator of the world.[9] The particular beauty of this conception is that the poet, by carving himself, inevitably carves the shapes of other men. He is entirely personal, yet general. Since it is really the poet's aspiration toward a higher poetry that resembles the aspirations of all men, there

---

9. The concept of central man and poet as hero is an important one in all of Stevens' work. Major considerations of it include Harold Bloom, "The Central Man: Emerson, Whitman, Wallace Stevens," in *The Ringers in the Tower* (Chicago: University of Chicago Press, 1971), pp. 217–233; Robert Pack, *Wallace Stevens: An Approach to His Poetry and Thought* (New Brunswick, N.J.: Rutgers University Press, 1958), pp. 145–165; Alan Perlis, *Wallace Stevens: A World of Transforming Shapes* (Lewisburg: Bucknell University Press, 1976), pp. 50–75. Helen Vendler draws the comparison to Shelley on p. 109.

need be no actual statue. As Stevens says in "Examination of the Hero in a Time of War":

> How could there be an image, an outline,
> A design, a marble soiled by pigeons? . . .
> We have and are the man, capable
> Of his brave quickenings, the human
> Accelerations that seem inhuman.
>
> [CP, pp. 278–279]

The Romantic heaven, "the deepest dome," is in reality "the future," or, more precisely, a constant movement toward the future. Heaven is an aspiration rather than a place as art is the artist creating and not the product of creation. Therefore, the poet's yearning for the clarity of that Romantic heaven is of historical and political importance, since it represents the yearning of groups for a better future. And since the emphasis is on the process of creation, this yearning never solidifies into monuments but remains fluid and organic like the paramours at their best.

But if this solution does away with statues it also seems to do away with poems. There is only the great wheel of time "with interruptions by vast hymns, blood odes. . . ." The image of the poet as hero somehow does not answer the question "How shall we face the edge of time?" The idea of poetry as process rather than as individual poems leaves these questions:

> Where shall we find more than derisive words?
> When shall lush chorals spiral through our fire
> And daunt that old assassin, heart's desire?

Stevens might be asking, when shall the poem come that will be more than aspiration, more than desire, a salve and a resolution of desire? Though the poet receives the "diamond crown of crowns" and begins a race of his own, his rule seems to be as joyless as Ananke's.

Therefore, in "Sombre Figuration," Stevens attempts to give a more complete account of the community possible between the poet and other people. He begins with a "subman under all / The rest, to whom in the end the rest return." In the letters, Stevens

identifies this man as the subconscious, and this connection is re-
flected in the fact that he is "Steeped in night's opium, evading
day." Stevens rather arbitrarily associates the subconscious with
the imagination and the conscious mind with logic (*LS*, p. 373).
But these two are not really separate. The subman "was born
within us as a second self, / A self of parents who have never
died." This doubling of the self recalls Whitman's "The Sleepers,"
where the poet flits above the sleeping forms, calling, "Double
yourself and receive me darkness."[10] As Whitman's sleepers be-
come unified in sleep and partake of the imagination of the poet
hovering above them, Stevens' "man and the man below" are
reconciled on certain nights, because there are "realities so closely
resembling the things of the imagination (summer night) that in
their presence the realist and the man of imagination are indis-
tinguishable" (*LS*, p. 373).

Night, which was indicative of a special mental bleakness in
"The Old Woman and the Statue," becomes the means of recon-
ciliation for imagination and reality, poet and people. It is also a
means of involving the poet in history. Stevens introduces a
"sprawling portent," a manifestation in the sky like the auroras of
autumn or the prophetic auroras Whitman sees when he turns
away from the monument in "Outlines for a Tomb." This is a
portent of the future, "something foreboded," and the subman
senses it first because his is a mind "through which a storm / Of
other images blows, images of time / Like the time of the por-
tent." The imagination senses change first. Its present is the future
of the conscious mind, just as the conscious mind retains sub-
conscious memories as its past. Thus the poet is the seer of the
future, forward-looking rather than passé, because a mind ac-
customed to images receives images of the future more quickly
than other minds.

On this basis, Stevens constructs a deity of the imagination:

> when the portent, changed, takes on
> A mask upgathered brilliantly from the dirt,
> And memory's lord is the lord of prophecy
> And steps forth, priestly in severity. . . .

10. Whitman, p. 426.

This is vatic poetry, having taken up the Yeatsian mask of its destiny and become a god. This is also much too florid and unbalanced a conception of poetry for Stevens to rest on. Stevens ultimately condemns, as Northrop Frye says, "the preference of the invisible to the visible which impels a poet to develop a false rhetoric intended to be the voice, not of himself, but of some super-bard within him."[11] The super-bard is a Romantic role that poetic momentum takes Stevens into in "Sombre Figuration" as it does in "A Duck for Dinner." But this masked god dominates reality, as did Ananke, rather than achieving interdependence with it. Its priestly indifference, represented by the mask, is another Symbolist cliché, used by poets like Yeats when they want art to free itself of petty realities. The unity it represents is not that of Whitman, who is willing to become any man, but a kind that requires every man to become the poet. The mask this bard wears makes him statuesque, as separate from everyday misery as the statue that began the poem.

Stevens recoils from this role, and *Owl's Clover* ends with "The statue scaled to space," reduced again to the size of the real. Here "the statue is not a thing imagined, a stone / That changed in sleep." Instead, "It is, it is, let be." Night becomes a time of imaginative penance. "To flourish the great cloak we wear / At night" is to be "without past / And without future," not to participate in the future as Stevens says earlier. This return to reality is a comforting thing, a "rapture," a "passion," but it is also "indifferent to the poet's hum."

As the poem comes to an end, Stevens begins to fiddle with paradox, especially in his use of the cloak. The shawl that is wrapped around one at night is, in "Final Soliloquy of the Interior Paramour," a symbol of the comforts of the imagination in a bleak world, what Marianne Moore calls a "happiness of the in-centric [that] surmounts a poverty of the ex-centric."[12] This very happiness is suspect, though, because of its effect of cloaking or hiding the mind from the real, as the draperies of the celestial paramours are a means of vanishing into the sky. The cloak wrapped around men at night, the subconscious, repository of the imagination, is an attempt to surmount this problem, to include everyone within

11. Northrop Frye, "The Realistic Oriole," *Hudson Review,* 10 (1957), 355.
12. Marianne Moore, *Predilections* (New York: Viking, 1955), p. 43.

the confines of the poet's imagination. Here Stevens speaks of a "passion to fling the cloak, / Adorned for a multitude . . . to be / The medium man among other medium men," and this sounds like the central aspiration of the poem, to find an imaginative enclosure that will unify the poet and the Depression unemployed, bringing them together in an imaginative concord. But this aspiration causes the "cloak to be clipped," to be reduced, as the land-breath of night is "stifled." "Night and the imagination being one" is an expression of defeat. It was the aspiration that began the poem, when the bleak night of the old woman could not be reconciled to the imagination represented by the statue. But here night and the imagination are one in that they are equally bleak, as if the only central desire among "medium men" is to live in a real world, to enjoy a "gaudium of being," to be free of the imagination. The only way the poet can be medium among them, can offer them a medium, is to make his art as small and black as the real. Thus the statue that aspired to fly when the poem began is earth-bound at the end, and the poet is reconciled to seeing it remain on earth.

He is not entirely reconciled, however, since this is hardly the last poem Stevens will write in an attempt to join the imagination and reality. He has, in Marianne Moore's words, a "hope that in being frustrated becomes fortitude."[13] But *Owl's Clover* shows Stevens determined to find some middle ground where the private and the public can meet and finding instead a momentum in his own materials that shoves him off the middle ground. The symbols that might replace the statue inevitably become absolutely private and end up reproducing the rigidity and isolation that made the statue unsatisfactory. And the communal symbols finally exclude the poet. In *Owl's Clover*, Stevens seems to take every poetic means left him by his Romantic and Symbolist predecessors in an attempt to realize the ideas of "The Noble Rider and the Sound of Words" and ultimately fails.

III

The basic attempt of *Owl's Clover*, then, is to replace the failed American monument of rhetoric and bombast with one fabricated

13. Moore, p. 36.

of modern materials. But since those modern materials exacerbate the very split on which the original monument founders, the outcome is not a happy one. Poetry, for all its power, and for all the augmentation of power received since the beginnings of Romanticism, cannot replace the monument. Emerson, in an entirely more hopeful tone, sees the poet taking the statue's place and clearing away monuments: "The true centre thus appearing, all false centres are suddenly superseded, and grass grows in the Capitol."[14] But Stevens does not see the poet replacing the gods, the legislature, or its statues: "we do not say that the poet is to take the place of the gods" (OP, p. 206). Owl's Clover is also clear about the fact that the poet loses something in trying to become Emerson's central man, the glass man of "Asides on the Oboe." Instead, Stevens' most persuasive considerations of the statue come when he is trying to describe a kind of monument that is truly public in that it is given neither by legislature nor by poet but by the common desire for a sovereign image. In this search for a collective imagery to replace the gods, Stevens looks for an imaginative abstraction so necessary and inevitable that it has the validity of natural fact.

"Lions in Sweden" ends with the assurance that "the vegetation still abounds with forms" that might serve to replace the faulty souvenirs in providing "sovereigns of the soul." In "Yellow Afternoon," Stevens calls this abstraction "the final sculpture" (CP, p. 236). In this poem the earth itself provides these sovereign images, becoming "the patriarch . . . that answers when I ask." The final sculpture is something enduring and central, that "reposes alike in springtime / And, arbored and bronzed, in autumn." The lines cleverly make bronze part of the endurance of nature, its natural sculpture, and not an artistic imposition. But the final sculpture is also something found among human beings:

> Of which one is a part as in a unity,
> A unity that is the life one loves,
> So that one lives all the lives that comprise it
> As the life of the fatal unity of war.
>
> [CP, p. 236]

14. Quoted in Bloom, "Central Man," p. 218.

Here is the same dream that motivates Yeats and Pound at times in their attempts to formulate monuments, the civic unity, a commonality in which the poet is simply a person among other people. The final sculpture arising out of this unity is a true public monument, truer than anything postulated in *Owl's Clover,* and yet the role of poetry in formulating it is so modest as to be doubtful. "Yellow Afternoon" also shows Stevens in an uncharacteristic mood, regretting change. One of the imperatives by which monuments are judged in *Owl's Clover* and in "Notes toward a Supreme Fiction" is their capacity to change. Here sculpture is defined as what does not change, either from season to season or from person to person. The poem seems simply to skirt the difficulties of *Owl's Clover,* but a number of other, later poems attempt to define the "final sculpture" in a way that resolves them.

Since the final sculpture is a product neither of artist nor of any other person, but of the context, what Stevens might call the weather, of a place, the recurrent imagery of these poems is not that of character but of setting. Several take place in a public square, a location of particular meaning for Stevens as the meeting place between the public and the private, the central space where crowds might gather around the central man, the spot for the noble rider. The public square is one of the purest examples of the monument, partly because it is not a true structure at all. Nothing more than a clear space in the center of things, it serves as a focus, the point at which all privacies converge. The public square at night represents the darkened, public mind, concentrated on one or two ideas, and these ideas are, given Stevens' assumptions about belief, often shaky and unstable. In "The Public Square" itself, the lantern of a janitor causes the "fractured edifice" to appear to fall: "the architecture swoons." The shaking of public structures is a commonplace in Stevens' work. The night of "The Public Square" is the same night as the one in "An Ordinary Evening in New Haven," "when the marble statues / Are like newspapers blown by the wind" (*CP,* p. 473). The wind also blows through "In the Element of Antagonisms," sweeping aside the "chevalier of chevaliers." At times Stevens gloats over the statues fallen from their pedestals, and at times he seems to feel regret, but he returns again and again to this situation in which the elements, the agents of change, destroy man's fictive constructions.

A large part of Stevens' aesthetic involves acclimatizing oneself to the facts of change, but public structures are, by their nature, slow to change and vulnerable to rapid dislocations. In other descriptions of the public square, Stevens stabilizes these images of destruction as a way of defining the final sculpture. In "An Ordinary Evening in New Haven" he describes a whole process of historical change that takes place in the public square. At the beginning of Canto XIX, "The moon rose in the mind," as night fell in the city, and "That which was public green turned private gray" (*CP*, p. 479). It soon appears that Stevens is using the past tense to place this moonrise in history as an occurrence in the general mind, when "the singleness" of the mind's will is so strong as to turn public things into private ones, darkening the square. In earlier times, "the radial aspect came / From a different source."

> A century in which everything was part
> Of that century and of its aspect, a personage,
> A man who was the axis of his time,
>
> An image that begot its infantines,
> Imaginary poles whose intelligence
> Streamed over chaos their civilities.
>
> [*CP*, p. 479]

Stevens' image of the past is of a steady "radial aspect," a light that, unlike the lantern of "The Public Square," shines in such a way as to solidify the public edifice, whose civility "streams over" and composes chaos. Identical to this light is the central man, who is as much an image, a sculpture, as a real hero. Above all, the light is "a sense in the changing sense / Of things," a steadiness amid change. Frank Doggett speaks of "*focal points* of traditional feeling,"[15] and his terminology is quite literally correct, because Stevens sees traditional feeling as focusing a single, steady ray of light and turning the private grey back into public green.

In such poems, Stevens disturbs any idea that the dichotomy of imagination and reality might be permanently expressed as one between the private and the public. In fact, the kind of imagination

---

15. Frank Doggett, *Stevens' Poetry of Thought* (Baltimore: Johns Hopkins University Press, 1966), p. 125.

he seeks is that behind public monuments, and, if anything, the
private nature of modern belief stands in his way. The lamp re-
turns in this connection in "The Sail of Ulysses":

> The quiet lamp
> For this creator is a lamp
> Enlarging like a nocturnal ray
> The space in which it stands, the shine
> Of darkness, creating from nothingness
> Such black constructions, such public shapes
> And murky masonry. . . .
>
> [OP, p. 100]

The steady ray of the lamp enlarges and constructs, whereas the
unsteady lantern of "The Public Square" toppled public shapes.
Comparison of the passages from "The Sail of Ulysses" and "An
Ordinary Evening in New Haven" makes it plain that the kind of
creator defined in the former poem is one who focuses, like the
"man who was the axis of his time," a time and a place into a
single spot of light. "Civility" is his hallmark because traditional,
unchanging patterns of belief and behavior make true cities
possible.

Thus the poetry returns to the public monument, seeking ways
to restore its sovereignty and to define that sovereignty in a way
that differentiates it forever from the productions of Clark Mills.
"The Role of the Idea in Poetry" concerns certain "patriarchs" like
the patriarch of "Yellow Afternoon" or the "sovereign images" of
"Lions in Sweden." Whereas "Lions in Sweden" mocks the un-
changing nature of humanity's sovereign images, "The Role of the
Idea in Poetry" makes its patriarchs inhabitants of "A time existing
after much time has passed" (OP, p. 93). Time, in this vision,
"settles and thickens round a form— / Blue-bold on its pedestal,"
defining the monument by sheer duration. The monument is
whatever endures, unchanging, and here Stevens seems much
closer to the more orthodox traditionalism of Yeats. Another
poem, "The Pure Good of Theory," shows a positive dread of
time, which is represented as battering; its beats are both a mea-
surement and an attack. So this poem proposes "A large-sculp-
tured, platonic person, free from time . . . A form, then, pro-

tected from the battering" (*CP*, p. 330). The monument fulfills its most orthodox function in this poem, protecting humankind's purest traits from decay.

Stevens' attempt to describe how this preservation can take place, how civility can exist without the solidification of the generals Jackson and DuPuy, constitutes his most sophisticated meditation on the monument. In a sense, he succeeds by abandoning the symbols of *Owl's Clover,* the paramours, the auroras, the subman, all of which veer off track for one reason or another, in favor of that genius of the soil he tries to describe in "Yellow Afternoon." Two poems that juxtapose the statue to a river of time exemplify the attempt. "This Solitude of Cataracts" places the poet beside one of his favorite symbols in his old age, the Heraclitean river, "Which kept flowing and never the same way twice" (*CP*, p. 424). The poet is quite open about his desire to elude this incessant change: "He wanted the river to go on flowing the same way." He wants to be "released from destruction, / To be a bronze man breathing under archaic lapis." The desire to avoid death, to acquire the immortality of sculpture is obvious. But "bronze" to Stevens is more than just durable metal. In "Yellow Afternoon" the final sculpture reposes "arbored and bronzed" in autumn as well as springtime, and the bronze stands for something burnished to endurance by the change of seasons. To become bronze, to breathe "his bronzen breath," is not so much to elude time as to live "at the azury centre of time." The very word "bronze" accepts the onset of autumn, and yet it characterizes the leaf that remains even after life is past. The poet becomes a monument and achieves endurance by staying at the very center of the change he fears. The civility of the monument, its centrality, is carried over from society to nature: the bronze man is the patriarch, the very center of his landscape.

"Metaphor as Degeneration," another poem juxtaposing statue and river, also belongs to Stevens' most ambiguous group of poems on the monument, those in which the marble idol is abandoned in the woods. In this poem, "there is a man white as marble / Sits in a wood," who is parallel to, though unlike, "a man in black space," who is "brooding sounds of river noises." The black man is the poet of "This Solitude of Cataracts," longing for the river to spare him its inevitable change. In the second poem, however, the river is double as well, both the river Swatara that it appears to be and a river twisting "among the universal spaces," which is finally "the landless, waterless ocean" (*CP*, p. 444). The mind's capacity to find this second river in the first gives it the power to defeat all "reverberation," all change. It is the power of metaphor, which, far from degeneration, constitutes the regeneration of things that incessantly die. Metaphor makes the man in black space into the "marble man" who remains "himself in space." But the two halves of the metaphor are locked together. Just as the river both is and is not Swatara, the marble man is and is not the poet, and endurance is inseparable from the depredations of time. The marble man is fallen and yet risen. It is the meditation on death, the sense of death in the simple flowing of a river, that makes simple men into marbles of themselves.

So it becomes one of the boons of the monument that the consciousness of death brings about its own kind of permanence. The marble statue is an image of fear and transcendence at the same time. It thus becomes for Stevens a version of the poetry that finds the unchanging within change, that stabilizes flux by going to its very center. Often, the marble idol in the woods is Stevens' example of lapsed belief. There is a "face of stone" in "Notes toward a Supreme Fiction" that represents man's propensity to humanize the face of nature to form a god (*CP*, p. 400). But this face is replaced by the figure of Christ as part of a fairly natural change, and the stone idol becomes a symbol of belief abandoned. Certainly, Stevens is relying on "Ozymandias" here, though the actual appearance of that figure in "Notes" seems to have little connection with the idol. Similarly, the statue of Jove is blown up in "An Ordinary Evening in New Haven" as an "escape from repetition," a desire for something new that statues prevent, purely by their persistence in space. Toward the end of his life, Stevens begins to imagine himself as one of these forgotten or destroyed idols, whose "marbles lay weathering in the grass / When the summer was over" (*CP*, p. 514). "Two Illustrations That the World Is What You Make of It" is, in fact, a sorrowful continuation of "Metaphor as Degeneration." In the later poem, the poet achieves the mastery over things that metaphor allows, and "master of the spruce, himself, / Became transformed." In this poem the poet's mastery does transform him into a marble man, but only as "fragments found in the grass." The poet is abandoned, and perhaps poetry also, and the solidity of marble metaphor becomes a mockery, as in "Ozymandias."

Yet this broken statue, forgotten in the grass, is the very genius of the wood. Broken statues and forgotten monuments are superior to Jackson and DuPuy because they do not pointlessly defy time but capitulate to it and return to the soil. It represents the patriarch, or sovereign image, acquiring a human and natural scale, as in "Conversation with Three Women in New England":

> And you, you say that the capital things of the mind
> Should be as natural as natural objects,
> So that a carved king found in a jungle, huge
> And weathered, should be part of a human landscape,
> That a figure reclining among columns toppled down,
> Stiff in eternal lethargy, should be,
> Not the beginning but the end of artifice,
> A nature of marble in a marble world.
>
> [*OP*, p. 109]

This is the paradox of the fallen idol, that it becomes part of "a nature of marble," that somehow it seems to bring the poetic idea down to earth and to find a place on earth for it. One of the "capital things," one of the examples of civility and centrality, it is nonetheless natural and ordinary. The fallen and broken aspect of the statue at the beginning of *Owl's Clover* is cleverly transformed here into the most humane, and therefore the most representative, aspect of the monument. The destroyed statue really is the "final sculpture," the monument that falsifies nothing on earth but stands as its most typical expression.

Thus "The Woman That Had More Babies than That" is figured finally as a marble Ozymandias who is also the very center of life:

> If her head
> Stood on a plain of marble, high and cold;
> If her eyes were chinks in which the sparrows built;
> If she was deaf with falling grass in her ears—
> But there is more than a marble, massive head.
>
> [*OP*, pp. 82–83]

The woman who had more babies is in fact a natural rhythm abstracted from particular examples or individuals. In the first section of the poem, she is the ocean, giving birth infinitely to wave after wave. Stevens sees her here as a marble head because he envisions that kind of recurrence in nature in monumental terms. The woman is the final sculpture, the genial genius of her soil and, in fact, of all soil. He sees her as a ruin, like the ruin left in the jungle in so many other poems, but she is the very principle of life. This is the basic paradox of the monument. It is stone dead, forgotten, aside from life. Yet the impulse that makes monuments continually recreates the world. It is fallen and risen, dead and alive, abandoned and teeming with children. It is the truest monument here because it is the very matrix of life, the massive structure within which life takes place. It is also the final patriarch, become a matriarch, the form of a single individual become the house of a population. The figure here is a kind of cross between Ozymandias and the pyramids, the forgotten colossus and the collective endeavor, and within this paradox a successful modern approach to the monument is finally visible.

CHAPTER

−9−

Boston Common

I

It is appropriate that two of the most complex modern poems on the monument should be set in Boston Common before Augustus Saint-Gaudens' relief commemorating Robert Gould Shaw. The Common itself is perhaps the most perfect example of the kind of public square that appears in Stevens' poetry as a focus for the imagination. Its name preserves the idea of public space as common land, of a square at the center of town owned by no one and thus representing, monument or no, the community itself. As a drilling ground, it also represents the community militant, and this image is reinforced by the motto and composition of Saint-Gaudens' work. And since it is in Boston, the Common is a focus for more than a single town; it is a public square for a vast geography, for the whole country once claimed by the Massachusetts Bay Colony.

The Shaw Memorial, as an American monument, carries much the same meaning. In the same spirit in which Robert Gould Shaw volunteered to lead the 54th Regiment during the Civil War, his survivors refused plans to erect an equestrian monument to him alone, so that Saint-Gaudens was forced, much against his will, to include a mass of black soldiers on a large relief.[1] The motto,

1. Steven Gould Axelrod, *Robert Lowell: Life and Art* (Princeton: Princeton University Press, 1978), p. 167. Axelrod's chapter on "For the Union Dead," pp. 156–176, is the most complete survey of the literary reactions to Shaw's death and his monument.

"Omnia Relinquit Servare Rempublicam," commemorates the sacrifice of Shaw and his soldiers but also enunciates the civic idea itself. When the memorial was unveiled in 1897, it was greeted by the speeches of William James and Booker T. Washington and by a seventy-line poem by Thomas Bailey Aldrich, the first of a long line of poetic responses to this central American monument.

As Steven Axelrod has shown, the monument is a kind of constant against which American attitudes can be measured. In the early days of its existence it "came to represent the North, and especially for New England, its own capacity for idealism and courage: [Shaw's] life and death were taken as justification for the Northern cause in the Civil War and, more importantly, as justification for the essential Yankee character."[2] Very quickly, though, the monument came to represent a standard from which the Union had fallen, as in William Vaughn Moody's accusatory poem on the Spanish American War. Still, for observers such as Henry James, the monument was so affecting as to be "outside articulate criticism." It represented for James one of the few true additions to the America he revisited at the turn of the century.[3]

Only later is the monument itself dissected and the very impulses of idealism behind it questioned. It is one of the purest examples of the deep divisions Scheyer notes in Saint-Gaudens' work, and as such it offers to poets like Berryman and Lowell a powerful image of the split between American idealism and American realism. It dramatizes better than any other actual example the continuing war between imagination and reality in the American symbol of nobility. The relief actually divides into three oddly discordant parts. Lowell and Berryman are much more conscious than either James of the unpleasantly anonymous nature of the black soldiers included beneath Shaw's horse. They are ideal portraits in the sense that they represent typical members of the regiment, who remain as a kind of backdrop to the equestrian figure. No matter how realistically they are portrayed, they remain abstract, and they vividly represent the way in which the collective abstraction evades and devalues its subject.

Above the colonel floats the celestial figure of an abstract angel

2. Axelrod, p. 164.
3. James, *American Scene,* p. 250.

of Victory. There was some controversy about including this di-aphanous vision. Paul Bion suggested that she was "as needless as 'Simplicity' would have been floating over Millet's 'Gleaners.' "4 But Saint-Gaudens was convinced that classical precedent justified the figure, and his decision was ratified by critics such as Royal Cortissoz. Nonetheless, the angel clashes both visually and con-ceptually with the rest of the piece. The bronze does such a good job of representing the clustered gun barrels of the regiment that the eye can hardly convert it again to gossamer, and the angel thus looks almost comically heavy above Shaw's head. The pathos of the monument also consists in its fidelity to the uniforms and accoutrements of the actual regiment. Nothing in this section of the relief is elevated, and nothing detracts from the scruffiness of the soldiers marching toward their deaths. The angel dissolves all this, softens it, distances it, while the whole effort of the lower half is to make it immediate. Between the two masses of bronze rides Colonel Shaw himself, looking, as Lowell realizes, terribly un-comfortable. He is suspended between two styles, two competing motives, between pure faithfulness to detail and idealistic gener-alization. He is suspended between the two poles of the monument itself, between the dusty crowd marching forward with him and the angel of ideal art. Even in bronze, the angel remains faithful to the art of fin-de-siècle France, and the connection Paul Leprieur draws between her and the women of Moreau reveals the true meaning of her mournful expression: privacy and obscurity.5 Like a woman in a poem by Yeats or Stevens, she closes her eyes against the men marching below, and it would be simply ridiculous for the men to take any notice of her. They cannot look at one another because they belong to different orders of being, and Shaw seems so alone because it is unclear which order he belongs to. His dis-comfort is the subject of the poems of Berryman and Lowell, both of which represent the contradictory pull of the angel above and the crowd below and in doing so try to define a poetry that would solve the contradictions and become a true monument.

4. Quoted in Scheyer, p. 221, as are the reactions of Saint-Gaudens and Cortissoz.
5. See Scheyer, p. 221.

John Berryman covers the same tortuous ground first plotted by Stevens in "Boston Common," a poem that begins, as *Owl's Clover* does, by opposing a statue to a destitute person abroad at night. A man, described as "the casual man," little more than "clothing and organs," is "slumped under the impressive genitals / Of the bronze charger."[6] He recalls both Stevens' old woman, whose thought "repressed itself / Without any pity in a somnolent dream," and his subman, "steeped in night's opium, evading day," in the way he is protected "by sleep from what / Assailed him earlier and left him here." The Saint-Gaudens relief functions here only as a shelter; its only use for the casual man is to keep out the wind.

This is a return to the situation of an earlier Berryman poem, "The Statue," in which a statue of Humboldt looks cynically across the "homosexuals, the crippled, the alone," and spares them "extravagant perception of their failure" by ignoring them. The favor is returned by the crowd, however, because they are not sure which Humboldt the statue is meant to represent. The situation is almost typically Stevensian in the picture it gives of monument and crowd at loggerheads. There is a similar irony in "Boston Common." The relief commemorates "immortal heroes," but, except for Robert Shaw, the faces are those of "Negroes without name." This reflects the fact that only the white officers of the regiment are named on the monument. The black enlisted men who died in the regiment's first and only battle will always be nameless, so their immortality as faces on the relief is somewhat hollow. For that matter, the faces are only representative, not specific. They have a "common character." The process of memorialization is presented as one of imaginative abstraction. The soldiers are "imperishable" only because they are "paradigm, pitching imagination where / The crucible night all singularity . . . burnt out." In "A Bronze Head," Yeats speaks of bringing "imagination to that pitch where it casts out / All that is

---

6. John Berryman, *Short Poems* (New York: Farrar, Straus & Giroux, 1967), pp. 59–64. All quotations from "Boston Common" and "The Statue" will be taken from this edition.

Augustus Saint-Gaudens' *Shaw Memorial* shortly after its dedication in Boston. Courtesy of Dartmouth College Library.

not itself" (*P*, p. 340). The imagination of the artist is like the war itself in that they are both crucibles wherein the idiosyncratic is burnt out and refined to the immortal.

This process is also described in sexual terms. War is "love in a mask," where the two partners are the casual man and the abstract angel who stands above Robert Shaw. The angel is the possible apotheosis, the possible heroism. She is the means by which statues are made, by whom war "gets a man of bronze," the ideal that the individual must meet in order to produce a hero. But, like the angels in "The Greenest Continent" or the celestial paramours, she is rendered ineffectual by the conditions of the modern age. Her function, which is the function of the imagination elevating the individual, has been taken over by war itself. The angel and the casual man never meet, "loose in the brothel of another war," but, as the word "brothel" implies, the kind of copulation they seek is promiscuously accomplished. In this kind of war

> tanks and guns,
> Move and must move to their conclusions, where
> The will is mounted and gregarious and bronze.

There is no individual will, just mechanical determinism. This kind of war ironically accomplishes just what Saint-Gaudens accomplishes. It produces abstract men, collective heroes without names, mounted and bronze like their weapons.

Berryman's angel is another celestial paramour, in a more literal sense than Stevens means. Though she represents the possibility of art made of the conjunction of the real and the ideal, the price of the ceremony is the life of the hero. Berryman warns,

> undergo no more that spectacle—
> Perpetually verdant the last pyre,
> Fir, cypress, yew, the phoenix bay
> And voluntary music—.

The perpetual greenery of hero worship, the art of statues and memorials, is simply an attempt to cover and ignore the pyre, an attempt to substitute what Lewis Mumford calls "a petrified immortality" for the life of the real.[7]

7. Mumford, p. 434.

Instead, Berryman proposes as hero "Jack under the stallion. . . . Who chides our clamour and who would forget / The death of heroes." When Berryman turns to the casual man as casual man, to the ordinary for its own sake, he is repeating Stevens' search for the subman. Like Stevens, Berryman finds a community and a better use for art at night, among those

> Who labour in the private dark
> And silent dark for birthday music and light,
> Fishermen, gardeners, about their violent work.

This is a version of Stevens' imaginative concord, with a valid place for the artist where he is not an enemy of the real. Those who work for music and light work alone, but their relationship to other workers is itself a better art than the statue's. The poet simply labors alone, but by doing so tills a "common garden in a private ground." He accomplishes what the poet accomplishes momentarily in *Owl's Clover* because of the analogy between his work and that of all workers who salvage sustenance from the physical world.

The private work of a poet, "tracing the future on the wall of a cell," becomes the work everyone must emulate, since it is the only work not based on "legends and lies." This small-scale elaboration of the "limited sick world" of the individual is also the only real heroism, because it does without heroes and without hopeful reference to any transcendent ideal. Though this solution gives the poet's imagination a central place in the real world, Berryman realizes that something has been lost. Having purged the world of heroes and eliminated the ideal has made the poet subject to the "turning world," a world that

> Brings unaware us to our enemies,
> Artist to assassin, Saint-Gaudens' bronze
> To a free shelter, images to end.

Reducing poetry to the small cell of the real world makes the artist an assassin, not a life-giver. It brings the bronze of the hero to be nothing more than a shelter, ultimately bringing images to an end, destroying poetry. This is Stevens' "statue scaled to space," and to scale it completely to physical space is to remove poetry altogether from consideration. This is the irreconcilable conflict of the poem, that "worship and love" are irreconcilable. To love Jack under the stallion is to hate the angel who rides above him and to worship the noble rider is to forget Jack. The diametrically opposed poles of Berryman's poem are the poles of the Saint-Gaudens monument itself, the straggling crowd and the angel above it, and Berryman can find no definition of poetry that might reconcile them.

Berryman follows Stevens in dramatizing the two poles of this problem by changing the poet's relationship to night and the statue. At first night is a bleak place, barely a refuge for the poor, and a place in which the statue is cold and indifferent, a symbol of the kind of art the poet hopes to avoid. As the imaginative ideal that the statue represents is rejected, night becomes the means of unifying the poet and a people in the community of "Sombre Figuration." But that night returns to its original bleakness when the poet realizes that making himself just a person among other people, with no particular relationship to a transcendent world, makes him no longer a poet. It is as if Berryman rejects the Romantic role that Stevens rejects because it is false to Jack under the stallion but finally finds Jack's world hostile and cold. The image of a concord between them hovers in the poem as something the poet desires but cannot achieve.

III

A similar rhythm is apparent in the poetry of Robert Lowell, where the statue is also an important figure. Lowell is a contemporary graveyard poet, whose poetry speaks of cenotaphs, gravestones, and memorials. Poem after poem places the poet at the foot of some stone monument: "The Quaker Graveyard in Nantucket," "Christmas Eve under Hooker's Statue," "In Memory of Arthur Winslow," "Winter in Dunbarton," "Between the Porch and the Altar," and "At the Indian Killer's Grave," from *Lord Weary's Castle* alone. Certainly the graveyard is in some way a formally necessary locale for Lowell. The graveyard poem can have the immediacy of the moment of mourning, and it can be primarily about the mourner's emotions, while still including as much history as the graveyard contains. For Lowell, for whom the past is a recurrent complaint, the graveyard is a fated location. But he is also concerned with statues as symbols of power, the misuse of power, and the possible nobility of its proper use. In his most manic moments, he fancied himself as an invulnerable statue, "one of Michael Angelo's rugged, ideal statues that can be tumbled down hill without injury," and he insisted, during a trip to Buenos Aires, on being taken to every equestrian statue in town, so as to mount up behind the rider.[8] This fascination with the power behind the ideal statue, mingled with Lowell's equally strong distrust of all such statues represent, produces in his poetry a version of the noble rider as ambivalent as that of Stevens, Berryman, and their predecessors.

The first and most obvious role of the public statue in Lowell's work is as representative of the past. But Lowell is ambivalent enough about the past to make the statue fill a dual role. His attitude toward it is the "awed contempt" he describes in "Between the Porch and the Altar."[9] For in some cases the monument represents ideals from the past to which the present has failed to conform. In "The First Sunday in Lent," the poet mocks his family's "weak-kneed roots," and wonders what will hold things together

> when the damp
> Aches like a conscience, and they grope to rob
> The hero under his triumphal arch.
>
> [*LWC*, p. 15]

The tottering monument is the glory of the past gone into decay. The family's relics are contemptible because their foundation is so weak, and also because they rest on such dubious ground, the "thankless ground" Lowell's grandfather "screwed from Charlie Stark" (*LWC*, p. 24). The shaken monument reappears in "Adam and Eve" and again in "For the Union Dead," where its founda-

8. Ian Hamilton, *Robert Lowell* (New York: Random House, 1982), pp. 227 and 301.

9. Robert Lowell, *Lord Weary's Castle* (New York: Harcourt, Brace, 1946), p. 42. All further reference to this work will be in the text, with the abbreviation *LWC*.

tions are again threatened by a weakness in the public itself. In such instances, the monument seems to represent certain ideals from which the present has fallen away.

A different use is visible in other poems such as "At the Indian Killer's Grave," in which the cenotaph confesses guilt instead of glory. In "Christmas Eve under Hooker's Statue," the figure of the hero stands paralyzed with the broken promise of America crushed between its iron gauntlets. He represents the paralysis of a culture, the iron aspect of a Santa whose "stocking is full of stones" (*LWC*, p. 17). This early poem resembles Berryman's "Boston Common" in several ways. There is another juxtaposition of night and the statue, another parallel drawn between an old war memorialized in bronze and the Second World War, a contemporary event for both poems. The failure of tradition is the problem of Lowell's poem, and Hooker's statue represents this failure because his rigidity is representative of the inability of the past to prepare a man or a country for challenges like the war.

These two different aspects of the statue are brought together in the second section of "Between the Porch and the Altar," subtitled "Adam and Eve." In this case the statue is Daniel Chester French's *Minute Man,* an even more obvious symbol than the statue of Hooker. Lowell allows the poem to enjoy two different attitudes toward the monument. It is at once "crisp and steady" and also perhaps "melting down like scuptured lard" (*LWC*, p. 42). For the most part, the soldier on the monument seems not shaken but oblivious: "He is content and centuries away / From white-hot Concord, and he stands on guard." The statue represents in this poem America's denial of its own sin, the mythography that chooses Concord instead of Lowell's own symbol, King Philip's War. He is what is "exempt," behind the "puritanical facade" that denies the serpent. Yet to deny sin is also to deny life, and the statue's motto is therefore "Never to have lived is best." His is the immortality of those who deny life:

> They lied,
> My cold-eyed seedy fathers when they died,
> Or rather threw their lives away, to fix
> Sterile, forbidding nameplates on the bricks
> Above a kettle.
> [*LWC*, p. 42]

They lied, and they are thwarted, because no such sacrifices can ever quash the serpent of sin. In "At the Indian Killer's Grave," Lowell asks,

> When the great mutation racks
> The Pilgrim Fathers' relics, will these placques
> Harness the spare-ribbed persons of the dead
> To battle with the dragon?
>
> [*LWC.* p. 56]

The answer to the rhetorical question is that little plaques and nameplates will not suffice against the dragon they were created to deny. Thus the statue of the Minute Man melts like lard in the hellish heat of Concord. He represents a specious innocence, a myth of innocence, created to obscure the guilt of King Philip's War. His separation from life and his specious sacrifice are prototypes of similar aspects of Colonel Shaw, and he is certainly the forerunner of the "wasp-waisted" Union soldiers of "For the Union Dead."

This juxtaposition of statue and serpent, ideal image and sinful reality, is a constant one in Lowell's work. But he does not always mock the distance of the ideal as he does in "Adam and Eve." In "Buenos Aires" he juxtaposes the "leaden, internecine generals" fomenting backstage rebellion and their "literal commemorative busts" to "a hundred marble goddesses." Fleeing the absurd revolution, he says, "I found rest / by cupping a soft palm to each hard breast."[10] These statues are Lowell's version of the celestial paramours, whose love he seeks when the grossness of life becomes overwhelming. The juxtaposition is made again in "The Neo-Classical Urn," in which "the caste stone statue of a nymph / her soaring armpits and her one bare breast / gray from the rain" stands next to a huge urn young Lowell fills with turtles, whom he feeds "gobs of hash." The corruption of flesh, here the flesh of turtles, symbolized in "Buenos Aires" by the "beefy breathing of the herds," is something from which Lowell flees to the arms of marble art. His love for the statues is based at least partly on the

---

10. Robert Lowell, *For the Union Dead* (New York: Farrar, Straus & Giroux, 1964), p. 61. The texts of "The Neo-Classical Urn," p. 47, and "For the Union Dead," pp. 70–72, will also be taken from this volume.

fact that he is himself implicated in the fleshliness he abhors. In "Buenos Aires" he wears a suede suit, pointedly identified as the skin of those beefy herds, and in "The Neo-Classical Urn" he is up to his elbows in turtle flesh. In "Adam and Eve" Lowell's own sinful nature is something that the Minute Man seems to deny, a denial for which he is mocked. Here Lowell veers toward the very distance he criticizes in the earlier poem.

Lowell's poems concerning monuments re-create over and over the same basic scene, as some ideal image is confronted with the realities of a sinful world. The Minute Man stands not in a park but in some modern garden of Eden, denying the fall that Lowell acts out before him. But Lowell himself sometimes seeks out the very relief that the distant ideal affords. As a body, Lowell's poetry attacks the pretensions of the ideal and demonstrates its appeal at the same time. This ambivalence, so like Berryman's and Stevens', and so like that embodied in the Saint-Gaudens monument, gives form to Lowell's finest poem, "For the Union Dead."[11] This poem begins with a scene from his own childhood, a visit to the Boston Aquarium where he longed to "burst the bubbles / drifting from the noses of the cowed, compliant fish." This is not entirely an experience from the past, however:

> I often sigh still
> for the dark downward and vegetating kingdom
> of the fish and reptile.

The word "downward" belongs to a phrase Lowell borrows from Milton for "The Quaker Graveyard in Nantucket": "upward angel, downward fish." In Milton, these are fallen angels, like his figure of Sin beautiful above the waist but loathsome below.[12] Lowell's longing for the touch of fish, like his wallowing in turtle

---

11. Studies of Lowell's personal involvement in his political poetry include Patrick Cosgrave, *The Public Poetry of Robert Lowell* (London: Gollancz, 1970), pp. 156–162; Alan Williamson, *Pity the Monsters: The Political Vision of Robert Lowell* (New Haven: Yale University Press, 1974), pp. 106–111; Dwight Eddins, "Poet and State in the Verse of Robert Lowell," *Texas Studies in Language and Literature*, 15 (1973), 371–386; Stephen C. Moore, "Politics and the Poetry of Robert Lowell," *Georgia Review*, 27 (1973), 220–231; Philip Cooper, *The Autobiographical Myth of Robert Lowell* (Chapel Hill: University of North Carolina Press, 1970).

12. Cooper makes the comparison to Milton on p. 3.

flesh or in beef, is an example of the downward pull of the flesh. It is related in "For the Union Dead" to a cowed compliance and to the "servility" with which the poem ends, a servility that contrasts unfavorably with the *servare* of the motto and that Lowell identifies with "grease." Flesh is not just a personal problem but stands, as it does in "Buenos Aires," for the push of history. Here "dinosaur steamshovels . . . cropped up tons of mush and grass" in the construction of the new parking garage on the Common. This particular kind of historic momentum leads to parking garages, to television, to the laziness of modern comfort embodied in the cars that cruise forth like fish at the end of the poem.

Opposed to this stands the statue of Robert Shaw, described in terms of physical refinement. His monument

> sticks like a fish bone
> in the city's throat.
> Its Colonel is as lean
> as a compass-needle.

Compass needles point the way, and this is a very accusatory needle, pointing a way no one else has taken. It can point precisely because it has lost its flesh, been refined away to bone. Lowell further describes Shaw's "wrenlike vigilance" and his "gentle tautness," which is "a greyhound's." The animal imagery is not meant to connect Shaw to the animal world, since the animals chosen are notable particularly for their leanness and speed. They are refined and unfishlike. Shaw is the "upward angel," barely connected to flesh, and as such takes a place beside the marble goddesses Lowell turns to in the other poems.

Shaw is Lowell's aspiration to a life free of the flesh and an art above the vileness of society. He is a celestial paramour, representing apotheosis, as does Berryman's angel. There is, in fact, a direct verbal parallel between Lowell's "He rejoices in man's lovely, / peculiar power to choose life and die" and Berryman's "flamelike, perish and live."[13] For both poets, Shaw achieves a suspension, a balance between immortality and death like that in Yeats's

13. The background of these statements in speeches by James Russell Lowell and Oliver Wendell Holmes is described by Axelrod, pp. 168–169.

"An Irish Airman Foresees His Death." But attractive as Shaw may be, his bias is toward oblivion. He longs to be released from existence even more completely:

> Colonel Shaw
> is riding on his bubble,
> he waits
> for the blesséd break.

He waits to be released completely by the end of all existence. Here Shaw resembles the Minute Man, for whom "never to have lived is best." Lowell also realizes, as Berryman does, the ironic fact that this yearning toward nothingness is satisfied easily and continually by modern war: "There are no statues for the last war." As he says in "Christmas Eve under Hooker's Statue": "The war-god's bronzed and empty forehead forms / Anonymous machinery from raw men" (*LWC*, p. 17). The conditions of modern war transform men into bronze, but only to annihilate them, not to immortalize them. Thus the ditch, which Shaw's father thought was a fitting enough monument for his son, becomes the ditch into which all will plunge in a nuclear holocaust. The ideal that Shaw represents is not just an alternative to the real but is the destruction of it.

This kind of statue represents escape into a purely imaginative world where only the poet lives, above the problems of the real as the statues of "Buenos Aires" stand above the troubled city. It is the kind of statue worshiped in poems like "La beauté" by Baudelaire, who is one of the most common sources of Lowell's translations.[14] Unlike Baudelaire, however, Lowell does not value the statue's indifference to life. The abstract Union soldiers of New England "doze over their muskets / And muse through their sideburns." Shaw himself is self-absorbed. He seems to "suffocate for privacy" even though "he is out of bounds now." The poem is full of images of isolation, the most poignant of which are the "drained faces of Negro school-children," which have no point of contact with the ideal soldiers of the war that was fought to free

---

14. See Irvin Ehrenpreis, "The Age of Lowell," in *Robert Lowell: A Collection of Critical Essays,* ed. Thomas Parkinson (Englewood Cliffs, N.J.: Prentice Hall, 1968), pp. 81 and 94–98, for a comparison of Lowell and Baudelaire.

them from slavery and no point of contact with the poet. The bubble on which Shaw rides and the bubble represented by the television tube cannot touch, and though Lowell may want to break the bubbles to come in contact with the real, his "hand draws back," as if he suffered also from Shaw's isolation.

Lowell presents another image of Concord in this poem, of "small town New England greens," which "hold their air / of sparse, sincere rebellion." There is a consistency there that Lowell might aspire to, a tradition that is under attack by the steam-shovels. But the way it holds its air shows that its faithfulness is also a form of isolation. It, like the poet, is enclosed in a bubble, unreal and useless. "For the Union Dead" is a satirical poem in which both the present age and the golden age are debunked, in which both the things of this world and the things of the imagination are equally dead. As R. P. Blackmur said in his famous statement about Lowell and religion, "in dealing with men his faith compels him to be fractiously vindictive, and in dealing with faith his experience of men compels him to be nearly blasphemous."[15] Lowell's experience tells him that the ideal is dead, but his poetic heritage provides him with a type of symbol in Baudelaire's statue that he knows to be inimical to the real. He longs to be alone with that symbol, with his art, as Baudelaire did, but he also fears his isolation and in the end is left, as Berryman was, alone with the sharklike cars.

"For the Union Dead" comes to an unhappy close much like that of *Owl's Clover* and "Boston Common." Lowell despises the idealistic art of the New England past, as represented by its statues, because such art is a lie; it does not make the confession of complicity that Lowell makes at the beginning of "For the Union Dead." Not to make such a confession is, in fact, to turn away from life, to long for the grave, and to reject the sort of connection Lowell longs for in this poem. Confession is a public act in such poems because it joins the confessing poet to those around him in the community of sin. This is exactly what Berryman proposes in "Boston Common," that those who "labour in the private dark" cultivate a "common garden in a private ground." The "limited sick world" of the individual thus becomes public; because it is so

15. R. P. Blackmur, Review of *Land of Unlikeness*, in Parkinson, p. 38.

common it replaces the Common as a civic symbol. Both poems therefore propose an alternative monument, a private dark that becomes a public space by rejecting the usual paths of idealization. Both suggest a way in which the obsessively private aspect of confessional poetry might be seen as its most public attribute.

But neither poet seems entirely comfortable with a definition of poetry that evades the ideal. As a public, satirical poet, Lowell calls on the very ideal he debunks. Shaw is the standard to which Lowell would hold everyone, and he is the agent of political criticism in the poem. Because he lacks complicity, he can function as such a standard, but not, oddly enough, as a civic symbol. His idealism is so exclusive as to be private, and he is obviously pained at his contemporary surroundings. Like the statues in Yeats's late poem, he despises the people among whom he finds himself. This is the double bind of "For the Union Dead," that community is to be found only in failure, heroism only in the rejection of the community. Blackmur's judgment of the doubleness of Lowell's attitude toward religion can also be applied to the politics of this poem, and this doubleness explains why the monument in it remains as ambiguous as those of his predecessors, Stevens, Yeats, and Pound.

Works Cited

Adams, Hazard. "Yeatsian Art and Mathematic Form." *Centennial Review* 4 (1960): 70–88.

Adams, Henry. *The Education of Henry Adams*. 1918. Reprint. Boston: Houghton Mifflin, 1961.

Agulhon, Maurice. *Marianne into Battle: Republican Imagery and Symbolism in France, 1789–1880*. Tr. Janet Lloyd. Cambridge: Cambridge University Press, 1981.

Anderson, Margaret, ed. *The Little Review Anthology*. New York: Hermitage House, 1953.

Appelbaum, Stanley. *The Chicago World's Fair of 1893: A Photographic Record*. New York: Dover, 1980.

Armstrong, Tom, et al. *200 Years of American Sculpture*. New York: Godine, Whitney Museum, 1976.

Arnheim, Rudolf. "Space as an Image of Time." In *Images of Romanticism*. Ed. Karl Kroeber and William Walling. New Haven: Yale University Press, 1978.

Axelrod, Stephen Gould. *Robert Lowell: Life and Art*. Princeton: Princeton University Press, 1978.

Bachelard, Gaston. *The Poetics of Space*. Tr. Marie Jolas. Boston: Beacon, 1969.

Bacigalupo, Massimo. *The Forméd Trace: The Later Poetry of Ezra Pound*. New York: Columbia University Press, 1980.

Banham, Reyner. *Theory and Design in the First Machine Age*. Cambridge: MIT Press, 1960.

Barthes, Roland. *The Eiffel Tower*. Tr. Richard Howard. New York: Hill & Wang, 1979.

Baudelaire, Charles. *Critique d'art*. Paris: Armand Colin, 1965.

——. *Oeuvres complètes.* Paris: Louis Courand, 1930.

——. *Selected Writing on Art and Artists.* Tr. E. Charvet. Harmondsworth: Penguin, 1972.

Baumann, Walter. "Secretary of Nature, J. Heydon." In *New Approaches to Ezra Pound.* Ed. Eva Hesse. Berkeley: University of California Press, 1969.

Beardsley, John. *Art in Public Places.* Washington, D.C.: Partners for Livable Places, 1981.

Benevolo, Leonardo. *The Architecture of the Renaissance.* Boulder, Colo.: Westview Press, 1978.

Berger, John. *Art and Revolution.* New York: Pantheon, 1969.

Bernhardt-Kabisch, Ernest. "Wordsworth: The Monumental Poet." *Philological Quarterly* 44 (1965): 503–518.

Berryman, Jo Brantley. "The Art of the Image: Allusions in Pound's 'Medallion.'" *Paideuma* 6 (1977): 295–308.

——. "Medallion: Pound's Poem." *Paideuma* 2 (1973): 391–398.

Berryman, John. *Short Poems.* New York: Farrar, Straus & Giroux, 1967.

Blackmur, R. P. Review of *Land of Unlikeness.* In *Robert Lowell: A Collection of Critical Essays.* Ed. Thomas Parkinson. Englewood Cliffs, N.J.: Prentice-Hall, 1968.

Blake, William. *Complete Works.* Ed. Geoffrey Keynes. London: Nonesuch, 1957.

Bloom, Harold. "The Central Man: Emerson, Whitman, Wallace Stevens." In *The Ringers in the Tower.* Chicago: University of Chicago Press, 1971.

——. *Yeats.* New York: Oxford University Press, 1970.

Bodenheim, Maxwell. "Isolation of Carved Metal." *The Dial* 72 (January 1922): 91.

Boime, Albert. *Thomas Couture and the Eclectic Vision.* New Haven: Yale University Press, 1980.

Brooke-Rose, Christine. *A ZBC of Ezra Pound.* Berkeley: University of California Press, 1971.

Brown, Malcolm. *The Politics of Irish Literature.* Seattle: University of Washington Press, 1972.

Burnham, Jack. *Beyond Modern Sculpture.* New York: Braziller, 1968.

Bush, Ronald. *The Genesis of Ezra Pound's Cantos.* Princeton: Princeton University Press, 1976.

Chambers, D. S. *Patrons and Artists in the Italian Renaissance.* London: Macmillan, 1970.

Clark, T. J. *The Absolute Bourgeois: Artists and Politics in France, 1848–1851.* Greenwich, Conn.: New York Graphic Society, 1973.

Clearfield, Andrew. "Pound, Paris, and Dada." *Paideuma* 7 (1978): 113–140.

Cooper, Philip. *The Autobiographical Myth of Robert Lowell.* Chapel Hill: University of North Carolina Press, 1970.

Cork, Richard. *Vorticism and Abstract Art in the First Machine Age.* Berkeley: University of California Press, 1976.

Cosgrave, Patrick. *The Public Poetry of Robert Lowell.* London: Gollancz, 1970.

Crane, Sylvia E. *White Silence: Greenough, Powers, and Crawford, American Sculptors in Nineteenth Century Italy.* Coral Gables, Fla.: University of Miami Press, 1972.

Craven, Wayne. "Henry Kirke Brown: His Search for an American Art in the 1840s." *American Art Journal* 4 (November 1972): 44–58.

Davie, Donald. *Ezra Pound.* New York: Viking, 1975.

———. *Ezra Pound: Poet as Sculptor.* New York: Oxford University Press, 1964.

Davis, Douglas. "Public Art: The Taming of the Vision." *Art in America.* May–June 1974: 84–85.

Devlin, D. D. *Wordsworth and the Poetry of Epitaphs.* Totowa, N.J.: Barnes and Noble, 1980.

Doezema, Marianne, and June Hargrove, eds. *The Public Monument and Its Audience.* Cleveland: Cleveland Museum of Art, 1977.

Doggett, Frank. *Stevens' Poetry of Thought.* Baltimore: Johns Hopkins University Press, 1966.

Drummond, John. "The Italian Background to *The Cantos.*" In *An Examination of Ezra Pound.* Ed. Peter Russell. New York: Gordian Press, 1973.

Eckhardt, Wolf von. "The Malignant Objector." *The Public Interest* 66 (Winter 1982): 22–24.

Eddins, Dwight. "Poet and State in the Verse of Robert Lowell." *Texas Studies in Language and Literature* 15 (1973): 371–386.

Ehrenpreis, Irvin. "The Age of Lowell." In *Robert Lowell: A Collection of Critical Essays.* Ed. Thomas Parkinson. Englewood Cliffs, N.J.: Prentice-Hall, 1968.

Ellmann, Richard. *The Identity of Yeats.* New York: Oxford University Press, 1954.

———. *Yeats: The Man and the Masks.* New York: Macmillan, 1948.

Emerson, Ralph Waldo. *The Conduct of Life.* Boston: Houghton Mifflin, 1904.

Engelberg, Edward. " 'He Too Was in Arcadia': Yeats and the Paradox of the Fortunate Fall." In *In Excited Reverie.* Ed. A. N. Jeffares and K. G. W. Cross. New York: St. Martin's, 1965.

——. *The Vast Design: Patterns in W. B. Yeats's Aesthetic.* Toronto: University of Toronto Press, 1964.

Epstein, Jacob. *An Autobiography.* New York: Dutton, 1955.

——. *The Sculptor Speaks.* Told to Arnold J. Haskell. London: Heinemann, 1931.

Espey, John J. *Ezra Pound's Mauberley.* Berkeley: University of California Press, 1955.

Fehl, Philipp. *The Classical Monument: Reflections on the Connection between Morality and Art in Greek and Roman Sculpture.* New York: New York University Press, 1972.

Fenellosa, Ernest. "The Chinese Written Character as a Medium for Poetry." In *Instigations,* by Ezra Pound. 1920. Reprint. Freeport, N.Y.: Books for Libraries Press, 1967.

Fletcher, Ian, ed. *Decadence and the 90s.* London: Arnold, 1979.

Foucault, Michel. *The Archaeology of Knowledge.* Tr. A. M. Sheridan Smith. London: Tavistock, 1972.

Frank, Ellen Eve. *Literary Architecture: Essays toward a Tradition: Walter Pater, Gerard Manley Hopkins, Marcel Proust, Henry James.* Berkeley: University of California Press, 1979.

Frank, Joseph. "Spatial Form in Modern Literature." *Sewanee Review* 53 (1945): 221–240, 433–456, 643–653.

——. "Spatial Form: Thirty Years Later." In *Spatial Form in Narrative.* Ed. Jeffrey R. Smitten and Ann Daghistany. Ithaca: Cornell University Press, 1981.

Frye, Northrop. *The Great Code.* New York: Harcourt Brace Jovanovich, 1982.

——. "The Realistic Oriole." *Hudson Review* 10 (1957): 353–370.

Gadol, Joan. *Leon Battista Alberti: Universal Man of the Early Renaissance.* Chicago: University of Chicago Press, 1969.

Gautier, Théophile. *Émaux et camées.* Paris: Flammarion, n.d.

Geist, Sidney. *Brancusi: A Study of the Sculpture.* New York: Grossman, 1968.

Glueck, Grace. "Serra Work Stirs Downtown Protest." *N.Y. Times,* September 25, 1981.

Goldin, Amy. "The Aesthetic Ghetto: Some Thoughts about Public Art." *Art in America,* May–June 1974: 30–35.

Gombrich, E. H. *The Image and the Eye.* Ithaca: Cornell University Press, 1982.

Gonne, Maud. "Yeats and Ireland." In *Scattering Branches.* Ed. Stephen Gwynn. New York: Macmillan, 1940.

Gordon, D. J. *W. B. Yeats: Images of a Poet.* Manchester: Manchester University Press; New York: Barnes and Noble, 1961.

Greenough, Horatio. *The Travels, Observations, and Experiences of a Yankee Stonecutter*. New York: Putnam, 1852. Reprint. Gainesville, Fla.: Scholars Fascimiles, 1958.

Hamilton, Ian. *Robert Lowell*. New York: Random House, 1982.

Harbison, Robert. *Eccentric Spaces*. New York: Knopf, 1977.

Harmer, J. B. *Victory in Limbo: Imagism, 1908–1917*. London: Secker & Warburg, 1975.

Hartman, Geoffrey. "Wordsworth: Inscriptions and Romantic Nature Poetry." In *Beyond Formalism*. New Haven: Yale University Press, 1970.

Haskell, Francis. *Patrons and Painters*. New Haven: Yale University Press, 1980.

Haskell, Francis, and Nicholas Penny. *Taste and the Antique: The Lure of Classical Sculpture, 1500–1900*. New Haven: Yale University Press, 1981.

Hawthorne, Nathaniel. *The Marble Faun*. Columbus: Ohio State University Press, 1968.

——. *The French and Italian Notebooks*. Ed. Thomas Woodson. Columbus: Ohio State University Press, 1980.

Heap, Jane. "Machine-Age Exposition." In *The Little Review Anthology*. Ed. Margaret Anderson. New York: Hermitage House, 1953.

Henn, T. R. *The Lonely Tower*. London: Methuen, 1950.

Holt, Elizabeth Gilmore, ed. *From the Classicists to the Impressionists*. New York: New York University Press, 1966.

——. *The Triumph of Art for the Public*. Washington, D.C.: Decatur House, 1980.

Honour, Hugh. *Romanticism*. New York: Harper & Row, 1979.

Hulme, T. E. *Further Speculations*. Ed. Samuel Hynes. Minneapolis: University of Minnesota Press, 1955.

——. *Speculations*. Ed. Herbert Read. London: Routledge & Kegan Paul, 1936.

Hunt, John Dixon. *The Pre-Raphaelite Imagination*. Lincoln: University of Nebraska Press, 1968.

James, Henry. *The American Scene*. Bloomington: Indiana University Press, 1968.

——. *The Art of Travel*. Ed. Morton Dauwen Zabel. Garden City, N.Y.: Doubleday, 1958.

Jeffares, A. N. *A Commentary on the Collected Poems of W. B. Yeats*. Stanford: Stanford University Press, 1968.

Jenkyns, Richard. *The Victorians and Ancient Greece*. Cambridge: Harvard University Press, 1980.

Jones, P. J. *The Malatesta of Rimini and the Papal State*. London: Cambridge University Press, 1974.

Kaplan, Julius. *Gustave Moreau*. Greenwich, Conn.: New York Graphic Society, 1974.

Kenner, Hugh. *The Poetry of Ezra Pound*. Norfolk, Conn.: New Directions, 1950.

——. *The Pound Era*. Berkeley: University of California Press, 1971.

Kermode, Frank. *Romantic Image*. New York: Random House, Vintage, 1964.

Koch, Vivienne. *W. B. Yeats: The Tragic Phase*. Baltimore: Johns Hopkins University Press, 1951.

Langbaum, Robert. *The Mysteries of Identity*. New York: Oxford University Press, 1977.

Le Corbusier. *Towards a New Architecture*. Tr. Frederick Etchells. New York: Brewer, Warren, and Putnam, 1927.

Le Corbusier and Amédée Ozenfant. "Purism." In *Form and Function*. Ed. Tim and Charlotte Benton. London: Crosby, Lockwood, Staples, 1975.

Léger, Fernand. "The Esthetics of the Machine." *Little Review* 9 (Spring 1923): 45–46.

Lewis, Wyndham. "The Rock Drill." *New Statesman*, April 7, 1951.

——. *Tarr*. London: Chatto & Windus, 1918. Reprint. Calder & Boyars, 1968.

——. *Time and Western Man*. New York: Harcourt, Brace, 1928.

——. *Wyndham Lewis on Art*. Ed. Walter Michel and C. J. Fox. New York: Funk & Wagnalls, 1969.

Lipke, William C., and Bernard Rozran. "Ezra Pound and Vorticism." *Contemporary Literature* 7 (1966): 210–219.

Litz, A. Walton. *Introspective Voyager: The Poetic Development of Wallace Stevens*. New York: Oxford University Press, 1972.

Lowell, Robert. *For the Union Dead*. New York: Farrar, Straus & Giroux, 1964.

——. *Lord Weary's Castle*. New York: Harcourt, Brace, 1946.

MacLeod, Robert. *Style and Society: Architectural Ideology in Britain, 1835–1914*. London: RIBA Publications, 1971.

Marinetti, F. T. "Futurist Manifesto, 1909." In *Futurist Manifestos*. Ed. Umbro Apollonio. New York: Viking, 1973.

Materer, Timothy. *Vortex: Pound, Eliot, and Lewis*. Ithaca: Cornell University Press, 1979.

Mathieu, Pierre-Louis. *Gustave Moreau*. Oxford: Phaidon, 1977.

Melchiori, Giorgio. *The Whole Mystery of Art*. London: Routledge & Kegan Paul, 1960.

Metzger, Charles R. *Emerson and Greenough: Transcendental Pioneers of an American Aesthetic.* Berkeley: University of California Press, 1954.

Millard, Charles W. "Sculpture and Theory in Nineteenth Century France." *Journal of Aesthetics and Art Criticism* 34 (1975): 15–20.

Mitchell, W. J. T. "Spatial Form in Literature: Toward a General Theory." In *The Language of Images.* Ed. W. J. T. Mitchell. Chicago: University of Chicago Press, 1980.

Moore, Marianne. *Predilections.* New York: Viking, 1955.

Moore, Stephen C. "Politics and the Poetry of Robert Lowell." *Georgia Review* 27 (1973): 220–231.

Morris, William. *Early Romances.* London: Dent, 1973.

Morse, Samuel French. *Wallace Stevens: Poetry as Life.* New York: Pegasus, 1970.

Mumford, Lewis. *The Culture of Cities.* New York: Harcourt, Brace and World, 1938.

Murray, Peter. *Architecture of the Renaissance.* New York: Abrams, 1971.

Norman, Charles. *Ezra Pound.* New York: Macmillan, 1960.

Novak, Barbara. *Nature and Culture.* New York: Oxford University Press, 1980.

Pack, Robert. *Wallace Stevens: An Approach to His Poetry and Thought.* New Brunswick, N.J.: Rutgers University Press, 1958.

Panofsky, Erwin. *Idea.* Tr. Joseph J. S. Peale. Columbia: University of South Carolina Press, 1968.

——. *Meaning in the Visual Arts.* Garden City, N.Y.: Doubleday Anchor, 1955.

Pater, Walter. *Greek Studies.* London: Macmillan, 1895. Reprint. Oxford: Blackwell; New York: Johnson Reprint Corp., 1967.

——. *Plato and Platonism.* London: Macmillan, 1910.

——. *The Renaissance.* Ed. Donald L. Hill. Berkeley: University of California Press, 1980.

Pearlman, Daniel D. *The Barb of Time.* New York: Oxford University Press, 1969.

Perlis, Alan. *Wallace Stevens: A World of Transforming Shapes.* Lewisburg: Bucknell University Press, 1976.

Pevsner, Nikolaus. *Pioneers of Modern Design.* Harmondsworth: Penguin, 1960.

Plato. *Philebus.* Tr. J. C. B. Gosling. Oxford: Oxford University Press, 1975.

Poulet, Georges. *Proustian Space.* Tr. Elliott Coleman. Baltimore: Johns Hopkins University Press, 1977.

Pound, Ezra. *The Cantos.* New York: New Directions, 1972.

———. *The Collected Early Poems*. Ed. Michael John King. New York: New Directions, 1976.

———. *Ezra Pound and the Visual Arts*. Ed. Harriet Zinnes. New York: New Directions, 1980.

———. *Gaudier-Brzeska*. 1916. Reprint. New York: New Directions, 1970.

———. *Guide to Kulchur*. 1938. Reprint. Norfolk, Conn.: New Directions, 1952.

———. *Instigations*. 1920. Reprint. Freeport, N.Y.: Books for Libraries Press, 1967.

———. *The Letters of Ezra Pound*. Ed. D. D. Paige. New York: Harcourt, Brace, 1950.

———. *Literary Essays*. Ed. T. S. Eliot. New York: New Directions, 1968.

———. "Paris Letter." *The Dial* 71 (September 1921): 457.

———. "Paris Letter." *The Dial* 74 (December 1922): 88.

———. *Personae*. 1926. Reprint. New York: New Directions, 1971.

———. *Selected Prose: 1909–1965*. Ed. William Cookson. New York: New Directions, 1973.

———. "Statues of Gods." *The Townsman*, August 1939, 14.

———. "Three Cantos." *Poetry* 10 (1917): 113–121, 248–254.

Praz, Mario. *Mnemosyne: The Parallel between Literature and the Visual Arts*. Princeton: Princeton University Press, 1970.

———. *On Neoclassicism*. London: Thames & Hudson, 1969.

———. *The Romantic Agony*. London: Oxford University Press, 1933.

Read, Benedict. *Victorian Sculpture*. New Haven: Yale University Press, 1982.

Read, Herbert. *The Art of Sculpture*. New York: Pantheon, 1956.

Reinach, Salomon. *Apollo*. New York: Scribner, 1924.

Rossetti, Dante Gabriel. *The House of Life*. Ed. Paull Franklin Baum. Cambridge: Harvard University Press, 1928.

Rowe, Colin. *The Mathematics of the Ideal Villa and Other Essays*. Cambridge: MIT Press, 1976.

Ruskin, John. *Seven Lamps of Architecture*. 1849. Reprint. London: Dent, 1907.

———. *The Stones of Venice*. London: Smith, Elder, 1853.

Russell, George. *The Living Torch*. Ed. Mark Gibbon. New York: Macmillan, 1938.

Ruthven, K. K. *A Guide to Ezra Pound's Personae*. Berkeley: University of California Press, 1969.

Sant' Elia, Antonio. "Futurist Architecture." In *Programs and Manifestos of 20th Century Architecture*. Ed. Ulrich Conrads. Cambridge: MIT Press, 1970.

Scheyer, Ernst. *The Circle of Henry Adams: Art and Artists.* Detroit: Wayne State University Press, 1970.

Schneidau, Herbert. *Ezra Pound: The Image and the Real.* Baton Rouge: Louisiana State University Press, 1969.

Seznec, Jean. *The Survival of the Pagan Gods.* New York: Harper/Bollingen, 1953.

Sharp, Lewis I. "John Quincy Adams Ward: Historical and Contemporary Influences." *American Art Journal* 4 (November 1972): 71–83.

Shaw, J. E. *Guido Cavalcanti's Theory of Love.* Toronto: University of Toronto Press, 1949.

Smitten, Jeffrey R., and Ann Daghistany, eds. *Spatial Form in Narrative.* Ithaca: Cornell University Press, 1981.

Stalker, Douglas, and Clark Glymour. "The Malignant Object: Thoughts on Public Sculpture." *The Public Interest* 66 (Winter 1982): 3–21.

Stallworthy, Jon. *Between the Lines.* Oxford: Oxford University Press, 1963.

——. *Vision and Revision in Yeats's Last Poems.* (Oxford: Oxford University Press, 1969.

Starkie, Enid. *From Gautier to Eliot.* London: Hutchison, 1960.

Stein, Richard L. *The Ritual of Interpretation: The Fine Arts as Literature in Ruskin, Rossetti, and Pater.* Cambridge: Harvard University Press, 1975.

Stevens, Wallace. *Collected Poems.* New York: Knopf, 1977.

——. *Letters.* Ed. Holly Stevens. New York: Knopf, 1966.

——. *The Necessary Angel.* New York: Random House, Vintage, 1951.

——. *Opus Posthumous.* Ed. Samuel French Morse. New York: Knopf, 1957.

Stock, Noel. *The Life of Ezra Pound.* New York: Pantheon, 1970.

Stokes, Adrian. *The Stones of Rimini.* 1934. Reprint. New York: Schocken, 1969.

Surette, Leon. *A Light from Eleusis.* Oxford: Oxford University Press, 1979.

Swinburne, A. C. *Poems.* New York: Harper, 1915.

Symons, Arthur. *Studies in Seven Arts.* New York: Dutton, 1925.

Thalacker, Donald W. *The Place of Art in the World of Architecture.* New York: Bowker; London: Chelsea House, 1980.

Tharp, Louise Hall. *Saint-Gaudens and the Gilded Era.* Boston: Little, Brown, 1969.

Tocqueville, Alexis de. *Democracy in America.* Tr. Henry Reeve. New York: Random House, Vintage, 1945.

Tomkins, Calvin. "The Natural Problem." *New Yorker,* March 29, 1982.

——. "The Urban Capacity." *New Yorker,* April 5, 1982.

Trapp, Frank Anderson. *The Attainment of Delacroix*. Baltimore: Johns Hopkins University Press, 1971.

Ure, Peter. "The Statues." *Review of English Studies* 25 (1949): 254–257.

van Doesburg, Theo. "Evolution of Modern Architecture in Holland." *Little Review* 11 (Spring 1925): 47–51.

Vendler, Helen. *On Extended Wings: Wallace Stevens' Longer Poems*. Cambridge: Harvard University Press, 1969.

Wagner, Geoffrey. "Wyndham Lewis and the Vorticist Aesthetic." *Journal of Aesthetics and Art Criticism* 12 (1954): 1–17.

Whitaker, Thomas R. *Swan and Shadow: Yeats's Dialogue with History*. Chapel Hill: University of North Carolina Press, 1964.

Whitman, Walt. *Leaves of Grass*. Ed. Harold W. Blodgett and Sculley Bradley. New York: New York University Press, 1965.

Wilde, Oscar. *Complete Works*. Garden City, N.Y.: Doubleday, Page, 1923.

Wilenski, R. H. *The Meaning of Modern Sculpture*. New York: Stokes, 1933.

Wilhelm, James. *Dante and Pound*. Orono: University of Maine Press, 1974.

Williamson, Alan. *Pity the Monsters: The Political Vision of Robert Lowell*. New Haven: Yale University Press, 1974.

Wilson, F. A. C. *Yeats's Iconography*. New York: Macmillan, 1960.

Winckelmann, Johann Joachim. *History of Ancient Art*. Tr. G. Henry Lodge. Boston: Osgood, 1872.

Wines, James. "De-Architecturization." In *Esthetics Contemporary,* ed. Richard Kostelanetz. Buffalo: Prometheus Books, 1978.

Witemeyer, Hugh. *The Poetry of Ezra Pound: Forms and Renewal, 1908–1920*. Berkeley: University of California Press, 1969.

Wittkower, Rudolf. *Architectural Principles in the Age of Humanism*. London: Warburg Institute, University of London, 1949.

——. *Sculpture: Process and Principles*. New York: Harper & Row, 1977.

Wordsworth, William. "Essay upon Epitaphs." In *Prose Works of William Wordsworth*. Ed. W. J. B. Owen and Jane Worthington Smyser. Oxford: Oxford University Press, 1974.

Worringer, Wilhelm. *Abstraction and Empathy*. Tr. Michael Bullock. New York: International Universities Press, 1953.

Wright, Nathalia. *Horatio Greenough: The First American Sculptor*. Philadelphia: University of Pennsylvania Press, 1963.

Yates, Frances. *The Art of Memory*. Chicago: University of Chicago Press, 1966.

Yeats, W. B. *The Autobiography of W. B. Yeats*. New York: Macmillan, 1953.

Works Cited

——. *Collected Plays*. New York: Macmillan, 1953.

——. *Essays and Introductions*. New York: Macmillan, 1961.

——. *Letters*. Ed. Allan Wade. New York: Macmillan, 1954.

——. *Memoirs*. Ed. Denis Donoghue. New York: Macmillan, 1972.

——. *On the Boiler*. Dublin: Cuala Press, 1939.

——. *The Poems*. Ed. Richard Finneran. New York: Macmillan, 1983.

——. *Reflections*. Ed. Curtis Bradford. Dublin: Cuala Press, 1970.

——. *The Variorum Edition of the Plays*. Ed. Russell K. Alspach. London: Macmillan, 1966.

——. *A Vision*. 1937. Reprint. New York: Collier, 1966.

Yeats, W. B., and T. Sturge Moore. *Their Correspondence, 1901–1937*. Ed. Ursula Bridge. New York: Oxford University Press, 1953.

Index

257

LIBRARY OF CONGRESS CATALOGING IN PUBLICATION DATA

North, Michael, 1951–
  The final sculpture.

  Bibliography: P.
  Includes index.
  1. American poetry—20th century—History and
criticism.   2. Monuments in literature.   3. Memorials in
literature.   4. Sculpture in literature.   5. Art and literature.   6. Yeats,
W. B. (William Butler), 1865–1939—Knowledge—Art.   I. Title.
PS310.M6N67   1985   811'.52'09357   84–17011
ISBN 0–8014–1725–2 (alk. paper)